X-Men®: The Characters and Their Universe

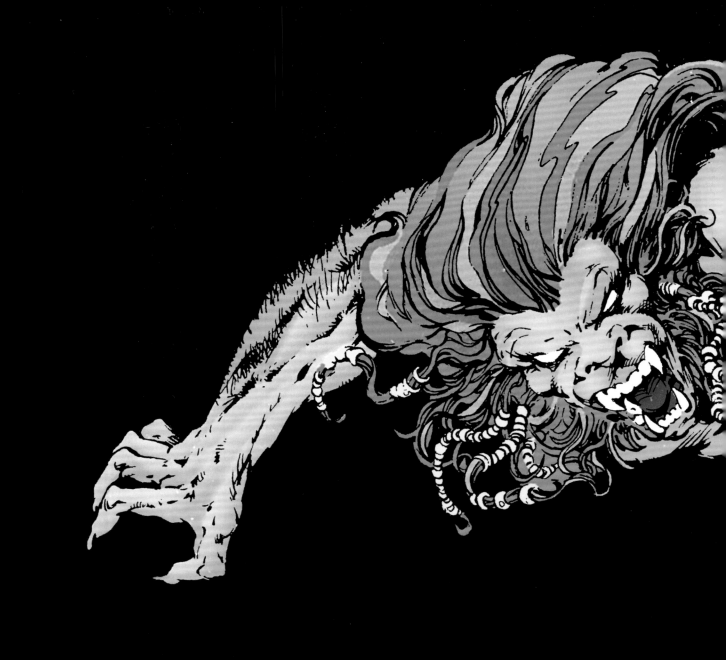

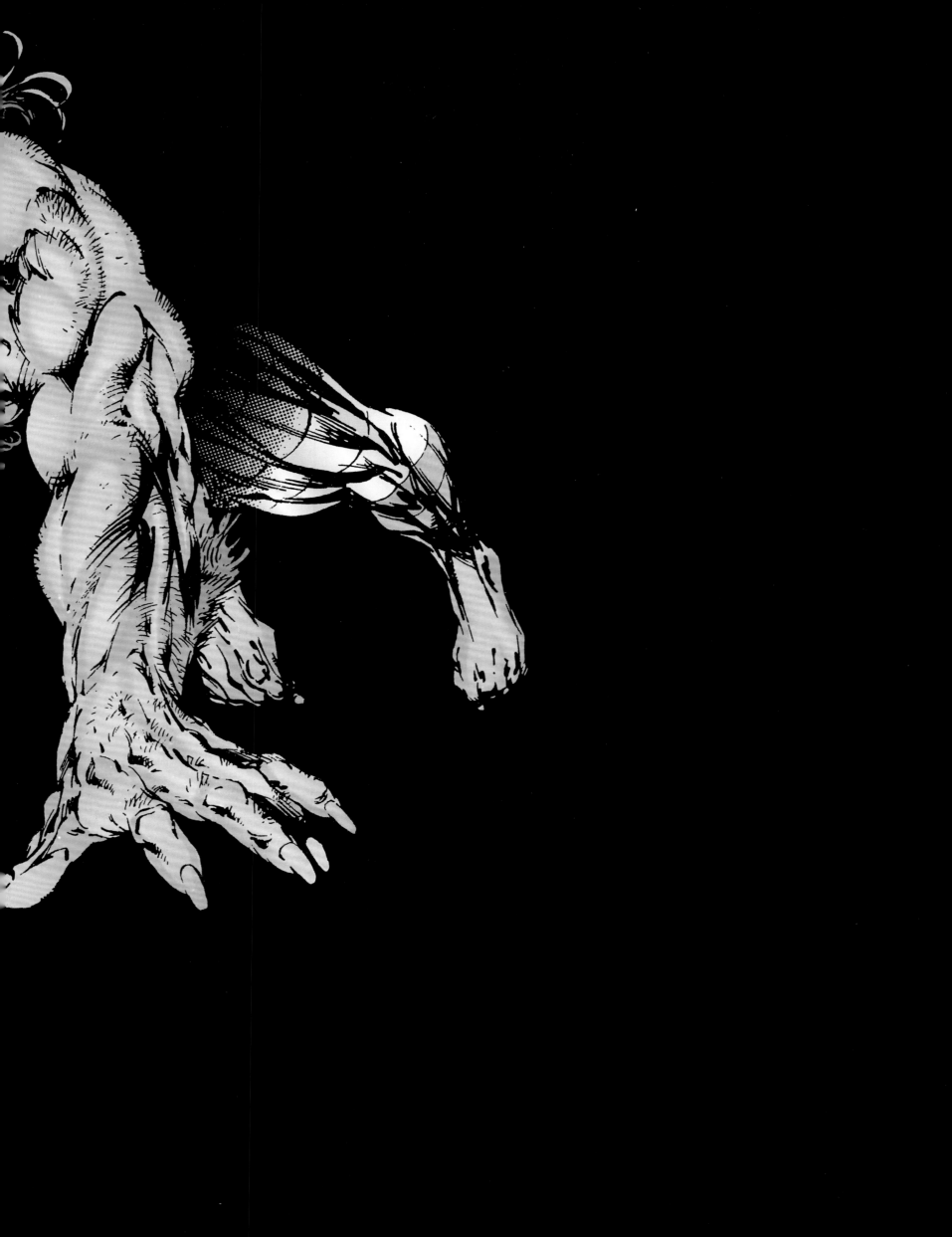

X-Me[n]

The Chara[cters]
and The[ir]

MICHAEL MALLORY

MARVEL CHARACTERS, INC.
BEAUX ARTS EDITIONS

Acknowledgments

The author would like to extend heartfelt thanks to the following individuals and companies who contributed to the creation of this book: Connie Ambrosch, Avi Arad, Jerry Beck, Halle Berry, Chris Claremont, Dave Cockrum, Adam Curby, Caitlin Cusick, Gloria Davies, Tom DeFalco, Mark Evanier, Jon Falkner, Tess Finkle, Toby Gibson, James Hinton, Hugh Jackman, Famke Janssen, Ruwan Jayatilleke, Greg Johnson, Neal Kirby, Boyd Kirkland, Craig Kyle, Michael Leavey, Kyle Ledyier, Hugh Lauter Levin, Margaret Loesch, Bruno Maglione, Sir Ian McKellen, JoAnn McLaughlin, Helen Mallory, Will Meugniot, John Morrow, Melissa Payne, Alex Plummer, Matthew Primack, Joe Quesada, Brett Ratner, John Rickard, Rebecca Romijn, John Romita, Ken Scaglia, Mickey Stern, Alberta Stewart, Carl Suecoff, and Roy Thomas; as well as Hollywood Book and Poster, Eddie Brandt's Saturday Matinee, and Jerry Ohlinger's Movie Material Store.

Special thanks go to Bryan Singer; to Rick Hoberg; to my research assistant Brendan Mallory; to Jim Muschett; to Marvel Enterprises; and, of course, to Stan Lee.

This 2011 custom edition is published exclusively for Barnes & Noble, Inc., by Universe Publishing, A Division of Rizzoli International Publications, Inc., 300 Park Avenue South, New York, NY 10010.

Design: Ken and Jan Scaglia
Text: Michael Mallory
Project Editor: James O. Muschett
Production Editor: Melissa C. Payne
Cover Art: Mickey Stern

ISBN 978-1-4351-3757-8

Manufactured in China

10 9 8 7 6 5 4 3 2

Contents

Foreword

Some people might not know this, but I arrived a little late for the X-Men party. It was already a crowded room, filled with white hair, bald heads, blue fur, and lots of yellow spandex. There seemed to be hundreds of mutants, while their fans numbered in the millions—and they were very, VERY passionate. This party was over thirty years old, and when I walked in, it felt like one of those classic moments where the record player scratched, the music stopped, and everyone fell deathly silent. All eyes were on me. Watching. Waiting to see what I would do.

It was awkward at first. I had never read an X-Men comic book. Back then, Nightcrawler was just another name for a worm. Wolverine and Sabretooth could have been sports teams, and Rogue and Mystique sounded like women's perfumes. And those were just their *codenames*, never mind their real names, histories, conflicts, and an endless amount of powers.

Unfortunately, there wasn't a family album or users manual to this complex universe, so instead of shyly standing in a corner, I dove in. I met everyone. I read the comics and watched the cartoons until I was as blue in the face as Beast. What I quickly discovered was that beyond the telekinetics, shapeshifters, and teleporters, X-Men contained a very poignant and relevant human story, one about outcasts.

There are times when we all feel like mutants. Whether it's the first day at a new school, a new job, or leaving the nest and venturing into the real world, our lives are dotted with periods where we just don't fit. For most, these awkward moments might be temporary, but for some, they seem to last a lifetime. In our world this isolation might be a matter of race, sexuality, or religion—various factors that cause us to feel like an outsider, even among friends and family.

These themes of identity and the struggle of a minority are what appealed to me the most. It gave the comic book a heart—a message. Something that made me feel oddly comfortable among these misfits. I saw a bit of myself in these characters, and in a way, I became one of them.

So while my introduction to the X-Men came a little later than others and might have been a little awkward at first, it was the beginning of a friendship that has lasted to this day. A book like this might have made the introduction a little easier, but whether you're a lifelong fan or a new recruit like I was, think of the following pages as the "X-Men family album" that I never had. Just don't be too surprised if you find yourself becoming one of them.

Bryan Singer
Director
X-Men, X2: X-Men United, Superman Returns

(Opposite) Director Bryan Singer gets Magneto's helmet in view in *X-Men*.

Mutants An

Mutants Among Us

In 2005, the planet Earth fell under the control of a mutant. He goes by the title "King Magnus," but that is not his real name. He is an uneasy mix of savior to his particular race and ruthless destroyer of anyone who stands in his way. He used to be known as Magneto (pronounced "mag-NEE-toe") because of his special ability to manipulate magnetic fields and use that power as both a defensive and offensive weapon. He will probably be known as Magneto again. But as of this particular moment in time he is Magnus Rex, ruler of the world—at least within that uniquely flexible reflection of reality called the Marvel Universe.

Magnus/Magneto's newfound power is being exploited through a massive, multi-issue storyline called "House of M," which has all but overtaken the Marvel Universe. It wipes clean the existing slate as comic book readers know it starts over again, with the core idea being that normal human beings—those without mutant abilities—are now the minority, while mutants are the dominant race. Those who are familiar with the character of Magneto, even if it is only through his animation and feature film appearances, know that he has dedicated his life to making certain that *homo superior*—his term for mutantkind—shall inherit the earth. On the surface of it, some might think that his ascension to the world throne at long last in this particular storyline is the end game in a long and complex saga, and that there is nowhere for the story to go from here. But it is not the end. It cannot be. The Marvel Universe, and specifically, the X-Universe within it, simply does not work that way.

The X-Universe does not expand, it inflates and deflates, turns inside-out, upside-down, becomes a black hole and then a blazing nova; it twists and turns, torques, and pulls and pushes like so much Silly Putty. It goes backward and forward and sideways. It turns in on itself and back out again like taffy on a pulling machine, each time reshaping itself within itself.

(Opposite) The X-Men have arrived. L-to-R, The Beast, the White Queen, Cyclops, Wolverine, Kitty Pryde, and Colossus. (*House of M #1*, July 2005; pencils Olivier Coipel, inks Tim Townsend)

Similarly, the characters of the X-Universe are not simply beings that are born, live, and die. Only their living can be accepted at face value. The X-Universe is an incredibly tangled web of characters and relationships that involve multiple identities, secret pasts, even more secret futures, which sometimes take place on alien worlds and in parallel time tracks or different planes of existence. Individual characters have frequently undergone transitions that go far beyond a new costume design. Some have died, only to return; some have leapt into other bodies; others have been cloned; quite a few of them have changed color, and a few have turned out to be neither mutants nor humans at all, but rather robots, or, more precisely, "techno-organisms." Virtually all have had their entire known histories rewritten at some point or other. Keeping the players straight throughout four decades of X-Men adventures takes more than a program, it takes a book. (And to help the reader chart the frenzied course that follows, any reference to "X-Men" that is un-highlighted refers to the group of characters in general, whereas any reference that it italicized—*X-Men*—refers specifically to the comic book title. Similarly, the first time a character's name is introduced it will be listed in "quotes," but in subsequent references it will not.)

Through it all, the central theme of the X-Universe is that its most important inhabitants are mutants, beings born with the mysterious "X-Gene," which makes them different from "normal" people and gives them supernatural powers or abilities that they themselves must decide how to use. Some mutants see their emergence as the inevitable result of natural selection, the next stage of evolution in human history, and are thus ready to take charge of the planet as completely as did the mammals after the age of dinosaurs. Magneto and his ilk stand steadfastly in this corner.

However, to much of baseline humanity within the X-Universe, those born without the X-gene, mutants are little more than freaks, creatures that are not special, just different, and therefore beings to be feared and hated. To

(Previous spread) Magneto enthroned in the House of Magnus royal portrait. (*House of M #6*, October 2005; pencils Oliver Coipel, colorist Frank D'Armata)

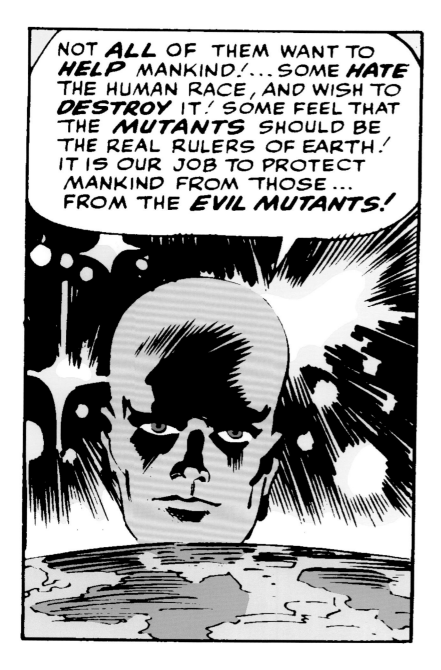

Professor X proclaims the X-Men's mission statement in *X-Men* #1. (September 1963; pencils Jack Kirby, inks Paul Reinman)

them, human mutants are like two-headed calves; oddities that, after the novelty of seeing it has passed, just become creepy and unnatural. For people of this mindset—who in the X-Universe are frequently involved with the government—the only good mutant is a dead one. Fanning the fires of this conflict is the knowledge that mutants are not as passive as poor deformed calves: they can think and fight, sometimes alarming well, and with weapons that stagger the imagination of conventional humanity. They will not go down without a battle.

The ongoing conflict between *homo sapiens* and *homo superiors* is one of the key factors that have allowed *X-Men* and its various spin-offs to become the most successful comic book franchise in history. Mutantcy has become an open metaphor for societal oppression and the underclass, and it has been presented in such a way as to allow the reader to fill in his or her own blank. "I've heard people describe the idea of the mutants in the Marvel Universe as sort of the class race wars that happened here in the states, or the idea of homosexuality, or just being different in general," says Marvel editor-in-chief Joe Quesada. "What a lot of our younger readers read into it is the idea that becoming a mutant at a certain age, and developing these powers that you don't know how to use, is a perfect metaphor for puberty. The characters lend themselves to so many wonderful interpretations."

X-Men did not start out with such large allegorical goals in mind. At its inception, it was another Super Hero book hoping to find favor with readers (who in 1963 tended to be considerably younger than today's comic book audience, which is largely comprised of young adult men) by giving them as much action and fantasy excitement as could be packed onto brightly colored wood-pulp paper and sold for twelve cents. These were grand tales of boys and girls in tights who saved the world from the machinations of dastardly and dangerous villains time and time again. Only after *X-Men* was up and running did the writers and artists who turned it out realize that they had the potential of creating something that was several notches above the standard comic book level. As years went on, the envelope would be pushed continually, to the point where in terms of character complexity, breadth of plot, and the willingness to address serious subjects, many bestselling novels looked simplistic in comparison.

Political themes, particularly how political power can be wielded to oppress the underclasses in America, increasingly informed the saga of the X-Men, and those critics who dismissed any kind of literature or entertainment they did not like as "comic-book storytelling" were clearly not reading comic books. And as time went on, the most popular members of the X-Men team, such as the wild and feral loner "Wolverine," would become such a part of the pop culture base that one did not even have to read comic books to know who he was. Nor did one have to have a subscription to *X-Men* or an open account at a comic book store to understand that mutants walked among us.

So where did mutants come from in the first place?

Like most everything within the X-Universe, the answer to that keeps changing. In his first appearance in *X-Men* #1, in 1963, the dour, bald and crippled organizer of the team, "Professor Xavier," refers to himself as "possibly the first such mutant," and believes that his powers of telepathy were the result of his scientist parents having worked on the world's first nuclear tests. In fact, he dubs his young X-Men "children of the atom" (exposure to radiation was a very common explanation for the genesis of Super Hero powers within the Marvel Universe). His claim to be first might have simply been a touch of pomposity, or he might not yet have learned about the existence of "Prince Namor, the Sub-Mariner," who as a born amphibian was clearly a mutant on some level. But decades later this theory was contradicted with evidence that mutants had been around as long as civilization. In fact, they may have been among the very first non-indigenous people in America.

Prince Namor, the Sub-Mariner (with flat top) is arguably the Marvel Universe's first mutant. (from *Marvel Comics Presents #7*, 1989; pencils John Buscema)

1602, an eight-part miniseries written by Neil Gaiman and drawn by Andy Kubert, which was published between November 2003 and June 2004, examined what might have happened if mutants had been among the very first Europeans to arrive in the Virginia colonies. It is a classic Marvel-style revisionist tale that turns known history on its ear. Set in the palaces of Europe as well as the struggling Roanoke Colony, *1602* chronicles a story of political intrigue that hinges around the death of old Queen Elizabeth, and the imminent ascension to the throne by James VI of Scotland, a psychotically religious man who believed that evil and witchcraft abounded in his realm. (The reign of the real James was indeed marked by religious struggles, though the fact that Elizabeth died and he was crowned in *1603* implies that we are dealing with an alternate version of history.)

Witchcraft to James and to the Grand Inquisitor of Spain, who is also seen to be on the prowl for evil, real or imagined, translates into anybody behaving differently, or possessing strange and unreal characteristics…in other words, *mutants*. Under Good Queen Bess, the "witchbreed," as they were then known, had been tolerated. There is even a special place for them: "Master Carolus Javier's Select College for the Sons of Gentlefolk" in Warwick, England, where pupils

(Above) Mutants in the age of Elizabeth depicted as prototypes for their 20th century versions, from *1602* #4 (January 2004; artist Andy Kubert).

(Opposite) The colonial version of The Angel suffering the fate of the "Witchbreed" in *1602* #1. (November 2003; artist Andy Kubert)

with special abilities are trained and kept out of the eyes of the superstitious public. In his first group of students are a young man named "Roberto," whose body can freeze; "Scotious Somerisle," whose eyes project a dangerous power force; the bestial "Master Henry McCoy"; "Werner," who has white angel wings, and as such is the most physically obvious among the witchbreed; and young "Master John Grey," Javier's page, who in best Shakespearean fashion turns out to be a girl. Anyone familiar with *X-Men* will see the parallels to Professor's X's first team.

Not surprisingly, the man who became King Magnus also shows up in this time, though the manner in which he does so is startling: it is revealed that *he* has been posing as the aged Grand Inquisitor, and as such has been engaging in unnatural selection: consigning only those mutants who were marked physically as different to the flames, while harboring those who could pass for human. When the truth of his background is discovered, that he is a man named "Enrique" who is in reality a ghetto-born Jew, he finds himself on the stake, charged by the maniacal King James with rejecting the "true church." Enrique breaks loose from his fiery stake and rises recognizably as Magneto.

But it is not simply the X-Men who show up in this bizarre version of history: virtually the entire Marvel Universe is caught in this expressionistic time warp. "Sir Nicholas Fury," the 17th-century ancestor of "Nick Fury, Agent of S.H.I.E.L.D.," plays a central role as a spy to the dying Queen Elizabeth, while "Dr. Stephen Strange" ("Dr. Strange") is her mystical court physician, who was unable to prevent her death at the behest of the corrupt ruler of Latveria, "Count Otto von Doom" ("Dr. Doom"). In Fury's employ are young "Peter Parquagh," who has an altercation with a spider in the course of the tale, and "Matthew Murdoch," a blind bard with a *daredevil* personality, while "Rojhaz," the giant Native American protecting Virginia, turns out to be the 17th-century version of "Captain America." Even "The Watcher," the strange, otherworldly being who keeps an eye on Earth from a vantage point on the moon, is represented here.

1602 (which has continued on in a second comic book series) is a perfect demonstration of the sheer tensile strength of the X-Universe, showing how it can be pushed and pulled and twisted into any direction, or even any number of directions at one time, without compromising its basic structure. By the time the saga concluded and time itself was righted (for now) the very existence of the world had been threatened. That is not an uncommon threat in the X-Universe, though such devastattion would not happen as a result of an actual world cataclysm or deadly disease epidemic, but rather by the joint whim of an editor, artist, and writer. Even so, it would be back. The world will always exist, as long as there are X-Men around to protect it, and as long as there are people in the world who are hungry for unique, emotional, and exciting stories. Whether they are told in a magazine, a book, a television show, a movie, or a video game, the X-Men will be there to intrigue, challenge, incite, alarm, occasionally mystify, but always satisfy them. "People care about the lives of the characters," says writer Chris Claremont, whose tenure with *X-Men* spans thirty years. "These are people that they like and they want to know more about. It's the same driving force that led people in New York to line up at the docks every month for the ship from England carrying Charles Dickens's latest chapter a hundred years ago."

These are the stories of the children of the atom, the mutant X-Men.

And this is their story…

(Above) The Professor X of *1602*, "Carlos Javier," also had his name rendered in the comic as "Carolus Javier" (then again, Shakespeare spelled his name different ways, too).

(Opposite) Artist Andy Kubert's depiction of the tortured Jew "Enrique" revealing his true *magnetic* mutant personality in *1602 #7* (April 2004) draws upon Crucifixion imagery.

Birth of a L

Birth of a Legend

It was 1963: JFK was president, and the country was enjoying its last shining moment of Camelot; gas was cheap, bad guys spoke Russian, the only mutant in sight was Godzilla, and everyone did their best to whistle past the nuclear plant. But in the late summer of that year, comic book readers across the country would learn that a strange and powerful sub-species of humanity walked among them. This revelation would be because of the combined efforts of two men who made their livings entertaining youngsters, and who, while no one was looking, would become two of the most dynamic creative forces in the history of American pop culture. Together, these two hard-working forty-somethings, Stan Lee and Jack Kirby, would create the seminal X-Universe.

(Above) Professor X's telepathic influence over the team is clearly depicted in this early group shot of the X-Men.

(Opposite) The very first appearance of the original X-Men, from *X-Men* #1, shows Cyclops, Iceman, the Angel, Professor X, and The Beast. Marvel Girl's entrance would take place mid-story. (Pencils Jack Kirby, inks Paul Reinman)

First, a word about creation: ask anyone who created Sherlock Holmes, and they will undoubtedly answer, Sir Arthur Conan Doyle. And they would be correct, since it was indeed that Victorian author who came up with the idea for Holmes and wrote his sixty adventures. There seems no way to dispute that fact. However, the *image* that we immediately recognize as Sherlock Holmes —the hawk profile, the deerstalker cap, the Inverness coat, the curved, calabash pipe—did not come from Conan Doyle at all, but rather from Sidney Paget, the man who illustrated the original Holmes stories for *The Strand* magazine. That iconic physical image has become so indelibly etched in the public consciousness that people who have never actually read a Sherlock Holmes story can still identify the legendary sleuth from his image alone.

What has this to do with *X-Men*? Quite simply, it describes the kind of collaborative method of creation that brings comic book characters to life, in which the question of who—"created"—whom is sometimes open to personal interpretation. This is all the more true for those working under what came to be known as "the Marvel method," a system of story plotting in which the artist would work from an outline, rather than from a

written script, and would therefore be allowed to devise a lot of the plot himself as he drew. Just as one could argue that Sidney Paget had a hand in "creating" Sherlock Holmes, comic book characters tend to have more than one, or even two, parents. In the case of *X-Men*, Lee and Kirby were the first in a long, long line of fathers and occasional mothers who contributed to the saga and its X-tensive cast of characters.

STAN "THE MAN" AND JACK "THE KING"

Given their status as Masters of the Marvel Universe, it is perhaps fitting that both "Stan Lee" and "Jack Kirby" started out as names that covered secret identities. Lee was born Stanley Martin Lieber in 1922 in New York City, and was the son of Romanian immigrants. Always a voracious reader, he had ambitions to be a writer, and at the age of seventeen he took a job with Timely Publications, which was run by his cousin by marriage, Martin Goodman. Timely was then making the shift from turning out pulp magazines—the popular 1930s format that offered an escape-hungry Depression-era public quickly-written, more often than not hack written, genre fiction published on cheap, rough paper— to the fledgling format of comic books.

Signing on as a coffee runner, errand boy, and occasional proofreader, Lieber soon received the comics industry's traditional newcomer assignment: writing the text filler pages in between the graphic stories that were a necessity in order for comic books to meet the U.S. Post Office's definition of second class (i.e., cheaper) mailing status. Usually skipped over by readers who were anxious to get to the next graphic page, text fillers nevertheless launched the careers of several notable 20th-century writers, including crime novelist Mickey Spillane and science fiction writer Harry Harrison. "Stan Lee," the name under which Lieber signed his first story, was derived through separating the syllables of his first name. Within a year, Lee would be moved into the editor's chair at Timely, which over the next two decades would transform into Atlas Publications, and then later into Marvel.

(Top) Stan Lee, seen here circa 1965, has good reason to smile: the renaissance of Marvel Comics was underway.

(Middle) Prose fillers like this one – Stan Lee's first comic book story – were necessary for comics to qualify for reduced postage rates. Lee's debut tale appeared in *Captain America* #3 (May 1941).

(Bottom) The protean Jack Kirby hard at work on a panel in the late 1940s. (Photo courtesy John Morrow)

(Top) Jack Kirby during his Marvel years, in characteristic pose, but without his trademark cigar. (Photo courtesy John Morrow)

(Above) Stan "The Man," circa 1980, proudly shows off bits of his legacy.

Similarly, Jacob Kurtzburg was born of immigrant parents in New York City, in 1917. As a teen Kurtzburg worked in the New York–based Max Fleischer animation studios, which was then the short cartoon home of "Betty Boop" and "Popeye," as an in-betweener—an artist who fills in the drawings between key expression or movement poses. After a short stint drawing newspaper strips, Kurtzburg entered the comic book field in 1939 and stayed there for the rest of his life, mostly as a freelancer, though in the early 1940s he briefly served as Timely's art director. Always prolific, the young artist signed his work with several different pseudonyms, including "Jack Curtis" and "Jack Cortez," but "Jack Kirby" was the one that stuck.

While not a household name to the public at large, within the comics industry Kirby is considered a giant; the King of Comic Books and perhaps the most talented and influential graphic artist who ever put pencil to panel. "Jack had all the qualities you could want in a collaborator," says Stan Lee today. "He was the most dependable person you could ever find, and nothing was too difficult for him. No matter what the story was, no matter what had to be drawn, and no matter how complex it was, he found a way to do it. And he was fast! I don't think he ever turned in a job where I would say, 'Oh, gee, he must have batted this out.' Whatever he did, it was his best."

Writer and comic book historian Mark Evanier, who was both a friend and a fan of Kirby's, adds: "He had the most amazing brain and the ability to see through many levels and make odd connections and put things together. Ideas just poured out of the guy, so no matter what Stan and he decided the story was about, Jack would start throwing in new inventions, new villains, and supporting characters."

Kirby's graphic style set the pattern for Marvel in the sixties: vigorous, dramatic, and powerful. Kirby panels were so cleanly staged and focused and his characters so charged with kinetic energy, that reading

one of his stories was often a cinematic experience—
something that is no coincidence, according to his son,
Neal Kirby. "He kind of saw comic books as movies in
book form," Kirby says. "He probably wouldn't be
surprised about [Marvel characters] being successes as
movies." Kirby had an equal facility for creating inani-
mate objects, such as machines, vehicles, and devices.
Even the helmets on his characters costumes were
dramatically distinctive.

While they did not work together exclusively, the
teaming of Kirby and Lee was a meeting of two hugely
imaginative minds, and they sparked off each other.
While Lee would remain with the company to the close
of the century, his name becoming virtually synonymous
with Marvel Comics, Kirby's primary involvement with
Marvel lasted until 1970, at which time he walked out
of the company in a financial dispute. He would occasionally return for a project, most notably in 1978 when
he collaborated with Lee for last time on "The Silver
Surfer," a book-length work that pioneered the concept
of the graphic novel. When Kirby died in 1994, he was
secure in the knowledge that his contributions as an
artist would be recognized by legions of fans. "I don't
think there's any doubt that he understood his impact,"
says his son Neal.

THE BIG BANG

Back in the early sixties, that impact was just beginning
to be appreciated. The efforts of Lee and Kirby, along
with artists Steve Ditko and Don Heck, had pulled the
newly rechristened Marvel Comics out of the doldrums
of the 1950s—a time that was also marked by the punishing, and in retrospect ridiculous, Senate hearings that
strove to condemn comic books as a source for juvenile
delinquency. Starting with *The Fantastic Four*, which
appeared in 1961 and introduced the idea of a Super
Hero team with occasional personality conflicts, and
continuing with such characters as "Spider-Man," created by Lee and Ditko, "The Incredible Hulk" (Lee and

The King in Autumn: Jack Kirby in the 1970s poses next to one of his most enduring creations. (Photo courtesy John Morrow)

(Top) Stan Lee flashes the "X-salute" at the *X2* premiere in 2003. (Photo Steve Granitz/WireImage.com)

(Above) Jack Kirby's kinetic artwork sometimes threatened to burst through the panels.

Kirby), "Iron Man" (Lee, Heck, and Lee's brother Larry Lieber), and "The Mighty Thor" (Lee and Kirby again), Marvel sparked a Silver Age renaissance of comic books.

Lee had always been blessed with a fertile, facile imagination, but now he was spinning tales faster than Scheherazade. Still, nothing succeeds like success, so in 1963, Martin Goodman suggested to Lee that the sales of *The Fantastic Four* were good enough to warrant the creation of a brand new Super Hero team. "He probably said to me, 'Maybe lightning will strike twice,'" Lee recalls. There was only one problem: Lee dreaded developing teams. "I hate doing teams because if there are a lot of characters, you've got to figure out how each of them got his or her super powers," he says. "Now, 'The Fantastic Four' was easy, they were all hit by cosmic rays, but I couldn't have another team hit by cosmic rays." After thinking about it, Lee came up with a solution, or, as he jokingly puts it, "I took the cowardly way out." The new Super Heroes were simply born that way. They were mutants.

He then set out to find more ways to make the new team different. "I made them teenagers because The Fantastic Four were all adults," he says. "Now I had to find a way to bring them together. Then I figured: what if there was a man who gathers mutants together when they're young, and tries to teach them to live with their abilities?"

Building the idea little by little, Lee got a crucial piece of the puzzle by thinking about the characters' differences from the normal human race. Lee states, "The thought occurred to me, 'Wow, if they're different from other people, I'm going to let them be persecuted, and have people fear them and hate them because people generally end up fearing and hating anybody who's different, especially anybody who seems to have greater ability.'" This sentiment is presented in the very first issue of *X-Men*, which has the mysterious Professor X telling his teenage charges: "*When I was young, normal people feared me, distrusted me. I realized the human race is not yet ready to accept those with extra powers!*"

Lee went back to Goodman to pitch his concept. "When I told Martin about it, he asked what the name would be," Lee says. "I said I wanted to call it '*The Mutants.*' He said, 'You can't call it "*The Mutants,*" our readers won't know what a mutant is!'" Now Lee had to come up with a new name, and fast. Since he had decided that the leader of the group would be called "Professor Xavier," with the first letter stressed—*X-avier* as opposed to *Zavier*—he then made the connection that his mutant characters had an *X*-tra power over normal humans, and were under the tutelage of "Professor X" (whose given name of "Charles Xavier" would not be fully revealed for several issues) and therefore, the group became the X-Men.

Despite the fact that Kirby was already shouldering a near superhuman workload, regularly turning out stories for *The Fantastic Four, The Mighty Thor, The Incredible Hulk,* and *Sgt. Fury and His Howling Commandos,* Lee gave him the assignment for the new book, and the artist began designing the characters. First was the enigmatic Professor X, whose completely bald cranium held a powerful intellect and unique telepathic ability. The professor had one more signature trait: he was confined to a wheelchair.

"I figured, if he's going to have a mental power, but he's still just walking around like everybody else, it won't look as good visually," Lee says. "I thought the wheel-chair was very good for a guy who was really the most powerful of all the X-Men, because of his mental prowess, and yet he's physically the weakest. I liked that." His disability would be explained within the story-line with the revelation that he was injured while bat-tling a villain named "Lucifer." As for Xavier's lack of hair, baldness had long been considered a visual metaphor for genius, whether real and beneficent as in the case of William Shakespeare or fictional and evil, as in Sax Rohmer's diabolical Dr. Fu Manchu.

There were several possible precedents for Professor X floating around in the creative ether of the time. One was the 1932 horror film *Doctor X,* in which the myste-

(Top) The demure Jean Grey, a.k.a. Marvel Girl, reports for class in *X-Men* #1.

(Above) Lionel Atwill as the mysterious, mansion-bound Dr. Xavier in the classic 1933 shocker *Doctor X* may have been an influence for Professor X. (Photo courtesy Hollywood Book & Poster Co.)

(Opposite) The ominously named Lucifer – here seen fighting both the X-Men and the Avengers (in *X-Men* #9, January 1965) – was responsible for crippling Professor X. (pencils Jack Kirby, inks Chic Stone).

rious title scientist is really "Dr. Jerry Xavier" (played by classic movie villain Lionel Atwill), though he has nothing to do with mutants or special powers, beyond the heightened ability to look suspicious. His character would be exhumed—literally—in a nearly unrelated 1939 follow-up, *The Return of Doctor X*, which featured a pasty-faced Humphrey Bogart who might or might not be the regenerated form of the mad scientist. Some thirty years later, there was Roger Corman's highly regarded science-fiction film *X: The Man With X-Ray Eyes*, which featured Ray Milland as "Dr. James Xavier," who creates a serum that gives him vision extending into the cosmos. While sometimes cited as a direct source of inspiration for *X-Men*, particularly for the character of "Cyclops," who has a similarly penetrating vision, the connection may be more coincidental, since the film was not released until mid-September 1963, by which time the first issue of *X-Men* was already on the stands.

Whatever its derivation, the title *X-Men* resonated with the publisher – much to Lee's amusement. "When I told Martin the name he said, 'Okay, that's fine,'" Lee says. "And as I walked out of the office I couldn't help laughing to myself. I thought, if our readers wouldn't know what a mutant is, how would they know what an *X-Man* is? But I had my title, and I didn't want to make waves." The name also conveniently ignored the fact that not all members of the new team were men – and more than four decades later, it is still being ignored.

GIFTED YOUNGSTERS

From the beginning, Professor X operated out of the exclusive private school of his own creation where he teaches his "gifted youngsters" not only how to control and refine their powers, but how to use them for the benefit of mankind. While in the early years, the school's location was identified simply as in Westchester County, New York, over the years its address has become much more specific. The Xavier School for Gifted Youngsters can be found at 1407 Graymalkin Lane in the town of Salem Center, which is located forty miles north of

(Top) That's Humphrey Bogart looking uncomfortable under the clown white from the 1939 *The Return of Dr. X*, yet another take on the Dr. X character. (Photo courtesy Hollywood Book & Poster Co.).

(Middle) No, it's not Jean Grey and Scott Summers in middle-age, it's Diana Van der Vlis and Ray Milland in 1963's *X-The Man With X-Ray Eyes*. (Photo courtesy Hollywood Book & Poster Co.)

(Bottom) The face that launched a Super Hero? Hardly, though early film comedian Slim Summerville's name was borrowed for Cyclops' first secret identity, "Slim Summers." (Photo courtesy Hollywood Book & Poster Co.)

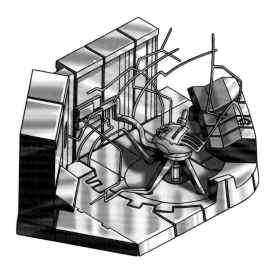

(Top) One of the many graphic interpretations of Professor X's mutant-locating device Cerebro.

(Middle) Scott Summers/Cyclops receives his official status as second in command.

(Bottom) The first class of Professor Xavier's School for Gifted Students get their diplomas in *X-Men* #7 (September 1964). Three guesses who was class president. (Pencils Jack Kirby, inks Chic Stone).

Manhattan, just this side of the Connecticut border, situated on an estate that was there before the Revolutionary War. Professor X identifies the prospective students through a machine called "Cerebro," which can detect mutant brain waves. Cerebro's other function is to serve as early warning system that a mutant menace is somewhere in the area.

The first recruited for this group is "Slim Summers," who emits a powerful single ray from his eyes, which must be covered at all times, either by a special visor or, when in civvies, heavy sunglasses, and goes by the code name Cyclops. "I loved the idea of the eyes," says Lee, "because the poor guy always had to wear those glasses, and he was afraid he'd accidentally hurt somebody, which gave him a little more dimension than the average cardboard hero. I always thought he would be second in command, he was the most sober and level-headed."

Slim would embody the very first of countless alterations that would characterize the X-Universe, becoming "Scott" Summers in issue #3 (January 1964). While "Slim" would occasionally appear in different contexts as either a nickname or alternate reality identification, he would remain Scott from that point on. The explanation, according to Lee, is that it was one of those confusing matters that sometimes occur while working at top speed turning out comic books stories. But the inspiration for the character's initial should be apparent to anyone of Lee's generation. "Years ago there was an actor and comedian named Slim Summerville, and when I gave [Cyclops] the name Summers, and I needed a first name for him, I thought, 'Why not?'" Lee says. Given that Slim Summerville, a former comic for Mack Sennett in the days of silent film, was not the heroic type—in fact, he resembled a basset hound with bangs—the name change was probably for the best. At various times throughout the decades, Cyclops would indeed take on the leadership role of the team, the first time in *X-Men* issue #7 (September 1964), after Professor X departs to take care of unspecified "unfinished tasks."

X-TREME CLOSEUP
Cyclops
THE INDISPENSIBLE X-MAN

"I'm an X-Man, pure and simple."
– Scott Summers, a.k.a. Cyclops

Despite his dangerous laser-like gaze, which can only be contained through a special ruby quartz lens, Cyclops is not the flashiest or most flamboyant of the X-Men. He is, in fact, the most adult of the group: solid, responsible, and dutiful to a fault, and not much in the humor department, as his teammates sometimes enjoy pointing out. But his constant presence throughout the various mutant teamings, often in a leadership position, and the fact that he has appeared in every film and television adaptation, make him the most ubiquitous of all the X-Men.

Scott's stability has stood him well, since an overview of his life and career reveals more endured trauma than can be found in a triage unit. His father, "Christopher Summers," was a major in the U.S. Air Force, where he served as a test pilot. While flying with his entire family—wife Katherine, Scott, and younger son Alex—Christopher's plane was shot down by representatives of the alien "Shi'ar Empire." The parents were believed killed, though the boys escaped and were raised separately. Even though Scott would eventually be reunited with his real father, who did not die in the crash, Professor X remains his true father figure.

Scott's affection for Jean Grey goes back practically to the moment they met, and endured throughout a never-ending parade of rivals. The most serious of these was "Madelyn Prior," a lookalike for Jean whom Scott would wed while Jean was believed dead. It would eventually be revealed, however, that Jean was not dead after all; what's more, Madelyn was not simply a double for her, but an actual biological clone! Upon learning all this Scott left Madelyn—who subsequently went mad and became the "Goblin Queen"—and returned to Jean, marrying her at long last in 1994.

Their attempt at happiness was ruined yet again when, under the influence of master villain "Apocalypse," Scott began an affair with "Emma Frost," also known as "The White Queen." Not long afterwards, Jean was killed in battle. Distraught, Scott nonetheless remained with Emma, who of late has been on the good side of mutantcy, and the two were put in charge of the Xavier School for Gifted Students.

X-Men come and X-Men go, but Cyclops remains the team's anchor.

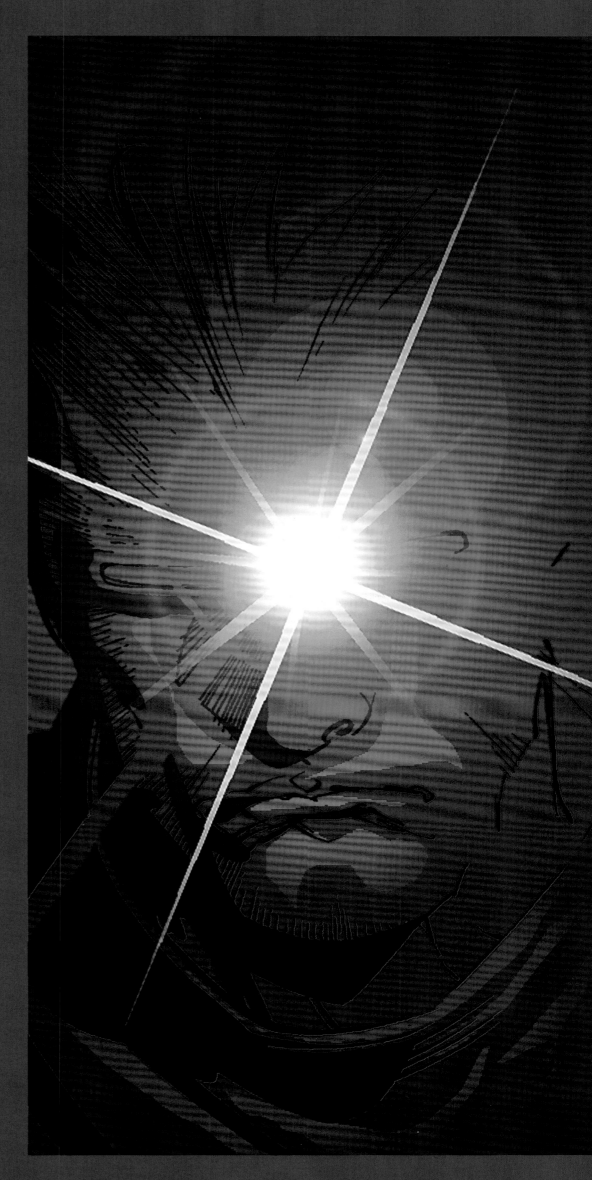

(Opposite) After the longest courtship in comics, Scott and Jean finally got married in *X-Men* (second series) #30. (March 1994; pencils Andy Kubert).

(Top) Cyclops charging into action.

(Above) Even comic characters have real life problems. Here Jean Grey catches Scott in a compromising position with Emma Frost, in *New X-Men* #139. (April 2003; pencils Phil Jimenez)

(Right) Cyclops fires his single-beam optic blast.

The sole X-*woman* in the beginning was "Jean Grey," a knockout redhead with strong telekinetic powers who went by the name "Marvel Girl." She had an equally powerful effect on her male teammates, much of whose juvenile banter was directed toward her (even Professor X found himself falling for her!) With time Jean would soon lose the Marvel Girl moniker and simply go by her real name, after which she would endure a long string of character and personality shifts that will be chronicled later. Jean would also set the record for the most deaths and rebirths of any character in the Marvel Universe.

Apelike "Hank McCoy," who is also known as "The Beast," a nickname he acquired as a high school football star because of his gigantic hands and feet and acrobatic agility, is the oldest of the teen group; presumably nineteen. In his first appearance, he speaks with the same kind of lazy, slangy English employed by the Fantastic Four's Ben Grimm, but that would soon change. Before long, the Beast would become the most intellectual of all the X-Men, rivaling even Professor X himself. "I wanted the Beast, who would appear to be the most bestial, to have a great vocabulary and be very erudite, intelligent, and well educated," Lee says. "I wanted him to be the opposite of his name." In time Hank McCoy would become less apelike and begin to wear glasses, and develop scientific specialties in biochemistry and genetics research. The biggest change for the Beast, however, would take place in *Amazing Adventures* #11 (1971), in an issue guest-starring the X-Men: while working as a staff scientist at an outfit called the Brand Corporation, which specialized in genetics research, Hank—now Dr. Henry McCoy—ingests a mutation-inducing serum that he had created, in order to prevent its theft. As a result, he turns gray, furry, and more bestial than ever. The gray quickly gives way to blue, and this image characterizes the Beast from then on, with degrees of ferocity depending on the artist. Only during his stint with the spin-off group "X-Factor" in the 1980s did he revert to human form, and then only briefly.

(Top) It sounded like a good idea: Dr. Henry McCoy ingests the chemical that transforms him into his blue and furry "New Beast" form in *Amazing Adventures* #11. (1971; pencils Gil Kane)

(Middle) The Beast at his most bestial, as rendered by artist Brian Hitch.

(Bottom) The original, happy-go-lucky Beast, whose feet were as big as his brain. (Pencils Jack Kirby)

(Opposite) Henry "the Beast" McCoy's brilliance as a chemist is captured in this moody rendering by Paul Smith.

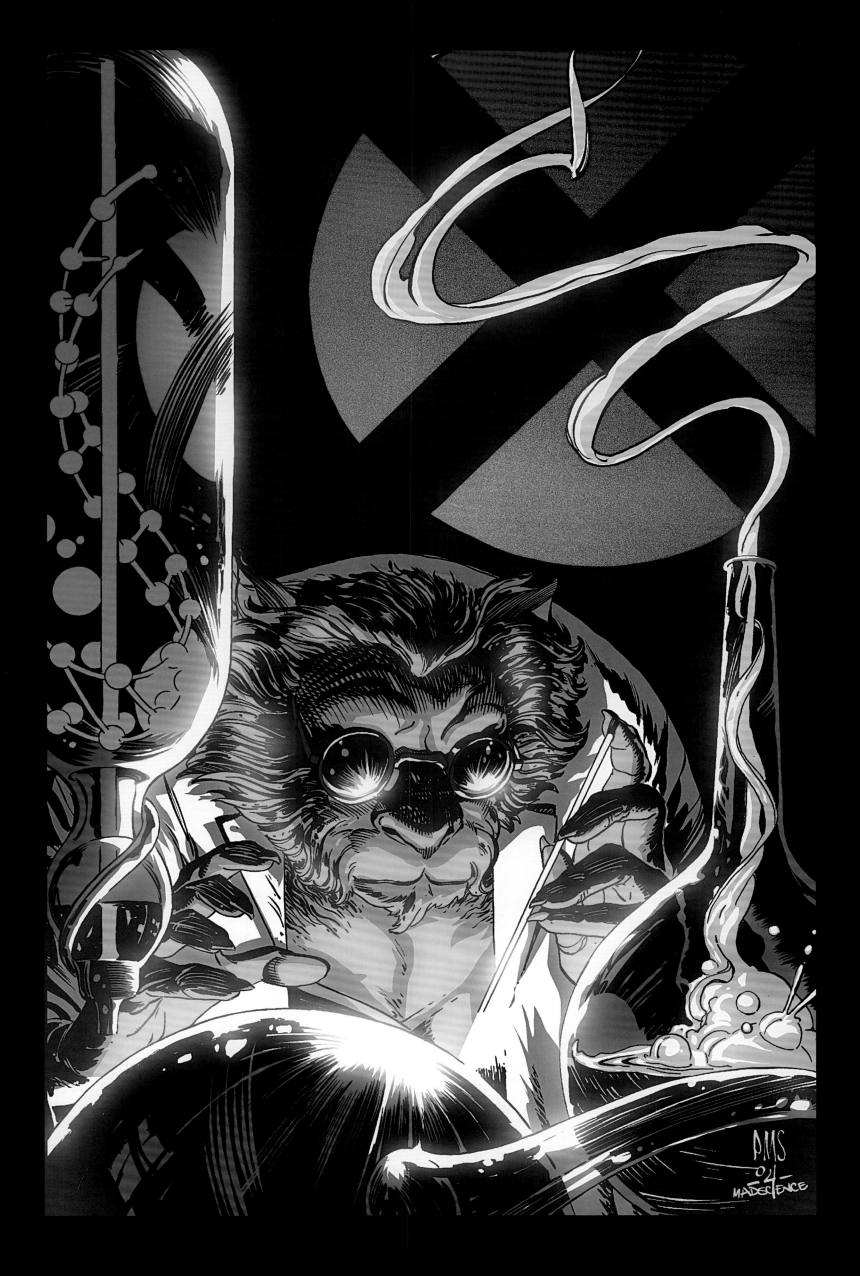

The youngest member of the original group was 16-year-old Bobby Drake, also known as "Iceman," and for good reason: he could transform his body completely into ice, use ice as a defensive weapon, and even freeze the air around him, making it uncomfortably cold for anyone within his proximity. Brash by nature, Iceman was also the most visually distinctive from his teammates: while they each wore variations on identical dark blue jumpsuits with bright yellow tabards and trunks, bound at the waste by a yellow belt bearing an "X" on the buckle, Iceman when powered up had no Super Hero costume at all, except for yellow topped boots. In the earliest issues he tended to resemble a humanoid pile of cottage cheese, but with time, he smoothed out and cast a sleeker, more ice-like figure. In later years, Iceman would also serve with secondary groups X-Factor and "The Defenders."

Every school, it seems, has to have an overbearing rich kid, and within the Xavier School it was Warren Worthington III, otherwise known as "The Angel." There had already been a Super Hero by that name that had appeared in *Marvel Comics* #1 in 1939. But outside of the fact that both wore costumes of blue and yellow, there was no similarity. The X-Men's Angel had two large, downy white wings growing out of his back, which enabled him to fly.

The first X-Men adventure featured another gimmick that would become as famous as the teammates themselves: the hyper-powered gymnasium where the team would train against surprise mechanical threats that appeared to come out of nowhere, known as the Danger Room. "The idea of the Danger Room was Jack's," Lee says. "I simply said they had a place where they would practice and work out, but when he actually drew the Danger Room with all those things, that was brilliant."

Just like the Xavier School in general was more than simply a safe haven for mutants, the Danger Room was for more that just a work-out gym. It was a training facility providing the necessary combat skills, both physical and mental, that they will need to face certain others

(Top) The early Iceman looked a bit like humanoid cottage cheese.

(Above) Under Cyclops' coaching, Bobby Drake/Iceman eventually learned to metamorphose into a sleeker, more crystalline figure.

(Opposite, top) Iceman propelled himself on a self-created ice slide.

(Opposite, bottom) A cool Bobby Drake demonstrates the freezing transformation into Iceman.

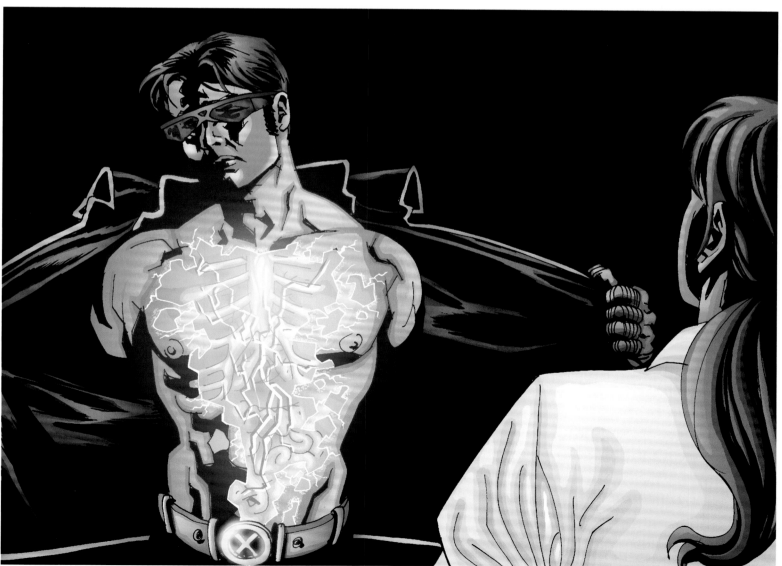

X-TREME CLOSEUP
The Angel
CHANGES FLY ON SWIFT WINGS

"Having a pair of wings can be more trouble than you'd guess."
— Warren Worthington III, a.k.a. The Angel

While not as well known or as frequently used as his teammates, the Angel remains one of Stan Lee's favorites, a fact that can be deduced by his name. Lee had a penchant for giving his primary characters alliterative names, as a way of remembering them: Reed Richards and Sue Storm (of The Fantastic Four), Peter Parker (Spider-Man), Stephen Strange (Dr, Strange), Bruce Banner (The Incredible Hulk) and Matt Murdock (Daredevil) are all in this club, as are X-Men's Scott Summers, and…Warren Worthington.

As his name—or at least his designation as "the Third"—implies, Worthington hails from a wealthy family. Handsome and carefree, he was also a bit of a show-off with a tendency toward overconfidence – a trait that sometimes hindered his performance as a hero. His body has birdlike characteristics as well as human, and not just his powerful, luxurious white wings. He also has lightweight bones that aid him in flight.

The Angel is something of a clotheshorse, which was reflected in the number of his costume changes. His early matching yellow-and-blue outfit gave way to more colorful variations, then to a more distinctive navy-and-white number with a halo emblazoned on the crest. By the time he reunited with his original teammates for the offshoot group X-Factor in 1986, his costume had changed to a red suit with a huge white X crossing his torso. More serious changes, though, would be in store. At one point the Angel's wings would be seriously injured during a battle, leading to their amputation. His super-identity gone, Worthington became desperately depressed, which opened the way for Apocalypse (who was always on the prowl for ways to gain control over individual X-Men) to provide "treatment" for him: a painful genetic process that did indeed produce new wings, albeit metallic ones, but it also turned his skin blue. After that, for a time, he was a fallen Angel, serving as one of Apocalypse's Four Horsemen under the name "Death." Later he emerged as "Dark Angel," and in yet another variation on the theme, appeared in the late 1990s alternate world storyline of Mutant X as "The Fallen," a leather-winged, fire-breathing entity. But it was not long before he rejoined the side of right, and in recent years he has regenerated natural wings out of the synthetic ones and has become flesh-toned yet again.

Today Warren Worthington III is better known under his new name, "Archangel," which proves that promotions can occur even in the realm of Super Heroes.

(Opposite, top left) While in street clothes, Warren Worthington bound his Angel wings in a harness. "That was Jack (Kirby)'s idea and it was brilliant," says Stan Lee. (Pencils Kirby).

(Opposite, top right) One of the many costume variations for the Angel—masked and multi-colored—as rendered by artist George Tuska.

(Opposite, bottom) The Angel, in his *X-Factor* costume, gets his wings clipped. His injuries would necessitate amputation.

(Top) No X-Man altered in appearance more than the Angel, who here is in his blue form with metallic wings.

(Above) The modern-day Angel as depicted in *Ultimate X-Men*.

(Right) The Angel transformed into Archangel, still blue, but once more with organic wings.

of their kind, who did not view conventional humans kindly in actual battle.

If the opposing mutants were evil, they were not entirely without provocation. "While the good mutants are mistreated by average humans, they're trying to figure out how we can all get along together," explains Lee. "But when the bad mutants are mistreated by average humans, they resent it, they want to strike back and punish the humans."

Magneto, who can control and emit waves of magnetic energy, is of course front and center in this class of mutant. In his first appearance, Magneto—clad in a crimson and purple costume, with a horned peekaboo helmet that protects his mind from Xavier's telepathy—is not shy about stating his superiority over the human race, whom he feels has lost the right to hold dominion over the earth. Referring to himself repeatedly as "the miraculous Magneto," he similarly declares Mutantkind to be a whole new species, *homo superior.*

To aid him, Magneto has assembled a team of his own, the Brotherhood of Evil Mutants, for which he was constantly recruiting. Even the Sub-Mariner got into the act in issue #6, having been convinced by Magneto to join his cause against humanity. While it was almost a requirement that every new Marvel Super Hero or team of the 1960s square off against Prince Namor, it was particularly fitting for him to face the X-Men, since for the first time, Namor's uniqueness was equated with mutantcy.

In many ways, Magneto is yin to Charles Xavier's yang. Of roughly equal power and intellect, their philosophies ultimately pulled them in opposite directions. Thinking ahead into the future, Lee had in mind a startling connection between the leader of the X-Men and the leader of the Evil Mutants: "I always thought I would end up having Professor X and Magneto turn out to be brothers," Lee reveals. Even without the blood relationship, though, it was clear that Xavier and Magneto shared some kind of common bond, despite their being

(Top) Jack Kirby had a particular talent for creating devices. Here he puts the Angel through his paces in the Danger Room.

(Above) Artist Jim Calafiore's depiction of a modern, state-of-the-art Danger Room, in which the mechanics are augmented by hologramic projections.

(Opposite, top) The Angel (rear left) in his bad period, as the Horseman "Death." (Pencils Patrick Zircher)

(Opposite, bottom) Hank and Bobby experience the dark side of human nature in *X-Men* #8 (November 1964), prompting Hank to leave the group...but not for long. (Pencils Jack Kirby, inks Chic Stone)

sworn enemies. As their personal histories evolved, it would be revealed that they had once been close friends.

MUTANTS WITH A MESSAGE

Over the years, some have read a socio-political meaning into this complex relationship between these two powerful leaders, seeing the struggle between non-violent cooperation and bitter confrontation as nothing less than a fantastical allegory to the then-growing American civil rights movement, with the passive, peaceful Professor Xavier representing the Reverend Martin Luther King Jr., and the righteous, but more militant, Magneto standing in for Malcolm X. Just the use of the letter *X* has fueled that argument over the years. But while *X-Men* in its various incarnations over the years would capitalize on politically charged subjects and storylines, Lee says that the civil rights analogy was not a conscious one … at least not at first.

"I was not influenced by that at all," Lee states. "However, once I had the characters worked out, and the minute I said I'm going to have society fear and hate them, I realized that this really was symbolic of the bigotry that is practiced in our society, and I thought this could be a metaphor for what was going on with the way people treated the blacks and the Latinos and the Jews and the Catholics and so forth. But I didn't plan it that way in the beginning."

Indeed, in the first issue of *X-Men*, the young heroes are greeted by the government and the public with awe and respect, as beings that are not so much threatening as "uncanny" – the adjective that would before long become part of their title. But as early as issue #8, (November 1964), Hank and Bobby are set upon and chased by an angry mob of mutant haters and barely escape.

X-Men was popular enough to go from a bi-monthly publication to monthly in late 1965. Shortly thereafter, Jack Kirby's direct involvement with the book, outside of cover art, largely ended. Kirby had created the look of

Pencils and Inks

Like animation, comic book art is created in stages: first in pencil, and then in ink and color. But unlike animation, comic book inking is not simply tracing over the drawn pencil line. Inkers are creative entities unto themselves.

The pencil artist is not simply responsible for drawing in the figures and action, he (or she) also stages of the story within the panels and selects the point-of-view "camera angles" from which it will be seen. Under the Marvel method, the pencilers contribute to the actual plotting and character population of the story, rather than simply illustrating a script.

The inkers then take those pencil drawings and render them in hard black lines and shading, and in the process add their own artistic sensibilities to the way a scene is detailed. It is quite possible for the artwork from one pencil artist to be rendered into two distinctive graphic looks by two different inkers.

In some instances, the inking greatly enhances the pencil art. "There are guys who really kind of draw in the ink stage and only become excited when they ink themselves," says comic book historian Mark Evanier. But time and money constraints usually did not allow for self-inked art pages, meaning that a different—and often brilliant—hand wielded the mighty pen.

(Above) The work of dynamic artist Jim Steranko was a welcome addition to the X-Universe in the late 1960s, but he stayed only three issues.

(Left) Artist Werner Roth's action work, such as this image of Banshee from *X-Men* #35 (August 1967; inks Dan Adkins), just wasn't up to Kirby fans' expectations.

(Above) Havok – in black costume and atomic crown – seen here in *X-Men* #138 (October 1980) was never part of the core group, despite being Cyclops' brother. (Pencils John Byrne, inks Terry Austin)

(Right) Polaris, a.k.a. Lorna Dane, was the longtime love interest of Havok. Some guys go for greenettes.

SO TELL ME, *TAI--* --THIS WHERE YOU CONSCIENTIOUSLY ROUND UP ALL THE "USUAL SUSPECTS"?

AN EXERCISE IN FUTILITY, FRIEND *PATCH--*

--EITHER AS SERIOUS SUGGESTION...

... OR AN ATTEMPT AT HUMOR.

IN THIS INSTANCE, I'LL WAGER WE COULD INTERROGATE EVERY "SUSPECT" IN MADRIPOOR...

...AND LEARN NOTHING.

AND PLEASE, SPARE ME THE TRADITIONAL: "I JUST HAPPENED TO BE IN THE NEIGHBORHOOD."

I MIGHT AS PERTINENTLY INQUIRE, ON THE OTHER HAND, WHAT *YOU* ARE DOING HERE?

HEARD THE RADIO CALL REQUESTING YOUR PRESENCE.

FIGURED ANYTHING WORTH DRAGGING YOU OUTTA BED WAS WORTH A LOOK-SEE.

ANY OBJECTIONS TO MY TAKING A GANDER AT THE BODY?

CHIEF-- WHY DO YOU ALLOW THAT FOREIGNER SUCH LIBERTIES?!

BECAUSE, DETECTIVE, IN MATTERS SUCH AS THESE...

"...PATCH HAS A SPECIAL-- I MIGHT SAY, UNIQUE-- EXPERTISE."

I LIKED RANJA.

HE KNEW MORE BAWDY SONGS EVEN THAN ME.

AND WAS AS DEADLY AT POKER...

... AS CHESS.

HE USED PEOPLE-- THAT WAS HIS JOB--

--BUT HE TRIED ALONG THE WAY TO HURT AS FEW AS POSSIBLE, AND HELP AS MANY.

HAD NO STYLE IN THOSE DAYS...

...AN' LESS KNOW-LEDGE.

FIGURED I'D KEEP POUNDING--HARD AN' FAST AS I COULD..."TIL SOMETHING BROKE.

K-R-U-S-H

NEVER IMAGINED IT'D BE ME.

NO UNBREAKABLE ADAMANTIUM REINFORCED BONES, THEN...

...NO CLAWS.

I WAS AS CLOSE TO HUMAN AS I EVER CAME.

BUT I WAS TOUGH.

AS WELL AS TOO FLAMIN DUMB TO REALIZE HOW MUCH TROUBLE I WAS IN.

MADE SABRE-TOOTH'S DAY...

ARRRRGH

...TO TEACH ME.

NOW

MEMORY HURTS MORE'N THE ORIGINAL WOUNDS.

NIGHT'S QUIET...

...AS THOUGH THE WHOLE CITY'S HOLDIN' ITS BREATH.

WE'RE ALL OF US WAITIN'.

THIS IS THE PART I HATE.

TOO MUCH IMAGINATION.

TOO MUCH EXPERIENCE.

SCREAM...!

X-Men and provided the original pencil artwork, which had been inked by such artists as Paul Reinman, Chic Stone, and Dick Ayers. But of late he had been turning his primary attention to other titles, while providing only layouts—sketched plot breakdowns, often with a first page and some individual panels drawn in detail—for *X-Men*. Other artists, such as Alex Toth and Werner Roth, would then take these layouts and finish them as the pencil artwork.

Kirby's departure in 1966 signaled the beginning of a slump in popularity for the original *X-Men*. Lee himself lost interest in writing the book when Kirby moved on and turned the scripting over to Roy Thomas, a young writer and first-generation comic book fan who had joined Marvel in 1965. Thomas was capable and creative, and soon found himself working with veteran artist Werner Roth. Roth, however, just wasn't up to paving the action-filled trails blazed by Kirby.

"Werner Roth was a fine artist, but he was also a guy who just did very simple work without a lot of that Kirby exaggeration," says writer/historian Evanier. "It wasn't just that he didn't draw like Jack, he didn't *think* like Jack." Roth's work was crisp and handsome, and he had a true talent for drawing women, but his pages lacked the kind of panel-to-panel forward propulsion that readers had come to expect. Compared to Kirby's hyperkinetic pages, Roth's looked like superbly rendered ViewMaster images. Other artists followed, including Don Heck and Jim Steranko, and some new characters were introduced to try and juice up the series, some of whom would become key players in the future X-Men tapestry. The most notable of these were "Polaris," a.k.a "Lorna Dane," who first appeared in *X-Men* issue #49, and "Havok," who was introduced in issue #54.

The green-haired Polaris had similar control over electromagnetism as had Magneto—in fact, for a while, she believed that she was his daughter. Polaris would hover in and around the X-Men, from then on, most often in tandem with Havok, with whom she would fall in love.

(Prevoius spread) Different inkers can sometimes provide entirely different looks to the same penciler's work. Artist John Buscema penciled both pages, but Al Williamson's crosshatch inking style (left, from *Wolverine* #4, February 1989), gives it a moody, almost noirish atmosphere. However, Bill Sienkiewicz's inks (left, from *Wolverine* #10, August 1989), give the pencils a sketchy, raw look.

(Below) Given this devilish-looking outfit, one might believe that Polaris was a super villain. But despite rumors that she was the daughter of Magneto, she remained on the side of good.

(Opposite) Havok's costume changed in later years, though his power—shooting blasts of heat from his hands—remained the same.

Havok, whose costume was a rare jet black color and included an atom-like crown around his head, was able to absorb cosmic energy and shoot powerful heat blasts from his body. That his powers were somewhat akin to Cyclops' is understandable, since Havok is in reality "Alex Summers," Scott's long-lost brother. The two had been separated as infants and raised separately after their father's plane crash, and would only rediscover each other as young adults. Alex's powers first emerged after being trapped by a villainous mutant called the "Living Pharoah," who used the power to turn into the "Living Monolith." It was a short-lived transformation, however, and Alex was ultimately released and signed up with the X-Men as an adjunct team member. Over the decades he and Lorna would have a long-running on-again-off-again relationship that almost, but not quite, made it to the altar.

THE END OF THE X-MEN?

As sales for the title waned, Marvel brought in artist Neal Adams to further energize the book. Adams had entered the comic book field while still in his teens (he was born in 1941 in New York) and would become one of the most accomplished comic book artists of all time, bringing a modern feel and a sense of photojournalistic dynamism to his panels. Under his tenure as penciler, the popularity and sales of *X-Men* did pick up a bit, but not to the level of the title's mid-1960s peak period.

After Adams left the series he was replaced by artist Sal Buscema (whose brother John was also a top Marvel artist), but by then the end seemed near. "Sal did one issue, but then they pulled the plug before we had a chance to show if we could survive without Neal [Adams]," says Roy Thomas. Publisher Goodman had decided that it was time to do what Magneto and his Evil Mutants could not accomplish: stop the *X-Men*.

Sort of.

In an unusual move, Goodman ordered that no new X-Men stories were to be created, but the title itself did not stop. Starting with issue #67 (April 1970), *X-Men*

(Above and opposite) Artist Neal Adams brought a dynamic, visceral graphic style to the pages of *X-Men* that was augmented by his revolutionary photo-montage manner of laying out the panels Four decades later the look remains startlingly modern. (*X-Men #60*, September 1969. Pencils Neal Adams, inks Tom Palmer)

consisted of reprints of earlier issues, mostly from the Lee/Kirby era. "Obviously it had been selling better at the end," theorizes Thomas, "because Goodman ordinarily didn't bring back things and start reprinting books he had just cancelled. He must have felt there was *something* there." Returning to a bi-monthly title, *X-Men* carried on as reprints (covering original issues #12 through #45) until issue #93. Then in 1975, the combination of a new creative team, new members, and a whole new thrust, brought the X-Men back … with a vengeance.

Professor X

"Mutation: it is the key to our evolution."
– Charles Xavier

Without Charles Francis Xavier, Ph.D., there would, of course, be no X-Men. Xavier comes from a family of scientists: his father, "Brian Xavier," was a nuclear researcher who was killed in the atomic blast at Alamogordo, New Mexico, which Charles remembers as a "fateful holocaust." An associate of the elder Xavier's, "Dr. Kurt Marko," married Brian's widow "Sharon" and raised young Charles, but not well. Marko, who was insanely jealous his colleague, was only interested in possessing what Xavier had – chiefly his wife and assets – though he was destined to lose both. It was Marko who first recognized Charles' powers, and acknowledged them as he, Marko, lay dying, and more or less repentant.

While a graduate student at Oxford (by which point he was already completely bald), Charles would meet a young Scottish noblewoman and propose marriage, but no wedding would take place. After graduation, as a young man, he developed his true calling as a mentor to mutants, while living and working in the Middle East, alongside the man who would become Magneto. In later years, it would also be revealed that during this time in his life Xavier had fallen in love with a woman named 'Gabrielle Haller" while in Israel, an affair that, unbeknownst to him for years, would produce a child.

During his X-Men years, Xavier would fall in love again, this time with "Lilandra," ruler of the intergalactic Shi'ar Empire (the same alien race responsible for shooting down the plane carrying the Summers family), who would likewise become a recurring presence in Xavier's life. In fact, Xavier has visited outer space more than most astronauts, and actually abandoned the X-Men for a time to live there.

Over the decades, Xavier's means of mobility have shifted from a conventional wheelchair to a hover pod, using Shi'ar technology, and on occasion he regained the ability to walk, though usually only temporarily. His emotional state has similarly shifted over the years, with the all-knowing, inscrutable,

What goes around comes around. (Top) Young Charles Xavier is bullied by his stepbrother, Cain Marko (from *X-Men* #12, July 1965, pencils Alex Toth, inks Vince Colletta), but (above) takes the upper hand years later through his telepathic powers (from *X-Men* #13, September 1965; pencils Jay Gavin, inks Joe Sinnott)

(Opposite) Charles Xavier lost the use of his legs in a battle with Lucifer, as recorded in *X-Men* #20 (May 1966), a fight that would prompt his creating the X-Men. (Pencils Jay Gavin, inks Dick Ayers)

"THEN, ROUNDING A CORNER..."

SO! IT IS YOU WHO HAVE TYRANNIZED THIS CITY! WHO ARE YOU--AND WHERE ARE YOU FROM?

MY TRUE PURPOSE YOU SHALL NEVER KNOW --BUT, ON THIS PLANET I CALL MYSELF ...LUCIFER!

AND NOW--THAT NAME SHALL BE THE FINAL THING YOU HEAR! PREPARE TO DIE--FOR DARING TO OPPOSE THAT WHICH NO MORTAL CAN COMPREHEND!

THAT GREAT SLAB--- RELEASED FROM ABOVE AT THE TOUCH OF A SWITCH! I-- CAN'T DODGE --IN TIME!

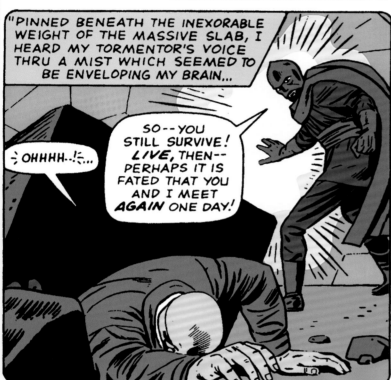

"PINNED BENEATH THE INEXORABLE WEIGHT OF THE MASSIVE SLAB, I HEARD MY TORMENTOR'S VOICE THRU A MIST WHICH SEEMED TO BE ENVELOPING MY BRAIN..."

SO--YOU STILL SURVIVE! LIVE, THEN-- PERHAPS IT IS FATED THAT YOU AND I MEET AGAIN ONE DAY!

OHHHH..!...

"BEFORE MY EYES, A MOMENT BEFORE I LOST CONSCIOUSNESS, LUCIFER DISAPPEARED--INTO THE VERY WALL ITSELF..."

BUT, REMEMBER THIS--IT IS EVER THE STRONG WHO ARE MEANT TO RULE! AND WE ARE THE STRONG!

WHO DOES HE MEAN BY "WE"? IS HE ACTU- ALLY THE HERALD OF A FAR GREATER MENACE--FROM THE STARS?

THEN, AS THE PARALYZED MENTAL MUTANT CONCLUDES HIS STARTLING NARRATION...

THEN--THAT IS HOW YOU LOST THE USE OF YOUR LEGS YEARS AGO!

YES, JEAN! AND, IT IS YET ANOTHER REASON WHY I FOUNDED THE X-MEN!

FOR, I KNEW THAT ONE DAY MANKIND WOULD HAVE TO MEET THE RENEWED THREAT OF LUCIFER!

BUT, EVEN XAVIER DOES NOT FULLY REALIZE JUST HOW URGENT MANKIND'S PLIGHT TRULY IS! FOR, AT THIS VERY SECOND, BENEATH THE SOUTH-WESTERN DESERT...

IT IS DONE! I HAVE CONQUERED THE ONE EARTHLY MIND WHICH MIGHT HAVE DIS- COVERED MY INTENTIONS IN TIME TO THWART THEM!

AND NOW, THE TIME DRAWS NEAR, WHEN MY RACE SHALL FULFILL ITS MISSION--- ITS MAGNIFICENT DESTINY!

Professor X

unflappable sage depicted in the earliest X-Men adventures giving way to an all-too-human figure whose pragmatism is often punctured by periods of anguish, doubt, or brooding. One of the bigger surprises for longtime X-Men fans in recent years would be the revelation that Xavier had a twin sister (whose psyche had managed to live on even after her body was stillborn), the mutant-hating "Cassandra Nova."

Through it all, though, one thing has never changed: Professor X's belief that it is *homo sapiens* and *homo superiors* ultimate destiny is to live together in peace, trust, and equality.

(Right) At times, Professor X traded in his wheelchair for a modernistic pod chair.

(Below) Xavier's lasting love was the alien Lilandra of the Shi'ar.

(Opposite) Oh, what power resides in that cranium…

X-Men

Revitalized

X-Men Revitalized

How fitting it is that one of the most notable characters ever to emerge from the X-Universe is named "Phoenix," since that could also be a metaphor for the series itself. Like that legendary creature, *X-Men* rose from the ashes—at least the doldrums—to become more popular than ever.

(Above) The new X-Men team featured (clockwise from top) Nightcrawler (upside-down), Storm, Wolverine, Kitty Pryde, Professor X, Cyclops and Colossus. (Pencils John Byrne)

(Opposite) Jean Grey rises from "death" to become a child of light and darkness called Phoenix.

This was the result of a confluence of factors, some creative and some purely business related. On the creative side were the contributions of Roy Thomas. Born in Missouri in 1940, Thomas was one of the first widely recognized comic book fans. Prior to his entering the field professionally at the age of 24, he was best known as the creator of the groundbreaking fanzine *Alter Ego*. Upon landing at Marvel in New York, he quickly impressed Stan Lee, who handed him the scripting duties for *X-Men* and *The Avengers*. By 1972, Thomas had ascended to the position of editor-in-chief, with Lee moving behind the publisher's desk. At that point, though, *X-Men* was on auto-pilot, still being put out each month but offering only reprints of stories from its early years. Still, Thomas was unwilling to write off *X-Men* and was looking for ways to bring the characters back, experimenting with ideas such as trying the team in plain clothes for a 1972 issue of *Marvel Team-Up*.

The business impetus came from Al Landau, who was then president of both Marvel and TransWorld, a company that successfully exported comic books to other countries. Landau's idea was to devise a book featuring characters who originated from each of the countries in which the comics were selling well, and then market them directly to those countries. "He said, 'If we could break even with it in this country [the U.S.], we could make decent money by selling to these four or five other countries, like Germany and Canada,'" Thomas recalls. "I had been looking for various ways to bring back the X-Men, so I immediately suggested taking a couple of the old characters and add two, three, or four new ones from these different countries we were looking to sell to, and that way they could wander around these countries looking for mutants." Both Lee and Landau

liked the idea and in 1974 gave Thomas the green light to develop it. He subsequently assigned writer Mike Friedrich and artist Dave Cockrum to get to work on the project, which he described as a "mutant *Blackhawk*," referring to the Golden Age comic book that featured a military hero who was supported by an international (mostly European) group of cohorts.

CALLING ALL MUTANTS!

Cockrum would become a key player in the revitalization of *X-Men*. Of the same comics-loving generation as Thomas (he was born in 1943), Cockrum's pages were filled with clean, dynamic staging that brought out maximum dramatic impact. He also possessed a facility for portraying people in the heat of extreme emotions: Cockrum's figures might be joyously exuberant, or they might be torn with mental or physical anguish, or they might just be enraged, but they were hardly ever passive and placid. *Blackhawk* had actually been one of Cockrum's favorite comics growing up, and he had already worked at D.C. on *Legion of Superheroes*. In fact, he had pitched a new character for the series, a devilish figure called "Nightcrawler." "I had created Nightcrawler when I was still a fan, about three years before he turned up in *X-Men*," Cockrum recalled in a 2000 interview. "The content altered a little, but his creation was totally independent of the X-Men."

Meanwhile, Marvel already had in its ranks a small pool of multi-national characters, which mostly functioned either as opponents to the main heroes or

(Top) Thunderbird (middle), Banshee (second from right), and Sunfire (right) were also part of the revitalized X-Men grouping in 1975, but none of them stayed around for very long. (Pencils John Byrne)

(Above) Before joining the X-Men as Nightcrawler, Kurt Wagner suffered a career as a circus freak. (Pencils Darick Robertson)

(Top) Kurt, in his first appearance in *Giant-Size X-Men* #1 (May 1975), is saved from a mob by Charles Xavier's mental powers of persuasion. (Pencils Dave Cockrum)

(Above) The Japanese Super Hero Sunfire was an early burn-out for the revitalized team.

supporting characters in the stories. An Irish-born mutant called "Banshee" had shown up in *X-Men* issue #28 (January 1967), and a Japanese character named "Sunfire" had appeared in issue #64 (January 1970). Banshee, who under his real name "Sean Cassidy" had worked as an Interpol agent and detective, was blessed with a supersonic scream and a brogue so thick it could mash a potato. Sunfire, a.k.a. "Shiro Yoshida," was the son of a woman who was radiated in 1945 when the American military dropped the atomic bomb on Hiroshima, which in turn led to his developing the power to super-heat air (and which makes him more a traditional Marvel Super Hero, one that is affected by radiation rather than born with a mutant gene). Because he blames America for his mother's subsequent death, he is not really a friend of the United States, but on occasion has been an ally to the X-Men. Both would make their way into the new team.

Then there was a mysterious being from Canada—a country that was one of the prime target markets—who, even as Cockrum and Thomas spoke, was just about to debut in *The Incredible Hulk* issues #180 and 181 (October/November 1974). His name was The Wolverine. "When I suggested Wolverine to Len Wein [who was then writing *Hulk*], he wasn't even necessarily a mutant," says Thomas. "I just wanted a guy named Wolverine, I wanted him to be Canadian, and I wanted him to be a little, short, mean-tempered character." Wein developed the angles that Wolverine was a Canadian secret agent and that he had retractable claws made of a mysterious, nearly indestructible alloy called "adamantium," and artist Herb Trimpe penciled the *Hulk* story in which the character first appeared. It was not, however, Trimpe who actually designed the first version of Wolverine, but rather Marvel veteran John Romita.

"All they gave me was, 'We want a character called Wolverine,' and I was under the impression that a wolverine was a female wolf!" Romita recalls with a laugh. "We had an encyclopedia in the office and I

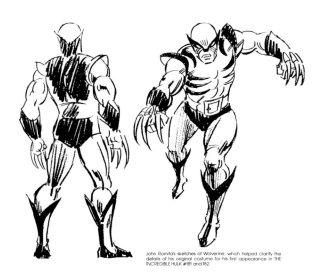

John Romita's sketches of Wolverine, which helped clarify the details of his original costume for his first appearance in THE INCREDIBLE HULK #181 and 182.

(Top) The very first appearance of Wolverine in *The Incredible Hulk* #180 (October 1974), in which he was an antagonist. (Pencils Herb Trimpe.)

(Top, right) John Romita's original design sketches for Wolverine emphasized his cat-like qualities. These would quickly disappear once he became an X-Man.

(Above) Barroom brawls were a specialty for Logan, a.k.a. Wolverine. (Pencils John Bolton)

(Opposite) Wolverine clearly demonstrates why it is virtually impossible for him to be outnumbered in the first issue of his own magazine (*Wolverine* #1, November 1988).

looked up 'wolverine' and saw a little drawing in there of a small cat-like animal, very ferocious, with tremendous claws. I changed my approach and put in cat-shaped ears, and even had the suggestion of whiskers in the costume design. I wrote down on the original sketch that he was about 5'4", which meant that this would make him distinctive, since every other Super Hero was so tall and heroic looking."

At some point in the course of development, the notion of fashioning the characters in order to sell them to specific foreign markets ebbed away, and characters were instead being created for their own intrinsic worth. "For the most part, we really had a free hand," Cockrum says. "I was told, 'Go home and bring us some designs.'" Among these were sketches for a Russian powerhouse called "Colossus" (proof that the cross-cultural comic sales scheme had been abandoned, since the USSR in 1974 was hardly a viable market for US goods); a Native American mutant named "Thunderbird"; a sleek woman who could change into any kind of feline from a panther to a house cat, named "Black Cat" (who also wore a belled collar around her neck); and a male character with distinctive white hair, who was a weather changer, named "Typhoon." At Thomas's suggestion, elements of the latter two would be combined into a single character called "Storm."

Before long, the Marvel Universe had its new team. What it did not have, however, was Roy Thomas, who left the company in late 1974, before the revitalized X-Men could appear in print. He turned the project over to Wein, who wrote the introductory story, which was penciled by Cockrum and inked by Bob McLeod and appeared in *Giant-Size X-Men* #1 (May 1975).

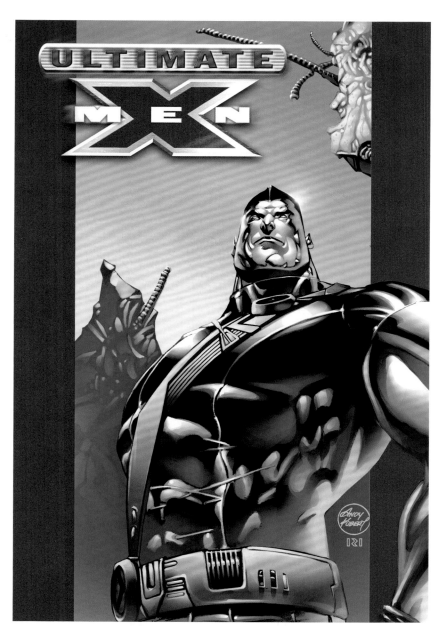

--AND, WITHOUT HESITATION, PETER RASPUTIN IS RUN-NING, LEGS PUMPING, HEART POUNDING--

--THE VERY AIR AROUND HIM CRACKLING WITH THE ENERGY OF HIS EXERTION--

--ENERGY RELEASED IN A MOST ASTONISH-ING MANNER!

(Top) Peter Rasputin, a.k.a Colossus, is reputed to be the strongest of all the X-Men, as evidenced by this cover from *Ultimate X-Men #5*.

(Above) Peter Rasputin in the process of changing into the metallic Colossus.

(Opposite) Artist Chris Bachalo's rendering of Colossus may suggest a robot, but he was essentially a flesh and blood giant.

THE ALL-NEW X-MEN

The first third of *Giant-Size X-Men #1*'s story was devoted to Professor X's travels around the world, approaching and recruiting the new mutants whom he identified through Cerebro. The first to be found is the midnight-blue "Kurt Wagner," a.k.a. Nightcrawler, a circus acrobat from Winzeldorf, Germany, who is the perfect picture of a Hell-born demon, complete with an arrow-tipped tail, pointed ears and teeth, and talon-like hands with only two fingers and a thumb. Kurt has the ability to "teleport": disappear and reappear elsewhere at will, a stunt accompanied by the sound "BAMF" and a trace of brimstone. Professor X arrives on the scene just as a mob of superstitious villagers is about to drive a stake through the "monster's" heart! Xavier rescues the young man by psychically "pushing" the minds of the mob into complacency—a skill he would resist using in future years for ethical reasons.

From Kenya comes "Ororo," the great goddess of the weather, who takes her title seriously, believing she really is a goddess. She isn't, even though she has the god-like power to affect the weather—hence her code name Storm.

In Osaka, Japan, Xavier convinces Sunfire to join the new team. Then skipping over to Lake Baikal, Siberia, he finds "Peter Rasputin" (later "Piotr Nikolaievitch Rasputin"), the huge son of peasant farmers, and also a good son to Mother Russia, who has the power to armor plate his body to near invincibility and become Colossus. Considered the strongest of all the X-Men, he is able to lift more than ten tons.

Closer to home is "John Proudstar," a Native American self-styled warrior from Camp Verde, Arizona, who possesses the speed and strength to outrun and bulldog a buffalo. If anything, Proudstar, who takes on the code name Thunderbird, is more unpleasant than Wolverine. He responds to Xavier's offer to join him by saying, "You can stuff a cactus, Custer!" Only when Xavier goads him with the implication of native cowardice does he agree to come, just to prove his mettle to the strange white man.

Banshee is tracked down not in his native Ireland, but in Nashville, of all places, and decides that, having walked on both sides of the law at various points in his life, going straight might do him some good.

Wolverine, meanwhile, has been tracked down by Xavier in a military installation in Quebec, where he is registered with the Canadian government as "Weapon X." Now appearing much less cat-like than in his *Hulk* appearance—Cockrum redesigned the mask to give him longer "ears" and took away the whisker effect— he compensates by acting even more pugnacious. Wolverine jumps at Xavier's offer to get out from under the bureaucracy under which he is currently serving, and threatens to harm a government military official on the way out, just for good measure.

For the rest of the story, the newbies are joined by most of the original X-Men (only the Beast is missing in action, though his likeness appears in peripheral artwork in the headings), but there is no longer any attempt to make them wear matching uniforms. Instead their costumes represent their own individuality. But even if they are not dressed alike, the team manages to channel their disparate, and sometimes conflicting, personalities enough to learn how to work together, long enough to jointly defeat the bizarre, radiated living island "Krakoa."

It was a show of unity that would not last long.

BACK IN ACTION

Giant-Size X-Men #1 was a dynamic restart of the classic title. While it incorporated a few darker-hued shades, mostly emanating from personality conflicts within the expanding group, it was overall an example of old-fashioned feel-good superheroics. With issue #94 (August 1975), *X-Men* resumed publishing original stories again, though immediately, the now-thirteen-member team began thinning out, with Sunfire declaring that he had had enough of the X-Men and

(Top) John Proudstar, a.k.a. the doomed Thunderbird, outrunning a stallion in his first appearance in *Giant-Size X-Men* #1. (Pencils Dave Cockrum)

(Above) Artists John Byrne (left) and Dave Cockrum (right) were instrumental in the revitalization of *X-Men*. (Photos courtesy John Morrow)

(Opposite) Storm demonstrates her name. The former "goddess" has evolved into one of the most forceful and most compelling of all the X-Men. (Pencils Greg Land)

leaving to return to Japan. A bigger surprise, at least for Professor X, was the defection of the original team members, who declare that it is time to move on in their lives…all of them except for Cyclops. On the surface, the ever-responsible Scott Summers is duty bound to remain an X-Man, even if it means watching the love of his life, Jean, walk out and leave him behind. Privately, however, Scott agonizes over the fact that he does not have the options that his compatriots enjoy: Jean, Bobby, and Warren can all control their mutant powers and hide them from the public at large, but Scott can only pray that his is never accidentally exposed in a situation where innocent people will end up hurt, or dead. Swallowing his anguish as the team he has grown up with walks away, Cyclops throws himself with renewed vigor into properly training the new members.

The team would lose another member in issue #95 in dramatic fashion, as declared by a cover sunburst reading: *Not a hoax! Not a dream! This issue an X-Man dies!* The doomed hero is the headstrong Thunderbird, who had remained a problem member since his recruitment. In his final attempt to prove himself a worthy warrior, Thunderbird latches on to the small airborne plane of villain "Count Nefaria" and destroys its cockpit with his bare hands. He and Nefaria are killed in the resulting explosion. Xavier is surprisingly distraught, though Cyclops accepts it stoically: "It comes with the uniform," he tells the others.

Readers of the time were not accustomed to comic book characters dying. Marvel had done it once before, dramatically killing off Peter Parker/Spider-Man's girlfriend "Gwen Stacy" in 1973 and leaving her dead. But according to Cockrum, there was a purpose behind the sacrifice. "When we put together *Giant-Size* number one, a subtext of the story was that it would be an entrance exam for new characters," he says. "We brought in Banshee and Sunfire because we figured that some people are going to have to fail the test. Then it turned out we all liked Banshee, and didn't want him to fail. Theoretically, Thunderbird was supposed to fail the test,

(Top) After a trip to Japan, Storm affected a radical new look in the 1980s.

(Above) Only Logan's supernatural healing powers allowed him to endure the horrific "Weapon X" experiment, in which he acquired an adamantium-infused skeleton.

(Opposite) The new X-Men team bursts forth from their introductory issue in 1975.

X-TREME CLOSEUP
Wolverine
TROUBLE IN TIGHTS

"I'm the best there is at what I do."
—Logan, a.k.a. James Howlett, a.k.a. Wolverine

The philosopher Thomas Hobbes famously described life as solitary, brutish, nasty, and short. He could have been talking about Wolverine.

One of the most mysterious and fascinating of all comic book heroes, this bad-tempered Canuck goes by the name of "Logan," and for decades that was the extent of the common knowledge about him. In fact, Wolverine's true background has long been a mystery even to himself. He is a puzzle inside an enigma, wrapped in yellow spandex.

In a field filled with behemoths and giants, Wolverine is a runt, though his sheer volume of attitude compensates for his lack of height. While he has an aggressive disrespect for authority, he nevertheless tolerates—and is tolerated within—the X-Men because of his value to the group. He can forge close friendships, such as one he enjoys with Nightcrawler (whom he affectionately calls "Elf"), though he is more often at odds with his teammates, particularly Cyclops. This fire is fanned both by Cyclops's leadership position and Wolverine's clear interest in Jean Grey. Wolverine is also the only X-Man with the temerity to flippantly call Professor X "Chuck" and get away with it.

Outside of sheer brute strength and razor-sharp metal claws, which produce the sound "SNIKT" when extended, Wolverine's chief power is the ability to quickly heal from the most serious of wounds, making him nearly invincible. As a boy he had been found living like an animal in the woods and was taken in by the Canadian government. Because of his toughness and healing ability, he was deemed a good subject for the horrific "Weapon X" experiment in which his skeleton was infused with adamantium in the hopes of creating a barely human fighting machine.

Wolverine is not simply ferocious in battle, he sometimes descends to the level of a bloodthirsty berserker, though he still manages to retain touches of humanity, such as a wry, sardonic sense of humor, and a surprising paternal affection for some of the young female members who have joined the X-Men

(Right) Presumed dead, Logan went undercover for a time as the laconic "Patch."

(Below) Wolverine practically leaps off the page, courtesy of penciler Frank Miller, in the 1987 graphic novel *Wolverine*.

over the years. He is also fascinated with Japan and Japanese culture, particularly the code of the Samurai. The love of Logan's life, in fact, was a Japanese woman called "Mariko Yashida," the daughter of a crime family, to whom he was once engaged!

For a while, the world at large believed Wolverine to be dead. During this time he went undercover (at least as much as was possible) using the name "Patch," and adopted a Mike Hammer-ish demeanor, complete with a battered fedora pulled down low and an eyepatch.

No one knows Wolverine's exact age, including him, though some believe he could be more than one hundred years old, a side effect of his regenerative powers. This facet of his character was exploited in a 2001 rewriting of Wolverine's origin story, titled, appropriately, *Origin* by Paul Jenkins, Bill Jemas, and Joe Quesada, which has him starting life in the 19th century as James Howlett, the son of wealthy Canadian parents, whose claws and powers emerged in adolescence as the result of natural mutantcy rather than a scientific experiment. Having inadvertently killed a loved one, James retreated to the wilderness and lived with the wolves.

But just as learning the true identity of Jack the Ripper or the actual whereabouts of D.B. Cooper would be less exciting than keeping their basic mysteries alive, it is likely that no amount of revealed truth about the man called Logan would eliminate the essential puzzle of his existence. It might even enhance it.

(Top) Onomatopoeia is a long and honorable tradition at Marvel: the sound of Wolverine's claws emerging is always rendered as "SNIKT!"

(Above) Canadian-born Logan has long harbored a fascination for the culture and philosophies of Japan. (Pencils Shin Nagasawa)

too, but then we liked him, too, and kept him around." Why, then, kill him off two issues later? "We didn't know what to do with him," Cockrum admits. "He duplicated stuff that some of the others could do, and he was an obnoxious loud mouth, and Wolverine already had the patent on that."

ENTER CLAREMONT

X-Men was about to take off like a shot, and one of the primary factors for that was the arrival of writer Chris Claremont, who would be responsible for propelling the book to new heights. Born in 1950 in England, Claremont initially had little intention of being a writer of any kind, let alone a writer of comic books; acting was his first career choice. But in 1969 he accepted an internship at Marvel and later began selling comic book stories simply as means of earning money. That was still his motivation in 1974, when he signed with Marvel as an assistant editor. The shake-up caused by Roy Thomas's resignation landed Professor X and crew in his lap, and at that point he left the theatrical stage for good. Claremont quickly put his stamp on *X-Men*, developing a tapestry of interconnected storylines and character evolutions that would become signature highlights for the title, as well as redefining and fleshing out the individual team members, creating complex and emotionally resonant character relationships.

When artist John Byrne took over the pencil reins from Cockrum two years later, the revitalization was truly underway (though Cockrum would return for a second run in 1981). Byrne, who was also born in 1950 in England, but was raised in Canada, shared with Claremont the conspiratorial-sounding title of "co-plotter," and brought a dynamic, cinematic sense of drama to the pages of *X-Men*. Through their efforts *X-Men* once more became popular enough to go monthly, starting with issue #112 (August 1978). Two issues later, the cover began bearing the legend "The Uncanny X-Men," replacing the not entirely accurate

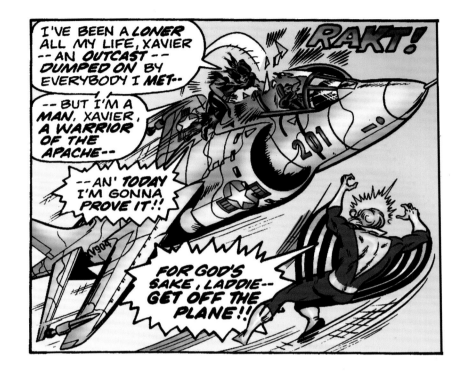

(Top) Thunderbird sacrifices himself in dramatic fashion and narrows the ranks of the new X-Men, in *X-Men* #94. (October 1975; pencils Dave Cockrum, inks Bob McLeod)

(Opposite) Now officially "The Uncanny X-Men," the team in the mid-70s tended to greet new arrivals (such as Kitty Pryde) with a hearty, "Hope you survive!" (Pencils John Byrne)

"All-New, All-Different" legend. While the adjective "uncanny" was first applied to the X-Men in their inaugural adventure, now it was part of their identity.

X-MEN ON A ROLL

The period of the next several years would be one of the most richly inspired and influential in *X-Men* history, with Claremont, Cockrum, and Byrne setting off a creative chain reaction. This happened in part, Claremont believes, because "nobody knew what we were doing. *X-Men* was a stealth franchise, a midlist title that had clawed its way into the top tier, and by the time anybody realized what they had, we were already rolling with incredible momentum."

A less heralded but important member of the creative team was series editor Louise Jones. "Weezie [Louise] bears as much responsibility for making *X-Men* what it is as John and Dave and I do, because she functioned as my conscience," Claremont states. "She knew how to cull the good ideas from the pile and how to focus them, and if I came up with a dumb idea, she would be the one who let me know it in a way that didn't freak me out. The focus that gave us the momentum that exists to this day came out of the synergy of the four of us." "Weezie" Jones would go on to marry artist Walt Simonson and receive greater acclaim as a writer under her married name, Louise Simonson.

Among the significant storylines that would emerge from the late 1970s to early 1980s was one that continues to resonate today as one of the most distinctive and important Marvel ever did, the "Dark Phoenix Saga." Novelistic in its approach, the story ranged over issues #134 to 138 (June through October 1980), and told the tale of Jean Grey who, having previously merged with the blinding "Phoenix Force" to become an enhanced version of herself called Phoenix, is subsequently transformed through the powers of darkness into a planet-destroying entity called Dark Phoenix. Because the denouement involved the sacrifice of a beloved

(Above) Nightcrawler passed for normal through the use of an ingenious "image inducer," which could change him into anyone, though he preferred Errol Flynn.

(Opposite, top) Jean Grey was psychically seduced by the inner circle of the Hellfire Club to become their Black Queen. This incarnation of Jean was an intermediate stage to her becoming Phoenix.

(Opposite, bottom) This image, from *X-Men* #137 (September 1980), of Jean Grey sacrificing herself to destroy her malevolent Phoenix incarnation not only shocked Cyclops, but fans as well, and marked a milestone in X-Men history. (Pencils John Byrne, inks, Terry Austin)

character turned menace, whose transgressions demanded the ultimate payment, even though she was not entirely responsible for them, it was an eye-opening, controversial storyline that propelled *X-Men* into the stratosphere in terms of reader interest and popularity. "We were off the radar for most of the time until the death of Phoenix," Claremont says.

Interspersed with the Phoenix saga were the ongoing machinations of "The Hellfire Club," a legendary organization steeped in Olde English debauchery that attracts some of New York's best, brightest, and richest—a sort of malevolent Studio 54. The public face of the Hellfire Club is that of a charitable, if eccentric, organization. But its inner circle, all of whom favor Georgian-era clothing and hair styles, is comprised of the evil mutants "Sebastian Shaw," "Jason Wyngarde"—known to charter *X-Men* readers as the nefarious "Mastermind"—"Harry Leland," and "Donald Pierce." From its lavish Hellfire Mansion on 5th Avenue, the club works toward its goal of world domination through the likeliest means of actually achieving it: manipulating political and financial power.

The X-Men become entangled with the club when Jean Grey is "psychically seduced" by Wyngarde (who manages to mask his naturally sleazy countenance with a dashing, rakish veneer) and convinced that she was "Lady Jean Grey," an 18th-century incarnation of herself, who was engaged to Sir Jason Wyngarde. Meanwhile, the club has also invaded the Xavier Mansion and bugged Cerebro so that they can receive any information on the mutants that Professor Xavier

X-TREME CLOSEUP
Phoenix
CHILD OF LIGHT AND SHADOW

"We're not children anymore…we have to live our own lives now."
—Jean Grey, a.k.a. Marvel Girl, a.k.a. Phoenix

Probably no one in comics history has had as many lives as Jean Grey.

The first, of course, was as Marvel Girl, the cute, bubbly feminine relief in the testosterone club of the initial X-Men grouping. All the X-Men flirted with her, but Jean only had eyes for the one who could not give her eyes back, Scott Summers.

Jean's second life was as Phoenix, the composite being who emerged in X-Men issue #101 (October 1976), a result of Jean's having piloted the space shuttle Starcore through history's worst solar storm in order to save the team. Only her love for Scott kept her alive through the solar flare, during which she was infused with the mysterious Phoenix Force and momentarily became an entity of pure thought. Experiencing rebirth as Phoenix, she was aware that she is different than the old Jean (so was Scott), but she nevertheless still operated in traditional superheroine fashion.

It did not take long, however, for absolute power to corrupt her absolutely, resulting in her becoming the lovely but lethal Dark Phoenix. When her power threatened the universe, Lilandra of the Shi'ar demanded her destruction as a preventative measure. At that point, enough of the old Jean returned to decide to end Phoenix's reign of terror by sacrificing herself. Jean remained "dead" for quite some time, but came back in the mid-1980s, after having been sequestered in suspended animation in an underwater construct at the bottom of the Hudson River.

Jean Grey's most recent demise occurred at the hands of villain "Xorn." With her last breath, she forgave Scott for his affair with Emma Frost, then died—or, as Wolverine has remarked, got "as close as she can get." Whether she will return is anyone's guess, though one thing is certain: death in the X-Universe not a black-and-white matter; it is rendered in hues of Grey.

(Top) This "pin-up" poster of Jean Grey appeared in *X-Men* #9 (January 1965). Clearly, Lee and Kirby knew their young boy audience.

(Above) Even before her personality began to change, Jean went through costume changes. Only her red hair remained consistent. (Pencils Barry Windsor-Smith)

(Opposite) Phoenix aflame, as rendered by Chris Bachalo.

locates and get to them first. Before she gets wise to Wyngarde's deceptions, Jean is warped into becoming the club's "Black Queen," which is the first step to her unleashing her deadly persona as Dark Phoenix. Fittingly, Wyngarde and Leland would number among her victims.

Of course, Jean was not the only one whose character underwent significant *X*-pansion. After his horror-movie-inspired introduction, Nightcrawler would lighten up and develop into something of the class clown of the X-Men, a carefree spirit whose life greatly improves when Professor X gives him a palm-sized "image inducer," a holographic projector that enables him to take on any shape he likes. He responds by casting himself in the image of a number of classic Hollywood stars (even Groucho Marx!) though his favorite likeness is Errol Flynn's. While the ability to alter his form is artificially induced, it is more than apt, since it would be revealed that he is the son of the bad mutant "Mystique," the shape-shifter supreme of the X-Men saga, who, like Kurt, is blue in her natural state. Speculation as to his father's identity has flourished, though it is now believed to be a demonic mutant named "Azazel." Ironically, the most evil looking of the X-Men would become its most outwardly religious member. Not only would Nightcrawler turn to the church, at one point, he would be accepted into the Catholic priesthood!

Storm, meanwhile, would be provided with one of the most detailed backstories in all of comic books. Shortly after she joined the group it was revealed that, not only was she not a goddess, she was not even a native Kenyan, but rather a child of Harlem named "Ororo Munroe," who was born in 1951. Her father, David Munroe, was a freelance photojournalist and her mother was a genuine Kenyan princess. While still an infant, the family uprooted from their home on 112th Street and moved to Cairo. Five years later, the Suez War caused the Munroes to flee. They plane they were on was shot down, and while Ororo survived, her parents were killed.

(Top) The young, orphaned Ororo Munroe was forced to live on the streets of Cairo and steal for survival. This basic background would be applied to several other X-Men in the future.

(Above) The adult Ororo genuinely believed she was a goddess, until Professor X set her straight.

(Opposite) Father and son separation is a common recurring motif throughout the entire Marvel Universe. Here Scott Summers/Cyclops is reunited with his long-lost father, Christopher Summers/Corsair.

As a young girl, Ororo made her own way through the streets of Cairo, surviving as sneak thief—she even picked the pocket of Charles Xavier, who was there in his nomadic wandering days. But at the age of twelve something awakened inside her and she felt compelled to walk two-thousand miles to the Serengeti Plain, suddenly finding "home." Living there, her powers emerged, and she attained her status as a "goddess," only to find out later that she was really a mutant.

With time, Storm's leadership qualities increasingly emerged, as would her ambition, which occasionally resulted in power struggles, even with Professor X himself. In the 1980s storylines she would be in charge of the team and drastically change her look (introduced by artists Paul Smith and Bob Wiacek in *Uncanny X-Men* #173, September 1983), adopting a sexier wardrobe and shearing down her long, flowing white hair into a Mohawk. In the alternate version of reality presented in *Mutant X*, which was created in the late 1990s, she would be cast—quite effectively—as a vampire!

The ongoing story of Colossus would strike many of the common X-Men themes: romance, family, loss, and temporary change of allegiance. The 1980s would see him falling in love with fellow teammate "Kitty Pryde," though the two would ultimately break up after Peter truly fell in love with – and ultimately lost – the white-haired alien "Zsaji." This was only the beginning of Peter's troubles.

His kid sister, Illyana, would similarly develop mutant powers, those of a sorceress, and would become part of a spin-off group called "The New Mutants" as "Magik." Illyana would tragically die from infection by the "Legacy Virus," a deadly disease that affects the X-gene. Taking the loss hard, the embittered Colossus went astray for a while and shifted his allegiance to Magneto, becoming one of his "Acolytes," though that was a brief association with the evil side of things. Like so many within the Marvel Universe, Colossus died for a noble cause—testing the vaccine for the Legacy Virus. But also like so many within the Marvel Universe, he came back (there is no word yet on Illyana).

Even the Gibraltar-like Scott would have his personal life buffeted by changes, and not simply because of Jean. Through his interaction with the Shi'ar Empire he would encounter a band of intergalactic pirates named "The Starjammers," who were led by the swashbuckling "Corsair," who is really Christopher Summers, Scott's father, long believed dead!

One of the more important non-mutant characters to emerge from the X-Universe was Moira MacTaggart, who was introduced in *X-Men* issue #96 (December 1975). The daughter of a chilly Scottish nobleman named "Lord Kinross," Moira first appeared in the saga in the guise of the housekeeper at the Xavier Institute. It would be revealed that she was really a brilliant geneticist, and the grad student to whom Charles Xavier had once been engaged, though the union would be thwarted by her inability to extricate herself from an existing marriage. Later she would become involved with fellow Celt Sean Cassidy/Banshee. A Nobel Prize winner for her work in genetic mutation research, she operates the Mutant Research Center, a facility on Muir Island, off the coast of Scotland, to study and house dangerous mutants. One of those was Magneto, who had been reverted to infancy, and who Moira tried to reprogram to grow up into a good mutant (it was only partially successful). Another was Moira's own son "Kevin MacTaggart," who as "Proteus" possessed the ability to alter reality. In later years, Moira would also raise a young Scot girl named "Rahne Sinclair," a mutant lycanthrope called "Wolfsbane," who would be part of the New Mutants.

Much later, Moira MacTaggart was killed in a battle at Muir Island with the reorganized Brotherhood, but not before revealing her final and lasting contribution to mutantkind: the cure for the deadly Legacy Virus.

During this classic period of *X-Men* the team itself enlarged as well, first to include thirteen-year-old "Katherine 'Kitty' Pryde," who first appeared in issue

(Top) Dr. Moira MacTaggart's Mutant Research Center located on Muir Island in Scotland would become an increasingly important location for X-Men adventures.

(Above) Once engaged to Charles Xavier, Moira MacTaggart later became cozy with Sean Cassidy/Banshee.

(Opposite) A mod Moira seems to have more on her mind than genetic research.

#129 (January 1980). Living with her family in Deerfield, Illinois, a suburb of Chicago, Kitty tries desperately to be a normal girl with an interest in dance, but it is impossible, having discovered the ability to pass through solid surfaces and objects, a talent she calls "phasing." She is scouted by both the Xavier School and Emma Frost's "Massachusetts Academy"—which is a front for the Hellfire Club—but decides to sign on with the X-Men, the announcement of which was heralded on the cover of issue #139 (November 1980). There she would be mentored by Storm. Kitty experimented with various code names over the years, first becoming "Sprite," then "Ariel," and then, abandoning the fairy motif altogether, settling for "Shadowcat." Casual readers would have had a hard time keeping track of her. Kitty is also master to the only animal sidekick in the team's history, a small, purple dragon named "Lockheed," who followed her home after an adventure in a strange alien realm called "Broodworld."

This same run of comics also introduced "Allison Blair," a.k.a. "The Dazzler," a Disco queen who can produce blazes of blinding, mind-blowing light which "dazzle" her adversaries. She helps the X-Men, but refuses an offer to join, though their paths will cross in the future. Alison would later fall in love with and marry another X-Man, the alien, but non-mutant, "Longshot." Never major forces within the team (but a good argument for mixed marriages), the couple eventually retired to Longshot's realm, called "Mojoworld."

The other A-list character to emerge during *X-Men*'s second decade was the mysterious mutant called "Rogue." Nobody knows her real name (in the 2000 film *X-Men*, Rogue, as played by Anna Paquin, reveals her name to be "Marie," which by *X3* had become "Anna Marie," but none of this is supported within the comics), but those within the mutant world realize her powers. In fact, many believe that Rogue is potentially the most powerful mutant of all, since she can absorb and use the powers of all others merely by touching them. Rogue hails from the Deep South, where she was ostracized in her home town after nearly killing her boyfriend with a kiss. She retreated to the woods and lived on her own for a while, eschewing human company (like the young Wolverine), but was eventually discovered by Mystique, who would become a surrogate mother to her.

Rogue was initially affiliated with the Mystique's Brotherhood of Evil Mutants, with whom she fought both the X-Men and the Avengers. But when she absorbed the powers of one "Carol Danvers," who was then known as "Ms. Marvel," she also got her memories and personality installed permanently, and began to lose control of her abilities. Despite her background, she appealed to Professor Xavier to help, and although it took some doing to convince the individual X-Men of her sincerity, she was finally accepted into the team. In particular she is able to break through Wolverine's growly reserve.

Eventually Rogue was able to cast off the Carol Danvers side of her psyche, though her problems were hardly over. The knowledge that the mere touch of her bare skin can be dangerous to anyone, mutant or otherwise, not only affects her dress—she must remain covered up head-to-toe at all times—but it leaves her with a level of sexual angst with which few, if any, can really empathize.

Operating below the surface of the X-Universe—in all regards—were the "Morlocks," a group of mutant outcasts who have taken to living deep underneath New York in an abandoned subway tunnel, who derived their name and basic situation from the sub-human underclass in H.G. Wells's novel *The Time Machine*. In their first appearance (Uncanny *X-Men* issue #169, May 1983) the Morlocks were led by "Callisto," a tough mutantatrix with an eye-patch and a shag haircut, and possessing hyper-sensitive senses. Through the Cerebro-like abilities of the monster-like mutant "Caliban" she has collected the other ugly and misshapen mutants for her underground band. Among them are the gigantic, thug-like "Sunder," the hideous "Masque," who can

(Above) This latter-day rendition of Kitty Pryde from artist Paul Smith is a far cry from her early, innocent teen days.

(Opposite) Kitty Pryde as "Shadowcat."

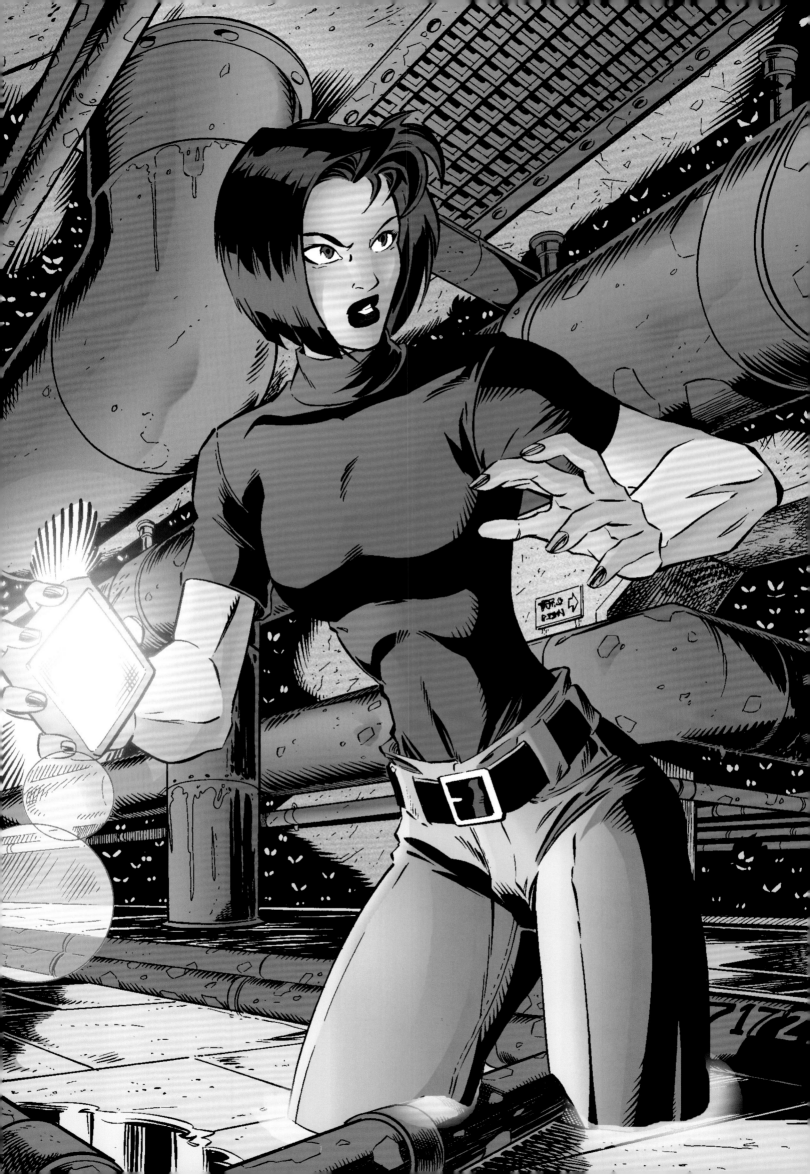

change any face except his own ghastly one, and green-hued "Leech," who can short out the superpowers of those around him.

At the time of the X-Men's first encounter with the Morlocks, they are completely under Callisto's iron-fist domination. The underground leader has also captured the Angel and plans to make him her consort. The rest of the X-Men come to the rescue, of course, and in the process Storm defeats Callisto in an old-fashioned knife fight, in which Callisto is injured but not killed. Storm then uses her newly acquired dominance over the Morlocks to demand that they act peaceably, and with time, they would become something akin to allies to the team.

Later in the saga, the Morlocks would be slaughtered by the minions of the evil mutant "Sinister," and the few survivors would become anti-human warriors led by "Mikhail Rasputin," the older brother of Colossus and Magik. One such future underclassling, a young girl named "Sarah," would grow up to be one of the more militant Morlocks and wreak havoc on humans under the code name "Marrow." The fact that the Morlocks were most often presented as antagonists rather than true villains served to further the shift within X-Universe from simple good-guy vs. bad-guy stories to more meaningful examinations of class, sub-classes, and outcasts within social structure.

X-PLODING UNIVERSE

Throughout the rest of the 1980s and into the 1990s, while still under the guidance of Claremont along with such artists as John Romita Jr., Barry Windsor-Smith, Jim Lee, and Marc Silvestri, the universe of the X-Men blasted into all directions. The fallout was the creation of off-shoot teams, new villains, old cast reunions, and, of course, a plethora of new characters.

Joining the main X-Men team was the young "Jubilee," short for "Jubilation Lee," a fifteen-year-old daughter of Chinese immigrant parents living in Beverly Hills, who can shoot fireworks from her fingertips.

(Above) Allison Blair, "The Dazzler," was an adjunct X-Man (or Woman) who never officially became part of the team.

(Opposite) Xavier's mutant brigade hardly ever held down day-jobs; one exception was The Dazzler, who was a Disco queen. (Pencil, John Romita Jr.)

(Following spread, left) The dynamic Rogue (whose real name never has been revealed in the comics), became a staple of the X-Men in the 1970s and grew popular enough to get her own magazine. (Pencils Mike Wieringo)

(Following spread, right) Rogue is easily recognizable by the white streaks in her hair (compare this image with the photo of Bogie on page 36). (Pencils Karl Moline)

Jubilee has followed what was becoming the standard path for a fledgling X-Man: orphaned when her parents were killed, abandoned, living on the streets, or in her case, a shopping mall, and stealing to survive. She was rescued from this life by the X-Men and joined the group, lending her acrobatic talents—which were not inspired by mutantcy but instead through training as a gymnast—to their fights. She also fulfilled the function once occupied by Rogue, which was as the humanizing sidekick to Wolverine, who developed a paternal fondness for her. Jubilee was introduced in *Uncanny X-Men* (issue #244, August 1989) though she would soon be transferred to the spin-off teen group "Generation X."

The first major X-Man of the 1990s was "Gambit," a New Orleans Cajun named "Remy LeBeau," who was also given the by-now familiar backstory (orphaned, lived on the streets, became a thief…), but who has the power to infuse objects with energy. While just about any object will do, Gambit has a particular fondness for charging playing cards. Like several other X-Men before him, Gambit has walked down the dark side of the street, at one time serving under the creepy Sinister, who had helped him gain control of his powers. Secretive by nature, like any good gambler, and not always given to playing by the rules, Gambit carries the air of a man whose allegiance is somewhat ambiguous (he was, in fact, originally created to be a traitor within the ranks of the X-Men, but that plan was abandoned). Not long after joining the team, Gambit becomes the object of affection for Rogue, proving perhaps that it takes one to love one.

"Bishop," who debuted in *Uncanny X-Men* #282 (November 1991), was unusual amongst his compatriots for two reasons: one is that his code name is also part of his real name, "Lucas Bishop," and the other is that he comes from the future, a particularly unpleasant one for mutants, who are branded in order to identify them. A huge African American, who wears his branded "M" over his right eye, Bishop had immersed himself in the lore of the X-Men, who were dead in his time, before

(Above) Rogue and Gambit remained an item for quite a number of years. (Pencils, Tom Raney)

(Opposite) The underground, underclass mutants called the Morlocks stand in the shadow of a robotic Sentinel. (Pencils, Shawn Martinbrough)

journeying back to the contemporary era through a time portal to join them. He possesses the ability to blast energy from his body, energy that he has absorbed like a power cell.

X-Men was hotter than ever in 1991, but that year would also see the end of an era for the book. After fifteen years of guiding the team through an arabesque of interconnecting storylines, character relationships, and alternate realities, Chris Claremont left Marvel (though he would come back in later years and once more pick up the *Uncanny X-Men* gauntlet). Claremont's tenure was one of the longest continuous runs of any comic book creator with a particular title and one of the most significant, marked by a seriousness of purpose and the desire to occasionally shock and awe.

By now the X-Universe encompassed a growing number of spin-off titles and cross-over storylines, and was branching into media adaptations. Not simply costumed action figures, many of the X-Men of this period were among the most complex and human fictional characters in any kind of literature.

And things would only get bigger.

(Top, left) The young girls of the X-Men team had a tendency to bring out Wolverine's paternal side. Here he welcomes Jubilee.

(Top, right) Jubilee, a Chinese American super heroine, was another break-out X-Man from the 1990s. (Pencils, Casey Jones)

(Above) Gambit aces his foes. (Pencils, Tom Raney)

(Opposite) The mysterious Cajun Gambit does magician Ricky Jay one better: his cards are not only lethal weapons, but highly charged as well.

X-Men in Love

It almost sounds like Hollywood.

Maybe it is to be expected, working together so closely under emotionally punishing conditions, in form-fitting costumes to boot, but over the decades, several X-Men have turned to each other for more than support in battle. Not all of the relationships are lasting ones...in fact, most don't last very long at all...but what some lack in duration, they make up for in intensity.

The most durable relationship in X-Men, practically in the entire X-Universe, is of course that of Scott Summers and Jean Grey, who have been together through sickness and in health, for better and for worse, till death them did part...again and again and again. Scott's brother Alex (Havok) maintained almost as long a relationship with Lorna Dane (Polaris), though the two eventually did break up after Polaris revealed a bit of a dark streak to her personality and had a flirtation with Bobby Drake/Iceman. Emma Frost, meanwhile, had a penchant for taking up with those with whom she served in the leadership of the Xavier school, first Banshee (a rocky relationship), and later Scott.

Living up to his early playboy image, Warren Worthington III became involved with one of the team's later members, British-born "Besty Braddock," also known as "Psylocke." This, too, was not destined for longevity, due in part of Psylocke's roving eye. She ultimately left Warren for a new recruit named "Neal Sharra," who borrowed the code name Thunderbird from its most recent owner.

The merry-go-round continued as Kitty Pryde and Colossus went at love hammer, sickle, and tong, but when that broke down Kitty had a brief fling with the mutant British spy "Peter Wisdom." Storm took up with the mutant known only as "Forge," who also forged a relationship with Mystique. Perhaps the strangest coupling was not between actual X-Men, but between the Avengers' "Janet van Dyne," a.k.a. "The Wasp," and...Magneto! The (pardon the expression) attraction was short lived.

Various X-Men have also had relationships with non-mutants over the years. The Angel, for example, had a fling with a woman named "Candy Southern," and Nightcrawler met a flight attendant named "Amanda Setton," which prompted him to forget about the priesthood.

(Top) Look again: this is not Jean that Scott is kissing, it's Madeline Pryor, whom Scott married while under the belief Jean was dead.

(Above) Wedding photos of Scott and Jean, who finally tied the knot in 1994, much to the distress of the dumped Jean-clone Madeline.

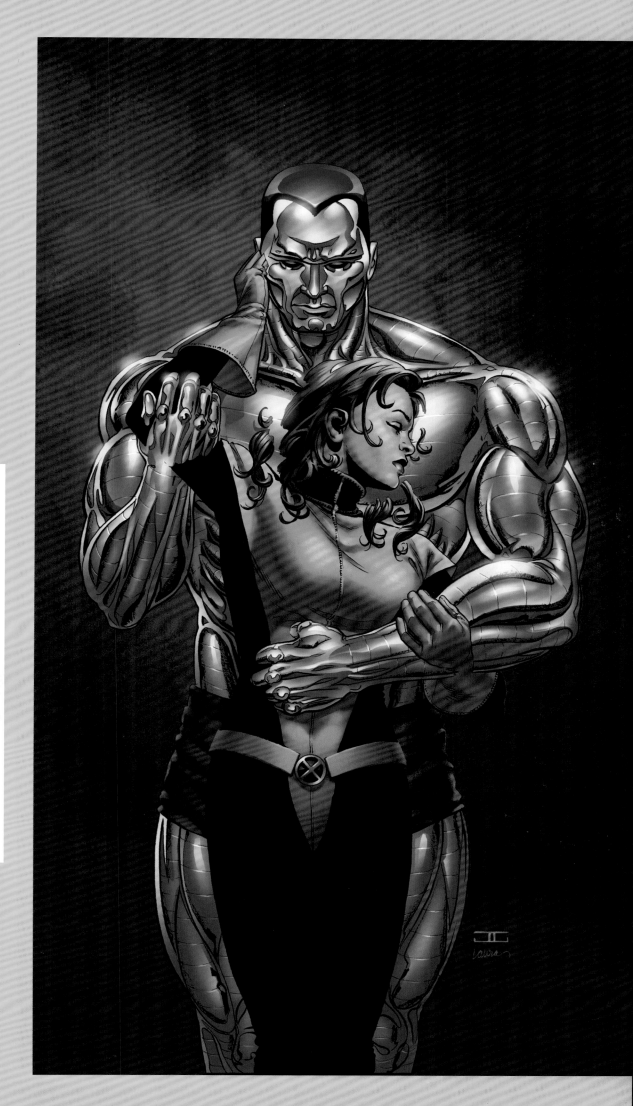

(Top) Captain Britain and Meggan, of the English Excalibur team, get married in an elaborate ceremony.

(Above) The edgier side of love: Rogue and Gambit.

(Right) Brawny Colossus was young Kitty Pryde's first love. In one time stream they are married.

(Left) X-Men has long been the most racially diverse team in comics, and African American Bishop became one of its leading heroes in the 1990s. (Pencils, Alan Davis)

(Opposite) Bishop proved to be a notable character, but he was hardly the last X-Man.

X-MEN

MARVEL COMICS

SEPT #92

WWW.MARVEL.COM

APPROVED BY THE COMICS CODE AUTHORITY

BISHOP is BACK...

...BUT IS HE the LAST X-MAN?

Andy Kubert

Jesse Delperdang

Magneto

THE ATTRACTION OF EVIL

"Extremism in defense of one's race is no evil!"
—Magneto

The motives of most villains are base and self-centered, ranging from the quest for power, wealth, or revenge. Magneto, however, is a rebel with a cause: the continued survival, if not dominance, of his *homo superior* race. He is a throwback to the anti-heroes of Jules Verne, such as Captain Nemo and Robur the Conqueror; a figure whose dark, twisted nobility informs his outwardly evil activities. In short, Magneto is a thinking man's bad guy.

Time has had a refining effect on Magneto. In his very first appearance, in *X-Men* #1, he was presented as a raving megalomaniac who could hardly bring himself to accept that he had been thwarted by a bunch of meddling kids and their professor. Since then his motives, his complexity of character, and his grim personal history have all been revealed.

The man known as Magneto is really "Erik Magnus Lehnsherr" (though in later years that name was rumored to be an alias). As a boy during World War II he was interned in the horrific Auschwitz concentration camp in Poland, and that experience fueled both his hatred for conventional humanity and his crusade for mutant dominance. He married a woman named "Madga," another survivor of the death camp, who bore him a daughter "Anya," but the girl died in a fire that even his powers proved unable to prevent. When the fearful Magda later left him, she was again (unbeknownst to him) pregnant. She would die delivering twins, a girl named "Wanda" and a boy named "Pietro," who grew up to become part of Magneto's Brotherhood of Evil Mutants. It would, however, be years before Magneto would learn of his paternity, and his subsequent relationship with his children would be difficult, to say the least.

Magneto's relationship with Professor X is even more complex. At one time they were close friends, having met in Israel as young men, and they remained allies until their philosophies ultimately pulled them in opposite directions. Fate (and an

(Above) Magneto, sans helmet, attempts to protect his wife and daughter from a deadly fire. (Pencils, John Bolton)

(Opposite) Magneto was always one villain who knew how to make an entrance.

X-TREME CLOSEUP
Magneto
THE ATTRACTION OF EVIL

alien threat) would bring them back together to fight a common enemy in writer Jim Shooter's now-classic Secret Wars storyline that began in 1984, with the unpredictable result of a reformed—or at least softened—Magneto taking over leadership of the X-Men and New Mutants team in Xavier's absence! His tenure as a benevolent leader and friend to the X-Men was destined to fail on both an organizational and inspirational standpoint. In fact, it splintered the group, resulting in the creation of a new team called "X-Force." Abandoning control of the team, Magneto later retreated to devote his energies into creating a haven and sanctuary for mutants on his outer space base of operations, "Asteroid M" (which he would rechristen "Avalon"), and on the island of "Genosha," which he controlled. As has been previously noted, in 2005 he became the ruler of the Earth, though it proved to be a short reign.

(Above) Magneto ruling over his island nation of Genosha.

(Left) A dying Charles Xavier begs a stunned Magneto to take over the X-Men! Time would prove, however, that neither Magneto's reformation nor Xavier's death was permanent.

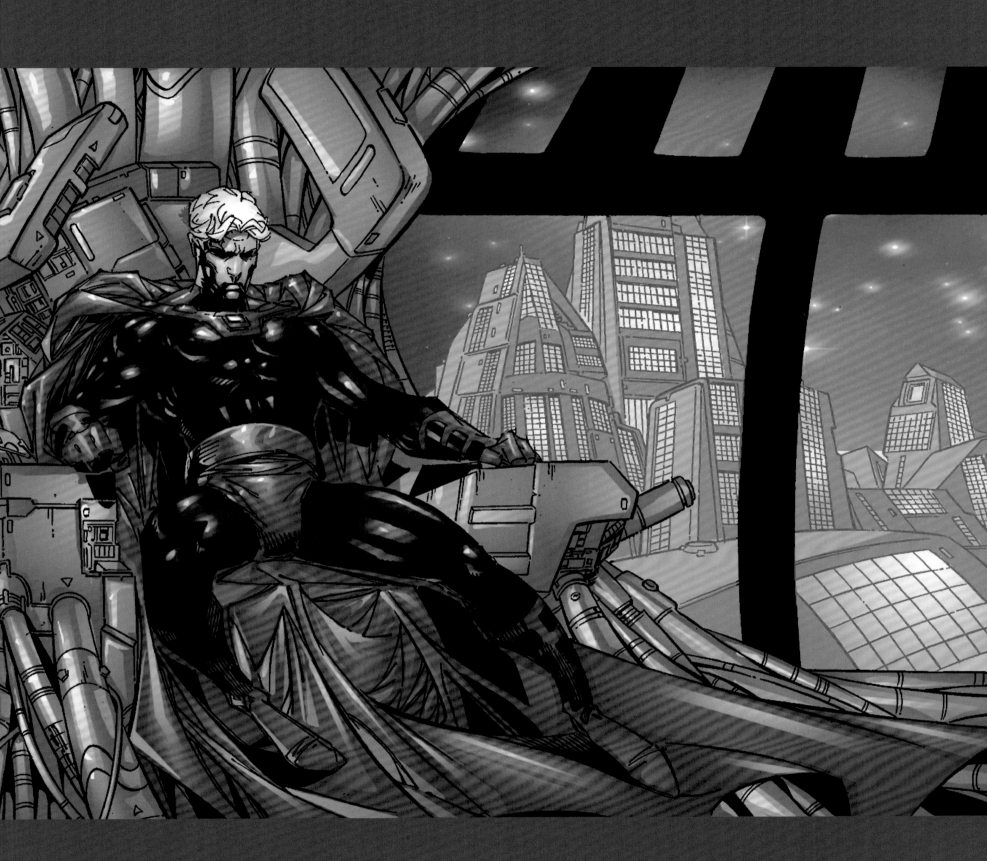

The Dark

Evil Mutants

The Dark Side of Mutantcy: Evil Mutants

The list of unheroes and antiheroes within the tapestry of X-Men is a long and varied one, even for a comic book mythology. Not only does the villain roster cover some seven-thousand years of history here on the Earth, but it branches out into different galaxies, worlds, dimensions, and realities.

(Above) Magneto's Brotherhood included the dwarfish Toad, the sleazy Mastermind, and the twins Scarlet Witch and Quicksilver, who would later be revealed as his children.

(Opposite) Magneto appears to have gained the upper hand over the X-Men...but not for long.

Magneto operated alone in the premiere issue of *X-Men*, but before long he had returned with his own fighting team, the Brotherhood of Evil Mutants, which consisted of the leaping, medieval-garbed "Toad"—real name "Mortimer Toynbee"—who looks like he dropped off the façade of Notre Dame Cathedral, and who serves as Magneto's whipping boy; the seedy-looking Jason Wyngarde, who as the Mastermind can project illusions; and the siblings, Wanda and Pietro, who are better known as "The Scarlet Witch" and "Quicksilver." The Scarlet Witch's hand gestures unleash a chaos-creating "hex power," which will later be redefined as having control over the possibility and probability of events that are about to take place. Quicksilver is blessed with super speed and a cocky attitude. The two (whose family name would later be given as "Maximoff") joined the group after being rescued from a murderous mob in a village in Europe by Magneto. At the time, none of them realized they were related.

New recruits were sought for the group, though few became permanent members. "The Blob," a Sumo-sized, cigar-chomping carnival performer named "Fred J. Dukes," whose flesh is virtually impenetrable, would become a recurring *X-Men* villain, though his self-pitying loner nature prevented him from hooking up officially with the Brotherhood, at least in the beginning. Magneto also approached a professional wrestler named "Unus," who had a force field around his body that could ward off blows. The up side of this power was that he could not be touched, no matter how strong his opponent. The down side was that it also came to keep *him* from touching and holding anything, including food, which caused him to starve. Once Unus's power-turned-disability was cured by the X-Men, he reformed

with the promise to go straight, but since he showed up in the pages of *X-Men* again, he must have had his fingers crossed.

The Sub Mariner proved to be an even bigger disappointment to *X-Men*'s miscreant-in-chief. From Magneto's point of view, Prince Namor was the perfect Evil Mutant, since he had long disdained the human race. What kept Namor from becoming a card-carrying member of the Brotherhood (outside of the purely commercial reason that he was too big a star within the Marvel Universe to be relegated to a henchman role), was simple decorum and good taste: upon hearing Magneto berate and threaten the Scarlet Witch, the gallant aquatic prince declared that he could never associate with one who treated women in such a base fashion!

Another early villain, "The Vanisher," who had the power to teleport away, might have made a good Evil Mutant, but his career in crime was short—just one adventure—after which he seemed to vanish for good (though his teleportation power would later be appropriated for Nightcrawler).

Magneto's Brotherhood would eventually disband, though two decades later Mystique would revive the group under the same name, and this time enlist the Blob. His teammates would be "Destiny," whose real name is "Irene Adler" (presumably not the same one who bested Sherlock Holmes in "A Scandal in Bohemia"), a blind precognitive, which meant that she could "see" the immediate future, even though she was unable to actually see anything in the present; "Pyro," a.k.a. "St. John Allardyce," an Australian mutant who

(Top) Mystique's revitalized Brotherhood of Evil Mutants was even worse than the first. L-to-R, Destiny, Avalanche, Mystique, Pyro, and the Blob.

(Above) The Sumo-sized Blob, formerly circus performer Fred Dukes, was a formidable foe, due to his near invincibility.

(Top) Sightless but psychic, Destiny was not only a member of Mystique's Brotherhood, she was Mystique's lover.

(Above) The deadly Lucifer, who would later be revealed as an alien being.

could manipulate fire; and "Avalanche"—just Avalanche—whose earthquake touch disintegrated solid objects. A third version of the Brotherhood, this time under the inept management of Toad, would appear some years after that, which would reunite Blob and Pyro, and add to the roster the humanoid pterodactyl "Sauron."

Magneto was not the only one of the X-team's major antagonists who would have personal ties to Professor X. The bearded master criminal who calls himself Lucifer would have an even greater impact on Xavier's life and activities. It was he who crippled Xavier by dropping a slab of stone on his legs during an altercation in a mysterious walled city at the base of the Himalayas in Tibet, and it was the deadly activities of Lucifer that convinced the Professor to organize a group of trained, combatant mutants in the first place.

When Lucifer reemerged in the early days of *X-Men*, Xavier took a sabbatical away from the group, leaving Cyclops in charge, to find and confront the evil mastermind, who was then operating out of a cave deep under the Balkans. The villain proves to be as diabolical as his name: he has anticipated the appearance of Xavier and has rigged a thermo-nuclear bomb to detonate if his heart stops beating, meaning that if Professor X—or anyone else—kills him, nuclear devastation will result! Xavier, of course, incapacitates Lucifer (who, unbeknownst to Xavier, is a creature not of this world) with sheer brain power, while Cyclops uses his vision to destroy the bomb's fuse.

From Lucifer's first appearance in the saga (*X-Men* issue #9, January 1965), readers were teased with speculation regarding his real identity. Over time this speculation would be put to rest as his singular backstory was revealed: Lucifer would turn out to be a member of an ancient alien race whose goal is to try and take over the universe. When Lucifer fails, his leader, the "Supreme One," banishes him to a nameless dimension, devoid of time and space.

Even closer to Xavier than either Magneto or Lucifer, though, is "Juggernaut," who is in reality "Cain

Marko," the natural son of Dr. Kurt Marko, and Professor X's stepbrother! Like his namesake, this Cain would like nothing better than to slay his brother, but he cannot truly be called an evil mutant, since he is not a mutant at all. Cain Marko is an "External," having received his powers of incredible strength and unstoppability from the mystical "Ruby of Cyttorak," which had been placed in its temple in Korea in ancient times by an extra-dimensional entity (like most bullies, Cain is a coward—he stumbles across the ruby after deserting from the military during the Korean conflict; Charles, of course, musters out with honors). The gargantuan Juggernaut wears an oversized nose-cone-shaped helmet, which prevents his stepbrother from psychically pushing his mind, meaning that the only way he can actually be stopped is through the removal of his helmet.

Xavier was not the only X-Man to have a bad penny in the family. Banshee's cousin, "Black Tom Cassidy," was himself a denizen of the dark side. Headquartered in the family pile, the thousand-year-old Cassidy Keep, which is located high atop a craggy cliff in Ireland, Black Tom for a time worked in tandem with Juggernaut (for whom Cassidy is his only real friend) to destroy the X-Men.

Among the most dangerous – certainly the most persistent – threats the X-Men would face came from the "Sentinels," a group of giant, marauding robots created by "Dr. Bolivar Trask," an anthropologist who was among the first of the well-known and respected figures to take a stand on the perceived dangers of mutantcy. Unfortunately, robotics was not Trask's field of expertise, so he created an army of Frankenstein monsters led by his prototype Sentinel, the "Master Mold," who decides that Sentinels are superior to humans—including their creator—and sets about to enslave humanity. Realizing what he has done, Trask blows up his own lab, destroying the Sentinels and himself. History would be repeated when Trask's son "Larry" would later create a new line of Sentinels as weapons against the X-Men, whom he believes were responsible for his father's death. Once

(Top) Xavier's half-brother Cain became the invincible Juggernaut, whose only weakness was exposed upon removing his helmet. (Pencils Werner Roth)

(Above) The creations of mutant-hating humans, the Sentinels invariably became Frankensteins and turned on their creators as well. (Pencils Brent Anderson)

(Opposite) Every family has a black sheep: evil Black Tom Cassidy was the cousin of Banshee, while his partner Juggernaut was the brother of Xavier. (Pencils Mark Texeira)

The Hellfire Code

The X-Men's Hellfire Club was based on a real 18th-century secret society of the same name, which also attracted the upper crust of the time, including artist William Hogarth, politician John Wilkes, and even Ben Franklin, whenever he was in England. But there may have been another inspiration for the comic book treatment of the club: a notorious episode of the cult television series The Avengers, which alarmed the censors of the time so greatly that it remained unshown in the United States for many years. Titled A Touch of Brimstone (The Hellfire Club was its working title), the 1966 show also featured a modern-day neo-Georgian debauchery society. Series heroine "Emma Peel" (played by Diana Rigg) was enticed into the gathering and appeared as the "Queen of Sin," a progenitor to Jean Grey's Black Queen. Most intriguing of all is that Brimstone's guest star was a British actor named Peter Wyngarde, which echoes the club's Jason Wyngarde. This is all the more intriguing since Jason Wyngarde had been created in earliest days of X-Men, several years before A Touch of Brimstone was filmed (though perhaps his name was his entrée into its membership roster in the 1970s).

The tantalizing connections do not stop there. Further revelations about the comic book club's history would include the fact that its American branch founders were "Sir Patrick Clemens" and "Diana Knight." For any Avengers fan, "Patrick Clemens" cannot help but sound like a combination of Avengers star Patrick Macnee and the show's head writer/producer Brian Clemens, while hardcore fans will recognize "Diana Knight" as potentially a sly contraction of Diana Rigg and "Emma Knight," the latter having been established in the television series as the maiden name of Mrs. Peel. And, of course, the club's subsequent White Queen was Emma Frost.

Does this represent a real-life conspiracy of ideas, a tribute to a popular show, or just one of those strange strings of coincidence with which popular culture is rife? Or is it proof that, given enough time and inclination, connections can be made between two of anything?

Perhaps only the inner circle knows for certain.

(Top) Jean Grey as the Black Queen, under the control of maleficent mentor Jason Wyngarde. (Pencils John Bolton)

(Above) Diana Rigg as "Emma, Queen of Sin," in a 1966 episode of The Avengers, may have inspired Jean's Black Queen persona. (Photo courtesy Jerry Ohlinger's Movie Material Store)

(Opposite) One of the most malevolent of all villains in the X-Universe: the ancient Apocalypse.

more, creator and creations would perish together. That was not the end of the Sentinels, however. The U.S. Government would later sanction and fund the creation of a new "foolproof" series of Sentinels that were designed to serve as a kind of dystopian National Guard unit under the control of mutant-hating politicos in Washington, helping them solve the mutant "problem" once and for all.

The Hellfire Club was involved in this scheme… but then, in the X-Universe, the Hellfire Club's fingerprints are virtually everywhere. Its dark tentacles stretch into the highest reaches of the United States Government, and many of the top power-brokers inside the Beltway are either members or had ties to the club. When last heard from, the Hellfire Club was still up and running, and continuing to pull the strings of global finance and power.

The oldest evil mutant on record is among the most powerful: the shape-shifting Apocalypse, who is usually found in the company of his team of servants, the Four Horsemen—"Death," "War," "Famine," and "Pestilence." Apocalypse has been around since the earliest days of dynastic Egypt, some 5,000 years ago. Abandoned as a baby because he was deformed, he was rescued and raised by a desert nomad named "Baal," who gave him the name "En Sabah Nur," which means "The First One." It was from Baal (interestingly, many names within X-Universe have biblical inspirations: *Angel* and *Archangel*, *Baal*, *Cain* Marko, *Lucifer*, *Apocalypse*, and—though this is perhaps stretching the point—*The Beast*) that Apocalypse got both his pre-Darwinian conviction that only the fittest survive, and something of a god complex. For this reason he has spent millennia traveling the earth (punctuated by periods of suspended animation), trying to provoke wars between cultures and societies, and between humans and mutants, in hopes of conquering the victors.

As bad as Apocalypse is, his one-time ally Sinister— who also goes by the more formal handle "Mister Sinister"—might even be worse. Arriving within the saga

Around since the days of the Pharaohs, Apocalypse was then known as El Sabah Nur.

The appropriately named Sinister, with the Goblyn Queen, who was formerly Scott's wife Madeline.

of *X-Men* at roughly the same time (1987, in *Uncanny X-Men* #221), Sinister seems to possess almost unlimited regenerative powers, even more so than Wolverine, and is a telepath and telekinetic to boot. A genius in the field of genetics and a skilled surgeon who has had ties to every evil organization from the Third Reich to the Hellfire Club, Sinister has never failed to put his intellect and talents to evil use.

Sinister was born Nathaniel Essex in England in the 1800s, making him yet another supernaturally old mutant. He was a contemporary and devotee of Charles Darwin, but felt that Darwin's theory was not extreme enough and began experimenting on his own, forming a band of cutthroats called the "Marauders" to procure victims for his experiments. In the process, the body of Apocalypse, which was then lying in suspended animation in London, was unearthed and awakened, and the ancient revived evildoer saw a potential ally in the brilliant, driven, but demented Essex. Apocalypse was able to bring Essex's mutant powers to the surface, and as a result Sinister was born, though eventually the two would part company. Terrifying in his shadowy, lurking nature and often ghostly appearance, Sinister has wreaked havoc in the X-Men Universe. Among his major crimes against humanity were his sanctioned slaughter of the Morlocks and his unleashing of the Legacy Virus.

One vicious mutant who put in a stint with one of Sinister's Marauder packs was "Sabretooth," also known as "Victor Creed," who first appeared in 1977 in an issue of *Iron Fist*, and has since become one of *X-Men*'s most visible villains. He was a member of Mystique's reorganized Brotherhood, and some years earlier had been in a relationship with her, which resulted in the birth of a son. Having passed through the same Weapon X program that "created" Wolverine, Sabretooth can be though, of as Wolverine without the warm and cuddly qualities. He is a violent, bestial killer who has an almost Pavlovian trigger reaction of violence upon seeing the Canadian X-Man. Like Wolverine, Sabretooth has only sketchy memory of his own past life, though the same recent revision of Wolverine's history also hints that Sabretooth might be a character named "Dog Logan," a brutish, rather canine figure who killed Wolverine's father, and who might even be his half-brother! ("Logan," of course, is the name under which Wolverine has traveled for most of his life.)

The Weapon X experiment was responsible for the creation of one more antagonist who swore to bring an end to Wolverine's life: "Lady Deathstrike." Formerly "Yuriko Oyama," she was the daughter of the Japanese scientist who had created the adamantium fusing technology, which she believes was subsequently stolen and misused to create Wolverine.

There have of course been many more villains who have shown up over the years and influenced the X-Men Saga in a less iconic way, proving that like every other aspect of the Marvel Universe, evil is linked together into a dark, dangerous mesh of its own.

(Opposite) The bestial Sabretooth has a lot in common with his mortal enemy Wolverine: both are victims of the Weapon X experiments.

X-TREME CLOSEUP
Mystique
THE SHAPE OF EVIL

"Senator Kelly is fond of speaking of the mutant menace. My colleagues and I are that menace incarnate!"—Mystique

She is not the most physically threatening of villains, or the most ingenious, but it is hard to think of anyone who has caused more Pandora-like chaos within the X-Universe than the eerily beautiful, cyan-hued shape-changer Mystique.

Mystique remains a considerable mystery, in part because so much of her history is clouded by false identities. The best known of these is "Raven Darkholme," which was once thought to be her real name (and who knows?...it might yet turn out to be), but she has also been known at various times as "Ronnie Lake," "Mallory Brickman," "Raven Wagner," "Valerie Cooper," "D. Raven"—which was a male disguise—and "Leni Zauber," the name she was using when she bore Sabretooth a son, which she ostensibly rejected because of his non-mutantcy (though she also abandoned Nightcrawler, who was a mutant). Her limited maternal instincts finally emerged when she acted as the foster mother of Rogue, though this might hinge on the fact that Rogue was a woman.

From her introduction in *Ms. Marvel* #17 (May 1978) on, Mystique has been a true militant amongst mutants. In her Raven Darkholme persona she ascended to a position in the office of the Assistant Secretary of Defense for Research and Development, which gave her access to the nation's most sophisticated weaponry. But secretly, she is merely using her position as a platform from which she and her Brotherhood can assassinate the powerful U.S. Senator Robert Kelly. The plan fails, but that hardly stops her, or her infiltration of the U.S. government (in her Mallory Brickman guise she is the wife of another senator). Years later, another attack by Mystique and the Brotherhood on the Mutant Research Center on Muir Island, in an attempt obtain a strain of the Legacy Virus to use against humankind, would bring about the death of Moira MacTaggart. At one point during her long career in evil, which stretches back to the early days of the 20th century, she was also linked with the terrorist group "Hydra."

(Above) The question mark is more than apt, since Mystique remains one of the most mysterious figures in the X-Universe.

(Opposite, top) "Pardon me while I slip into something a little more dangerous..." Mystique changing form from Raven Darkholme to her natural state.

(Opposite, bottom) When the occasion calls for it, Mystique can disguise herself as a man. (Pencils Michael Ryan)

With so much blood on her blue hands, Mystique would appear to be last person who would actually be offered a spot in an X-Men team, but she was! Mutantcy makes strange bedfellows, and Mystique and the Brotherhood found themselves working for an increasingly suspicious U.S. Government as "Freedom Force," after which she was forced to join the group X-Factor. Her stint on the side of good was a short, uneasy one, however, and before long she was up to her old tricks.

Mystique's romantic life is one of the more interesting ones in the X-Universe. Over the years she has been linked with many men, both mutant and non, but her most lasting and most serious relationship was with Destiny/Irene Adler. Clearly it is not simply within the realm of good-vs.-evil that Mystique has swung both ways.

It Can Ho

1980:

THE BLIND PRECOG, *DESTINY*, HAS SENATOR KELLY CORNERED. BUT... IF SHE CAN PSYCHICALLY SCAN THE FUTURE, WHY HASN'T SHE SPOTTED ME?! UNLESS...

...THE TIMESWITCH HAS MADE ME SOME-HOW *INVISIBLE* TO HER PRESCIENT ABILITIES!

MY COLLEAGUES HAVE BEEN DEFEATED, YET VICTORY WILL STILL BE OURS-- WITH YOUR DEATH.

MURDERING ME WILL ACCOMPLISH *NOTHING.* TRUE, PEOPLE WILL FEAR MUTANTS, AS THEY FEAR *ALL* TERRORISTS --

--BUT THEY WON'T BE *COWED* BY THAT FEAR. THEY'LL FIGHT BACK. THEY'LL *DESTROY* YOU, DESTINY!

POSSIBLY. BUT YOU ARE A GREATER THREAT ALIVE.

DO NOT TRY TO EVADE MY CROSSBOW BOLT, SENATOR. I WILL SENSE YOUR PLANS A HEARTBEAT BEFORE YOU EVEN FORMULATE THEM, AND FIRE WHERE YOU ARE *GOING* TO BE.

I WOULDN'T GIVE YOU THAT SATISFACTION. IF I GOT MY HANDS ON YOU, MUTANT, I'D PROBABLY BREAK YOUR NECK...

...BUT I WON'T RUN.

DESTINY LAUGHS SOFTLY, AND TIGHTENS HER FINGER ON THE TRIGGER.

BUT, AS DESTINY FIRES, KATE "PHASES" WRAITH-LIKE THROUGH HER, CALLING UPON HER DECADES OF TRAINING AND EXPERIENCE TO ACT AS HER CHILD SELF COULD NOT...

MY-MY-- *MIND!*

THE TEMPORAL ANOMALY-- A PART OF ME-- CONSUMING ME!

SENATOR-- *DUCK!*

SHE WILLS HER SHOULDERS TO BECOME SOLID, BASHING THE OTHER WOMAN'S ARM AND THROWING OFF HER AIM.

IN THAT SPLIT-SECOND, AN ABYSS OPENS WITHIN KATE PRYDE. REALITY TWISTS INSIDE-OUT AND, SUDDENLY, SHE COMES FACE-TO-FACE WITH HERSELF AS A CHILD:-- SO INNOCENT, SO VULNERABLE, SO YOUNG.

IMPULSIVELY, SHE GIVES HERSELF A KISS...

...AND LETS THE WINDS OF ETERNITY SWEEP HER HOME.

It Can Happen Here

"It takes sophisticated technology and expertise to build a nuclear bomb…none at all to create a mutant. We have to be able—as a nation, and, perhaps, as a species…to defend ourselves."—Senator Robert Kelly

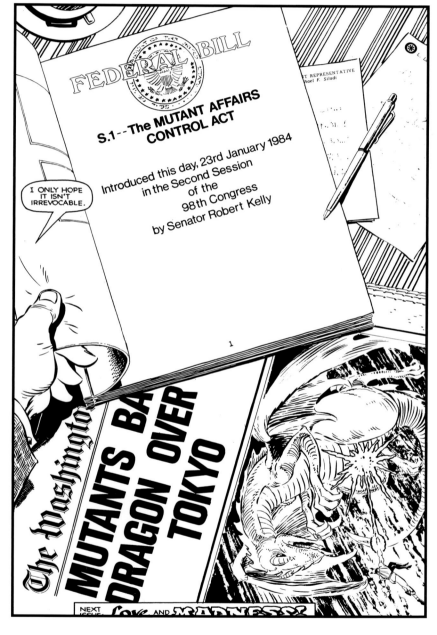

(Above) The start of all the trouble: The Mutant Affairs Control Act, introduced by Senator Kelly.

(Opposite) Senator Robert Kelly narrowly escaped assassination by the Brotherhood of Evil Mutants in another watershed moment of X-Men history, depicted in *Uncanny X-Men* #142. (February 1981; pencils John Byrne, inks Terry Austin)

On Monday, January 23, 1984, in the second session of the 98th Congress of the United States, Senator Robert Kelly introduced Federal Bill S.1: *The Mutant Affairs Control Act.* Its goal was to ensure that all known mutants were registered with the government and live under its explicit control, and that all unknown mutants be tracked, captured, and identified. A congressional colleague of Senator Kelly's declared that the act was nothing less than the officially sanctioned beginning of "legalized slavery," and vowed to fight it any way he could.

The framers of the United States Constitution might have written that all men are created equal, but the framers of the X-Universe have a different agenda. Their creations operate as a perpetual underclass who not only cannot expect equality from their government, but may be forced to fight for their very lives because of its fear, distrust, and hatred of them. In short, the story of the X-Men is not so much steeped in the fight for the American way, as the fight *from* the all-too-prevalent American way of discrimination, presented in allegorical fashion.

In the earliest days of *X-Men*, the government – which was most often represented by the military – was in support of the mutants. The generals who appeared in those first issues may not have understood the strange beings in "cornball" costumes who had unearthly powers, but they accepted them as benevolent. It was instead the ignorant citizenry who feared and harassed them. But by the time of the All-New X-Men of the mid-1970s, things had changed.

It is no coincidence that this running theme came to fruition in the years following the Watergate scandal. "The whole thing with Kelly and the Mutant Registration Act basically came out of the '60s and '70s and watching history unfold, the whole reaction of the

United States to the hostage crisis in Iran, and my thoughts of what the future might be," says Chris Claremont. "The advantage of *X-Men* is that it allows us to explore this territory quite openly and easily, because the X-Men are the all-purpose ultra-minority."

Even so, the way the government-versus-mutants storylines in *X-Men* played out seem not so much inspired by the activities of Richard Nixon's White House as those of Nixon's one-time mentor Joseph R. McCarthy, the junior senator from Wisconsin, who in the 1950s rode to fame and great power by stoking the fires of the rabid anti-Communism sentiment.

The first X-Men figure to take on the McCarthy mantle was, of course, Senator Kelly, whose home state was never specified. Neither was his political affiliation, and an argument could be drawn for membership in either party. Since Kelly was introduced in *X-Men* #135 (July 1980) as a presidential candidate with "a good chance of winning in November," and since then-President Jimmy Carter himself is depicted in the very next issue as the sitting president, one could speculate that Kelly was meant to be Carter's Republican challenger. On the other hand, the fact that the name "Senator Robert Kelly" is not that far removed from "Senator Robert Kennedy," who ran for president in 1968 only to be assassinated—as was Kelly in one version of X-Universe reality—perhaps he was meant to echo the Democrat. Or maybe he is an Independent—in the final accounting, it doesn't even matter. Whatever his party, Kelly is powerful and influential enough in the Senate to call hearings that take up the "mutant problem," hearings at which both Professor Charles Xavier and Dr. Moira MacTaggart testify (and the fact that he was still *Senator* Kelly in 1984 when he introduced his act implies that he never became president in any reality).

Despite his questionable actions, Kelly is frequently described—even by the mutants whose freedom he wants to curtail—as a basically decent person who just happens to have a different outlook on the world.

(Above) A wolf in sharp clothing: Graydon Creed.

(Opposite) The Terminator-like Henry Peter Gyrich, who represents the government at its worst.

"When we had someone like Kelly, or even, to a certain extent, like 'William Stryker' in *God Loves, Man Kills* [a 1982 graphic novel in which a media evangelist declares a Holy War on mutantkind], we had to make sure they were never portrayed as two-dimensional stock villains," Claremont says. "They always needed to have aspects of themselves, their characters, or their beliefs that were admirable, that they believed they were doing the right thing. The reader was left to judge from the context of the story and the circumstances whether they were."

While it is true that as time went on he increasingly became more rabid about his belief that mutantkind was a danger, Kelly never achieved the belligerent demagoguery of "Graydon Creed," who was not so much in favor of registering and controlling mutants as exterminating them altogether.

A virulent public opponent of mutant rights, Creed is also a man with a terrible secret: *he* was the son born to Mystique and Sabertooth! For obvious reasons, Creed made sure this information was never revealed publicly; in fact, a reporter from the *Daily Bugle*—the newspaper that employs Peter Parker/Spider-Man—who happened to stumble upon the secret, was murdered by a political supporter of Creed's in order to maintain silence.

It was the knowledge of his parents' identities, exacerbated by the fact that his mutant birth mother had abandoned him as a baby, which turned Creed into such a violent anti-mutant activist in the first place. He became the leader of an organization called "The Friends of Humanity," which on the surface was a group that strove to have "muties" branded as a sub-class of humanity that would be denied basic civil rights. Its secret activities, however, were more proactive and deadly, and included violent attacks on mutants.

Like Kelly before him, Creed ran for president, using the "mutant problem" as his central platform, and began to receive a good amount of support. But he was assassinated during the campaign. In time it would be revealed that his killer was his own mother, Mystique, who had led the 1980 assassination attempt on Kelly.

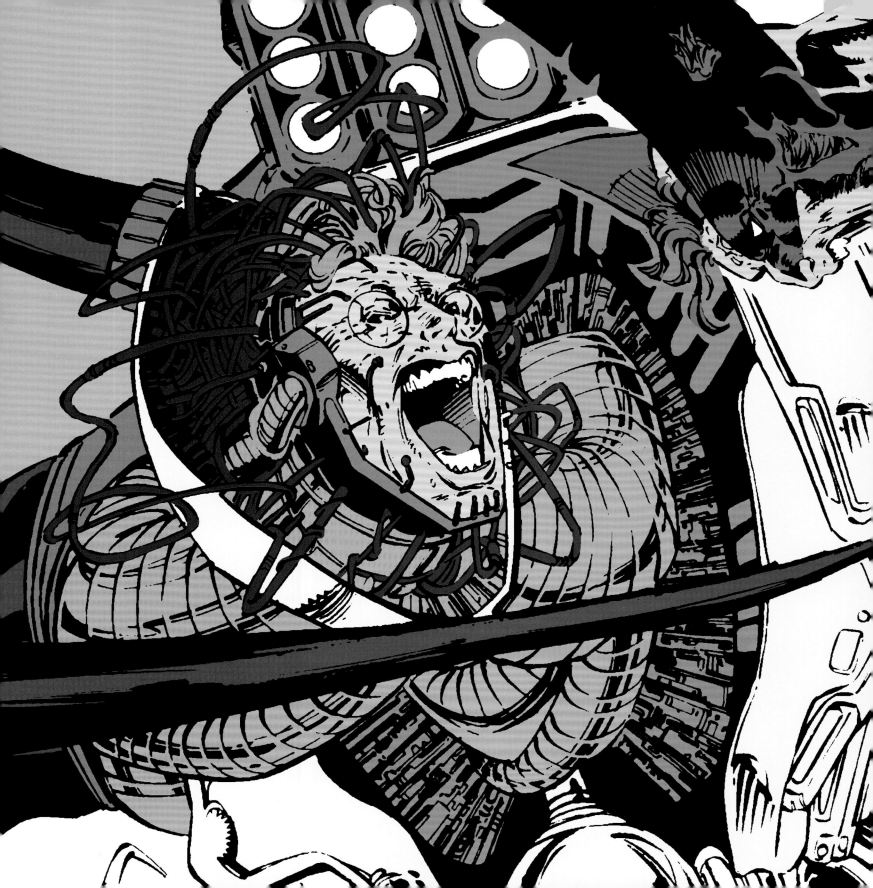

(Above) The ruthless, mutant-hating Bastion gathers his troops for attack.

(Opposite) Cameron Hodge plotted against Mutantkind under the guise of an ally. (Pencils Jim Lee)

This time her motive was different and much more personal: Mystique murdered Creed in retaliation for the death of the grandson of her great and good friend Destiny, who was killed as a result of an attack by the Friends of Humanity.

Things got no better with Creed out of the way, however. A buzz-cut, sunglassed government operative named "Henry Peter Gyrich" was stirring up trouble for mutantkind. Gyrich, who first appeared in the pages of *The Avengers* but was introduced into the X-Universe around the same time as Kelly, was the White House's point man overseeing the official (if clandestine) government response to the mutant problem. Even though he would periodically fall out of favor with the administration in charge, he never seemed to fall too far out of power. Just as dangerous to mutants was a man named "Cameron Hodge," an old friend of the Angel's who initially appeared to be completely supportive of the cause of mutant rights, and even put on a happy face before members of the Senate Committee on Mutant Affairs, all the while secretly working for anti-mutant causes.

These antagonists had all fallen into the category of smooth, business-suited professional nemeses, but a new, even more threatening character would eventually appear on the scene that had more of the trappings of a standard supervillain. This mysterious figure was called "Bastion" and he was behind "Operation Zero Tolerance," an organized, militaristic pogrom against mutants. Bastion had been a key supporter of Creed in his presidential bid—in fact, it had been Bastion who had murdered the *Daily Bugle* reporter—and the anti-mutant sentiment that had resulted from Creed's slaying only helped him promote his argument for staging a mutant final solution.

Bastion and his organization began hunting down and kidnapping the X-Men—including Professor Xavier—and launched an all-out invasion of the Xavier Mansion, absconding with all of computers and available information about the world's identified mutants. But it did him little good, since the cautious professor encoded his files in the Shi'ar language.

Ultimately, Bastion and his Operation Zero Tolerance team went too far even for the likes of Kelly and Gyrich, who began to get cold feet about his warlike tactics. The government put a stop to the operation and Bastion was taken into custody, where it was discovered that he was really a robot with an artificial intelligence and memory, who had been created from the remnants of Master Mold, the original prototype Sentinel!

These kinds of storylines are miles removed from the days when Captain America wrapped himself in the flag and fought the Axis powers and later the forces of Communism on behalf of his country, to the overwhelming thanks of his government. It is one thing to present such an ominous projection of society within an alternate reality storyline, where the reader can always hide behind the safety of knowing that, even within the fictional realm of comic books, it is meant to be a fantasy that will go away by the next issue or two. But placing it in a "real" storyline that holds a dark mirror up to the worst aspects of modern, contemporary society —the philosophies of hate that still proliferate in today's America—and show how it could easily lead to the formation of essentially a Fourth Reich, is to push the field of comic books to a whole new level. It was the beginning of an era when no subject matter was out of bounds to graphic lit, no matter how serious. At a time, for example, when many people were hesitant to talk openly about the AIDS epidemic, *X-Men* was exploring its ramifications metaphorically through its Legacy Virus storylines.

That political turmoil continues to rage within the X-Universe, and probably always will, is evidenced by the fact that five years ago, another assassination attempt was made on Senator Kelly, and this time it was successful. This time the X-Men were not on hand to save him.

(Above) The formidable Bastion would prove too extreme even for veteran mutant haters like Henry Gyrich.

(Opposite) The Sentinels were the government's official take against the "mutant threat," but before long the Sentinel threat became an even greater problem.

The Worl

of X-Men

The World of X-Men

Nothing exists in a vacuum, least of all popular culture. Just as the creators of *X-Men*, consciously or unconsciously, tapped into the creative ether of their time for inspiration, so has the *X-Men* phenomenon had an effect on the books and films that have since followed—even some of the highest profile properties.

(Above) The coat of arms for the Xavier School.

(Opposite) Without the Xavier Academy, where young people with special powers go to learn how to control them away from the fearful eyes of conventional humanity, would there be a Hogwarts?

Consider the basic premise: young people with special talents, who are perhaps having a particularly difficult time blending in with the world around them and being accepted by it, are drawn to a school that is far out of the public eye, a place where they can learn to control their gifts under the tutelage of a benign, if demanding, headmaster. Along the way they learn that there are others of their kind who are not so benign, who are, in fact, trying to use their talents not only to take control of their breed, but perhaps threaten the world at large. Clothe that idea in spandex suits and helmets, mansions and private jets, and it sounds an awful lot like the Xavier School for Gifted Youngsters, Professor X, Magneto, and the class struggles between *homo superiors* and *homo sapiens*. But now think about it clad in traditional British university robes and pointy hats, castles and trains, and the image that springs to mind is Hogwarts School for Witchcraft and Wizarding, with Dumbledore, Voldemort, and the class struggle between wizards and "muggles."

Even a figure as far removed from sci-fi Super Hero activities as comedian Jerry Lewis has tapped into the Universe. In describing the special magic chemistry he experienced in his partnership with Dean Martin, Lewis has written, "We had that X factor."

That *X-Men* has infiltrated the fabric of pop culture so completely is not surprising; what is, though, is that it appeared to do so in record time. For most of the X-Universe's existence, it was a phenomenon that was largely contained within the realm of comic book readers, as opposed to the wider public at large. For three decades, the X-Men remained one of pop culture's best kept secret.

That changed in the early 1990s, the result of the conjunction of occurrences, one of which had begun earlier. That was the system of distributing comic books, which in the 1980s had expanded to include the "direct market," a new marketplace that encompassed specialty comic books stores and hobby shops in addition to (or, frequently, in replacement of) newsstands and bookstores. "*X-Men* was the kind of book that really worked in direct market," says Tom DeFalco, who served as Marvel's editor-in-chief from 1987 to 1994. "As the direct market grew, *X-Men* grew."

There is also no question that the public profile of *X-Men* was raised enormously through the 1992 animated series, the first television show to star the characters. But something else was happening on another previously untapped front: toy store shelves. Prior to 1991, the X-Men had not been very visible as toys and games, certainly not achieving the ubiquity of Marvel's other superstars, such as Spider-Man, The Hulk, Captain America, and the Fantastic Four. But a dedicated line of X-Men action figures first released in 1991 by Toy Biz—a company that would soon become part of Marvel—in tandem with the animated series, served to introduce the characters to a whole new audience of youngsters. Even some "oldsters" within the toy industry itself took notice. "When we introduced our X-Men action figures all in poses and muscles, it really changed action figure history," says JoAnn McLaughlin, Senior Vice President of Product Development for Toy Biz. "They weren't stiff-looking figures like were being done by every other company, and previously by Toy Biz as well, which were done more in four, four-and-a-half-inch scale. We went five, five-and-a-half inches, built up their muscles, gave them great poses, and everybody followed."

That first grouping included something of the usual suspects team of heroes—Cyclops, Wolverine, Colossus, Storm, Nightcrawler, and Archangel—but also included three top villains, Magneto, Juggernaut, and Apocalypse. Each articulated figure came with accessories and a

(Top) Toy Biz's X-Men action figures, first released in 1991, helped popularize the franchise to a mainstream consumer audience.

(Above) One of the more accurate "character vehicle" toys around is this one with Logan astride his chopper.

(Opposite) Action figures remain one of the staples of the toy trade. Toy Biz's most recent line features articulated figures of the Angel (above), Cyclops (left), Nightcrawler (middle) and Mystique (right).

trading card. In the X-Men toy line's first year on store shelves, sales reportedly topped some $80 million.

Toy Biz followed that series with others, including a line of six-inch figures that reflected the likenesses and costumes of the actors from 2000's *X-Men*, and also a separate line that tied into the concurrent animated series *X-Men: Evolution*. However, it is not a requirement for an *X-Men* line to be tied to a particular film or television show for it to be a success. The company's recent series of X-Men figures were not endemic to a particular film or television show, but rather featured the characters in their classic comic book forms, and even reflect the different looks of different series (figures of Cyclops and the Angel, for instance, represent their *X-Factor* looks from the 1980s). These are targeted toward the niche collector's market.

Niche, though, might be too passive a word for a marketplace that has grown immensely over the last two decades, one that is not driven by toys, as such. While they represent images from comic books, which was once the most disposable of entertainment media, today's collectibles are more like portable, permanent works of art: statues, busts, even wall hangings that recall favorite characters or episodes within the comic book sagas. Real hard core collectors can even get replicas of Cyclops's visor or Magneto's helmet! "With the movies, and the dynamic growth of graphic novels in comic stores and book outlets, we're seeing exposure to many more new fans than I think anyone thought was possible," says Michael Leavey, Marketing and Sales Supervisor for Diamond Select Toys, which produces several lines of comics-related collectibles. "We've done several product lines geared around the X-Men Universe and many have been complete sell outs."

Leavey's company—a subsidiary of Diamond Comic Distributors, the largest comic book distribution house in the country—also produces action figures in addition to its numbered limited edition statues and busts; in fact, it is partnered with Toy Biz for the "Marvel Select" line, action figures that come in a setting. Often, these

(Top) Phoenix, with wings of fire, has joined the action figure lineup.

(Above) Action from the waist up: Professor X in his traditional wheelchair.

(Opposite) The Storm figure comes complete with a "weather" pedestal.

(Above) They say you've made it when your likeness appears on a toy: Hugh Jackman as Wolverine, as a 12″ action figure.

(Opposite) This Wolverine model kit lets the consumer build his own excitement.

settings represent particular scenes straight from the comic book pages. "Some of our more popular characters, like Wolverine and Spider-Man, we try to portray from some of their more popular storylines and time periods, so fans have as full a library of key moments as possible," Leavey says. One new collectible line features six different figures from the classic period which, when put together, create a famous scene from the Dark Phoenix saga.

Naturally, the likenesses of those within the X-Universe have been licensed for virtually every other kind of toy on the market, from plush dolls to pre-school figures to role playing toys to vehicle toys, to the product that stands as the symbol of a character's making in a crowded pop culture world: the Pez candy dispenser (the Wolverine Pez has become a perennial).

X-Men toys are popular in other countries as well, as evidenced by MediToy's "Kubrick" line from Japan, which are small, block-based articulated figures, similar but somewhat larger than the popular MiniMates toys, which feature X-Men as part of an entire Marvel Universe line.

If anything displaced action figures as the backbone of the toy industry in the 1990s, it was the rapidly

(Top) This Emma Frost figure is part of the "Marvel Select" line of toys, which come complete with a setting.

(Above) No mundane broomstick for the Scarlet Witch action figure!

(Opposite) Iceman action figure from Toy Biz.

(Above) Kids like to play with evil things, too, as evidenced by this Sinister action figure.

(Opposite) This towering Sentinel action figure cannot be bought separately, but is made up of bonus pieces that come within Marvel Legends figure sets.

growing electronic media area. Fortunately, X-Men characters and storylines were also natural candidates for the realm of video games. The first such video game translation came in 1993 and was simply titled *X-Men*. It involved the Xavierites facing off against a serious threat from what was normally a training tool: the Danger Room. This time Magneto had installed a virus in the computerized set-up, which meant that the various surprise challenges of the Danger Room were now playing for keeps, and it was up to the X-Men to stop it.

That was followed in 1993 by *Spider-Man and the X-Men: Arcade's Revenge*. The "Arcade" in question is a bizarre villain from the comics who pushes the concept of the Danger Room one step further by creating a deadly amusement park in which he traps Super Heroes. In the game, the X-Men are captured by Arcade, forcing Spidey to swing to the rescue. Then it is up to the gamers to bring each character out of the trap-laden park.

The X-Men franchise proved extremely popular in game form, prompting new variations, such as *X-Men: Children of the Atom*, in 1994—which utilized the services of the same Canadian voice actors working for the animated show—and Capcom's 1996 *X-Men vs. Street Fighter*, another teaming in which the goal was to stop Apocalypse. Then, in 2000, the first of a series of elaborate, state-of-the-art video games was released by Activision, operating on an exclusive deal with Marvel: *X-Men: Mutant Academy* was set back in the Xavier Mansion as the players took the roles of new recruits trying to make the team. A sequel, *X-Men: Mutant Academy 2*, followed in 2001.

X-Men: Next Dimension, released in 2002, featured a host of characters and promised free-form "super hero warfare." The voice cast for this game now included Patrick Stewart, reprising his role as Professor Xavier from the feature film. Stewart also lent his authoritative voice to *X-2: Wolverine's Revenge*, which headlined actor Mark Hamill as Wolverine. The storyline had Wolverine racing to find a cure for a deadly virus, which in the process leads him through an exploration of his

(Top and above) "Mini-Mate" figures of Phoenix and Cyclops.

(Top) "Super Hero Showdown Fighting Figures" pit one hero against another.

(Above) The Iceman Squirt Toy is another design for pre-schoolers.

(Top, left) The Japanese "Kubrick" series of small action figures have become quite popular and collectible in the US as well.

(Left) The Wolverine Disk Toss is designed for pre-schoolers.

mysterious and troubled past, including the Weapon X program in the wilds of Canada. By 2003, when the game was released, voicing video games had become a viable marketplace for name actors in Hollywood, and *Wolverine's Revenge* features several noted performers: in addition to Stewart and Hamill, the cast included Mayim Bialik (former star of the sitcom *Blossom*); Danica McKellar (*The Wonder Years*), who voiced Jubilee; Dorian Harewood, who was heard as "Shadow King"; and Lou Diamond Phillips, who played Forge.

2004's *X-Men Legends* featured the voice of Edward Asner (as a "Morlock healer"), in a cinematic, high-action storyline that pitted the X-Men against two menacing fronts: Magneto and his Brotherhood on one side, and the anti-mutant coalition employing the Sentinels on the other. The gamer could assemble a team from fifteen available X-Men, who here included the classic core team of Cyclops, Jean, Wolverine, Storm, Nightcrawler, Beast, and Colossus, along with the likes of "Multiple Man" and Magik. *X-Men Legends* went on to become the best-selling X-Men game to date.

Its follow-up, *X-Men Legends II: The Rise of Apocalypse* (2005), pushed the envelope even further in terms of personal player customization for role playing games (known in the gaming world as "RPG's"), allowing gamers to mix and match teams from a pool of sixteen characters. *X-Men Legends II* even had the capability of putting the game online so gamers could compete in cyberspace. The storyline places the X-Men once more in the situation of having allied with their traditional foes—Magneto and the Brotherhood of Evil Mutants—in order to defeat a common foe, in this case Apocalypse. The game's semi-mystical storyline has the ancient villain discovering the power of a secret prophecy that could give him dominance over the world.

One area in which comic books might seem a little out of place is the realm of books without graphics, but that has not proven to be the case. *X-Men* has inspired a series of original paperback novels that contain no pictures at all, other than those on the covers

(Top) A glowering digital Apocalypse is the star of Activision's *X-Men Legends II, Rise of Apocalypse* game.

(Above) Mystique, cyaned, rested, and ready for action in *X-Men Legends II*.

(Opposite) Players of this latest X-Men game iteration can choose between sixteen different characters to build fighting teams.

X-MEN LEGENDS II
RISE OF APOCALYPSE

and chapter headings. These include the *X-Men: Mutant Empire* trilogy by Christopher Golden, who also wrote *Codename Wolverine*, a book that chronicles the character's pre-X-Men stint as a secret agent; *X-Men: Smoke and Mirrors* by eluki bes shahar; a novelization of the 1980's spin-off comic *Generation X*, authored by Scott Lobdell, co-creator of the comic book series (with Chris Bachalo), and Elliot S! Maggin; and the trilogy *X-Men: The Legacy Quest*, by Steve Lyons.

Award winning science-fiction writer Kristine Kathryn Rusch along with Dean Wesley Smith wrote the official novelization of the film *X-Men*, which was released in 2000 (Smith had also previously written the novel *X-Men: The Jewels of Cyttorak*), while no less an authority on the subject than Chris Claremont wrote the novelizations of *X-2: X-Men United* and *X-3*.

One of the more intriguing books to emerge from the X-Universe is *Planet X*, a 1998 paperback by Michael Jan Friedman, which offers an historic teaming between two pop culture icons: *X-Men* and *Star Trek: The Next Generation*. The story takes place on the planet "Xhaldia," which is experiencing a sudden outburst of rapid mutations, causing a situation that the crew of the *Enterprise* cannot handle alone. While author Friedman could not have known this at the time the book was written and published, he came up with a novel that could not be filmed, at least not without some sense of confusion, since Captain Jean-Luc Picard, commander of the Starship Enterprise in *The Next Generation*, was played both on television and in film by actor Patrick Stewart, who, of course, went on to take the role of Professor Xavier in all three *X-Men* films. The leader of the *Enterprise* meeting the leader of the X-Men face to face, with precisely the same face, might be a conundrum that could not even be worked out within the Marvel Universe.

Then again, just about anything is possible with enough *X*-planation.

(Above and opposite) Character design and animation in video games, such as these for Wolverine, Beast, Magneto, and Storm from *X-Men Legends II*, have made a quantum leap in quality since the early days of the gaming.

Mutants in

Mutants in the Media

Timing, as they say, is everything.

Perhaps that explains why *X-Men*, which has become one of the most successful film franchises of the decade, actually took more than twenty years before being ready for its close-up. Other denizens of the Marvel Universe—even Howard the Duck!—had their media profiles raised far more prominently during the 1970s and '80s. Even though the core group we now recognize as the X-Men was in place by the early 1980s, media recognition was later in coming.

MARVEL SUPERHEROES

The very first television appearance for the X-Men took place in 1966, only three years after their creation, in the now-classic animated series, *Marvel Superheroes*. This syndicated show brought Captain America, the Sub-Mariner, the Mighty Thor, the Hulk, and Iron Man to the small screen in a series of five-minute cartoons that often used the original comic book art as the basis for their animation. Produced for only about $6,000 each by Hollywood-based Grantray-Lawrence Animation (though the *Thor* shorts were farmed out to the Paramount Animation unit in New York), these cartoons redefined the term *limited animation*: only what was absolutely essential to move did move, usually mouths, which were often animated on separate cels over the top of a stationery face.

Professor Xavier and his original team showed up in a three-segment episode of "Sub-Mariner," under the titles "Dr. Doom's Day," "Allies of Peace," and "The Tug of Death." Unfortunately, it was not a particularly auspicious debut. They are never identified collectively as the X-Men or individually by the code names—in fact, they appear in settings more applicable to the Fantastic Four—and some of the production staff seem to have been confused by the characters: in one shot, Iceman appears flesh-toned and wears blue trunks.

It would be another fifteen years before the X-Men would receive another shot at television, and again, it would again be in a guest star capacity.

(Opposite) It was in a 1966 "Sub-Mariner" cartoon that the X-Men made their media debut—doubling for the Fantastic Four, the rights to whom were then owned by a rival animation studio.

SPIDER-MAN AND HIS AMAZING FRIENDS

The Saturday morning cartoon *Spider-Man and His Amazing Friends*, which premiered on NBC in 1981, was the first show to appear under the Marvel Productions banner. Created in response to the success of ABC's *Super Friends*, a comedic take on DC's *Justice League*, the show sought to put together a new teenaged Super Hero team that operated under cover as students at Empire State University. Peter Parker was the centerpiece of the group, and Bobby Drake/Iceman was imported from the X-Men. Plans originally called for Johnny Storm/The Human Torch from Fantastic Four to be the third member of the group, which would have made perfect sense: in the comics they were roughly the same age, rather impetuous, and would be very believable as college students. In addition, Iceman and the Human Torch paired well as "fire and ice." Unfortunately, there were problems at the network level.

"Anytime there was an animation prospect for the *Fantastic Four*, the Human Torch was always a problem, because the feeling at the time was that the kids would be setting fire to themselves," says John Romita, who as art director for Marvel was involved in all of the early media adaptations of the characters. "The Saturday morning people were very, very skittish, very nervous. So just to keep the whole plan from dying, we came up with a character who would fly with heat power, and emit high temperatures in heat, but no flame." Romita went to work designing the new character, which was changed from a teenaged boy to a girl. She was initially called "Heatwave," then "Firefly," and ultimately "Firestar," and the artist took pains not to let her fire-colored costume look too much like flames.

Despite her having been created specifically for the show, within the context of the series Firestar (who was voiced by Kathy Garver, best known as the teenager "Cissy" from the 1960s sitcom *A Family Affair*) was a former X-Man, whose true identity is "Angelica Jones," the daughter of a poor but honest single construction worker. Angelica's powers slowly begin to emerge in

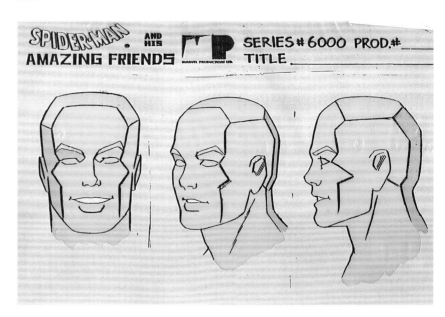

(Top) The cast of 1981's *Spider-Man and His Amazing Friends* included Peter Parker's Aunt May, voiced in the show by June Foray. (Image courtesy Jon Falkner and Adam Curby)

(Middle) The "Spidey-Friends"—Spidey, Iceman, and Firestar—face off against mythical monsters in *Spider-Man and His Amazing Friends*.

(Above) Model sheets such as this one of Iceman helped animators figure out how to pose the characters from different angles. (Image courtesy Jon Falkner)

(Top) Concept art by John Romita for *Spider-Man and His Amazing Friends*. Initially, Firestar was dubbed "Heatwave." (Image courtesy Jon Falkner)

(Above) A Firestar model sheet. (Image courtesy Rick Hoberg)

response to taunting from a particularly nasty classmate named "Bonnie," and usually in the most awkward situations. Her humiliation at a school dance, for instance, causes her to smolder and set off the sprinkler system. This leads to her cruel nickname, "Jinx Jones."

Angela does not make her official debut as a costumed superheroine until her reputation is threatened by Bonnie, who frames her for the theft of the school's homecoming trophy, which she has been entrusted with (of course, the real thieves are Bonnie and her boyfriend). Suspecting who the guilty parties really are, and desperate to clear herself, she flies overhead, spying on them, and gains the information she needs to prove her innocence. Angelica then goes home and creates her Firestar costume and then appears at the halftime show of the big game and forces Bonnie to confess. Meanwhile, her boyfriend is caught trying to sneak the trophy cup into Angelica's locker, and the two bad apples are expelled. But watching her dramatic entrance at the game carefully from the sidelines is Bobby Drake/Iceman (voiced by the prolific Frank Welker), who approaches her and tells her about the Xavier School for Gifted Students.

Later at ESU, Firestar's and Iceman's secret identities are discovered by Peter Parker, who captures their heroics on film, and he convinces them to join him as Spider-Man and form a new team. Making matters easier is the fact that Angelica and Bobby decide to board with Peter's Aunt May in a home that comes complete with a tricked up bedroom that transforms into a laboratory. The technology for that had been provided by "Tony Stark," who even the intrepid photojournalist Peter does not realize is Iron Man.

The second-season episode "A Firestar is Born" contains this origin story, along with a secondary story involving the rest of the X-Men team and Juggernaut. In it, Iceman and Firestar leave for the weekend to attend an "X-Men reunion" at Xavier's school. Never having been an X-Man, Spidey (voiced by Dan Galvizan) is not invited. But he ends up in Westchester soon enough to help the team when Juggernaut goes on the rampage and tries to wipe out Xavier and his students. It is, in fact, Spidey who gets the honor of pulling off Juggernaut's protective helmet so Professor X can telepathically incapacitate him. In addition to Iceman, Cyclops, Storm, the Angel, and Wolverine (sounding suspiciously Australian…but more of that later) make appearances in this episode.

Another second-season episode, "The Origin of Iceman," featured Kitty Pryde, who is represented here during her "Sprite" phase. Voiced by *Little House on the Prairie* star Melissa Sue Anderson, she would return in the third and last season for "The X-Men Adventure," and would be joined by a slightly different line-up of X-Men: Cyclops, Storm, Nightcrawler, Colossus and…Thunderbird! Long since dead in the comics, Thunderbird's presence demonstrates that fidelity to the characters often takes precedence over adherence to a particular mythology.

"You should keep in mind that the chronology of what happens in these cartoons and the chronology of what happens in the comic books are different things altogether," says Rick Hoberg, who finalized the character designs for the show and served as a storyboard artist. "When they go into another medium, they quite often have to change [chronology] for a lot of reasons, primarily that you have to bring a new audience up to speed on things that are already established, and many times you don't want to do that."

In this episode the villain is "Cyberiad," a half-human, half-cyborg maniac who, prior to being transformed in a science experiment gone bad, was a college boyfriend of Angelica's named "Nathan Price." With Spider-Man's help, Firestar and the team manage to prevent the vengeful villian from interfacing in a deadly way with Cerebro.

"The X-Men Adventure" is a prime example of the series' desire to provide action and excitement for the comic book fans, while putting in enough jokes and gags to satisfy the Saturday morning crowd that was more

(Above) Preliminary sketches by artist Rick Hoberg show the design phases Firestar passed through on the way to formalization. (Images courtesy Jon Falkner and Rick Hoberg)

(Top) A Rick Hoberg sketch of the "Spidey-Friends" group reacting to something unseen. (Image courtesy Rick Hoberg)

(Above) A demure, girlish Kitty modeled from three different angles for *Pryde of the X-Men*. (Image courtesy Rick Hoberg)

used to *Scooby-Doo* or *The Pink Panther*. At one point Cyberiad gloats to the trapped Kitty Pryde that she cannot use her phasing powers because, "I've grown accustomed to your phase." *Spider-Man and His Amazing Friends* in its various forms (for its second and third seasons it was packaged with episodes of *The Incredible Hulk*) was successful enough to remain on the air in reruns until 1985.

PRYDE OF THE X-MEN

Hoberg and fellow storyboard artists Will Meugniot and Larry Houston would remain at Marvel Productions (which had evolved out of the TV animation giant DePatie-Freleng) and would become the driving forces behind what might be considered the first real TV adaptation of the X-Men to date, 1988's *Pryde of the X-Men*. The half-hour show was produced by Marvel and Graz Entertainment as the pilot for a proposed *X-Men* segment for the syndicated series *The Marvel Action Universe*. The *Pryde* in question was, of course, Kitty, and the show, written by Larry Parr, details her entrée into the X-Men. "Larry, Will, and I totally agreed on bringing in that wonderful storytelling element of the outside observer, the child who is watching heroes, and Kitty was the perfect character," says Hoberg. "You see it from a child's point of view, so the heroes become more real. The audience would just slip into the suspension of disbelief about Super Heroes and take this seriously."

Inspired by the run of X-Men comics from issue #129 through 139 (1979 and 1980) in which Kitty was introduced into the saga, *Pryde of the X-Men* begins with Magneto held in the custody of the U.S. Army, represented by the brusque "Colonel Jaffe," who happens to hate mutants, particularly "terrorist mutants," i.e., the Brotherhood of Evil Mutants. "He's a mutant, a stinking mutant!" Jaffe rages. "He doesn't deserve to live on the same planet as normal, decent human beings!" Perhaps not, but Magneto soon escapes, and pretty much wipes out the normal, decent soldiers.

Meanwhile, fourteen-year-old Kitty is summoned to

the Xavier Institute through a letter from the Professor himself. Young and naive, she is also frightened, and particularly disturbed that a total stranger—Xavier—seems to know about her ability to phase through solid objects, which she has striven to keep secret. Once she arrives Professor Xavier does his best to put her at ease, and gives her a tour that includes both the Danger Room and Cerebro, and introduces her to his current team: Cyclops, Nightcrawler (who terrifies Kitty), Storm, Colossus, Wolverine, and, in a rare media appearance, the Dazzler. "She was included because New World [the entertainment company that then owned Marvel] thought they still might do a feature and/or get a recording contract for the Dazzler," says Will Meugniot, who along with Hoberg, Houston, and Parr produced the pilot. Jean, he adds, was left out of the lineup because of concerns that the cast was getting too big.

Unbeknownst even to Xavier, real trouble is afoot: Magneto has infiltrated the Xavier Institute and plans to steal the power circuit from Cerebro and use it to capture and control the orbit of the "Scorpio Comet," in order to send it crashing into Earth. As happened to the dinosaurs, the comet's impact would kick up such a cloud of dust that the sun would be blocked for decades, and all life on the planet would die (except, presumably, mutant life). When the plot is revealed a fight breaks out, and Xavier lobs the power circuit to Kitty and asks her to escape through the wall with it. She tries, but is caught by Magneto who, sensing her youthful confusion, even tries to woo her to his side. She spurns his offer, but loses the power circuit to him. Because of this, Wolverine is ready to write Kitty off as a failure, but the others on the team are not as willing to cut her loose.

Professor Xavier concocts a plan for the X-Men to travel through space to Magneto's Asteroid M, and retrieve the power circuit, though Kitty is ordered to stay behind. Foolishly, she stows away, out of sight…or so she thinks. Kitty learns the hard way that it is virtually impossible to hide from a telepath like Xavier. The team manages to break into Magneto's hideout on the aster-

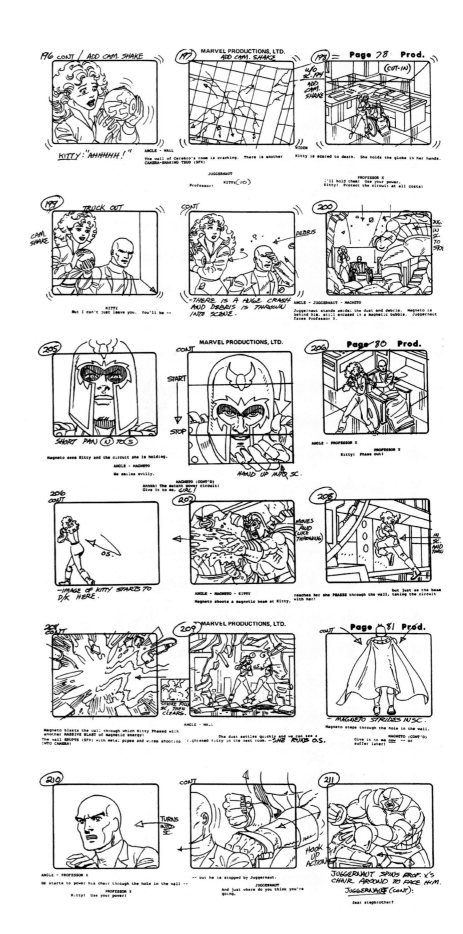

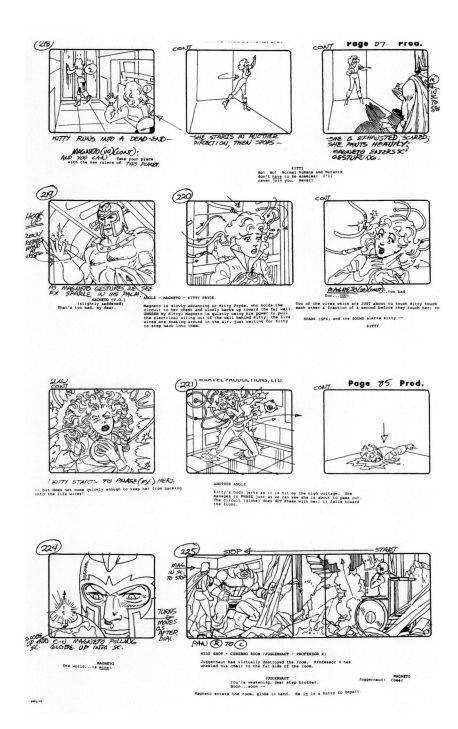

(Above and opposite) Artist Rick Hoberg's original storyboard for *Pryde of the X-Men* In animation, storyboards are commonly used instead of written scripts. (Image courtesy Rick Hoberg)

oid, which is also a haven for his Evil Mutants Toad, Blob, the White Queen, and Pyro, and a battle ensues. It is ultimately Kitty who defeats him, though she is aided by Magneto's white pet dragon (which is never specifically identified as Lockheed), who bites the villain in the leg at every opportunity.

The power circuit is retrieved, though in the process, the asteroid is now in danger of blowing up. Nightcrawler closes the circuit, formerly occupied by Cerebro's power source, with his body, at the risk of his own life. Xavier orders him to teleport out at the last possible second, while the rest of the X-Men escape, though it appears that Nightcrawler was too late. As the others mourn his sacrifice, he finally appears, tired and a little smoky, but intact. Embarrassed by her earlier feeling of revulsion toward him, Kitty now embraces Nightcrawler.

Despite disobeying Xavier's orders to stay behind, Kitty has proven her mettle in combat on her first time out. Even the grouchy Wolverine has to admit that Kitty has done a good job…but he still doesn't want her to be an X-Man. "Not yet," he growls, retreating.

Briskly paced and terrifically designed, *Pryde of the X-Men* packs a lot into its twenty-two minutes. While it is a more serious treatment of the characters than had previously been seen in animation (with only the presence of the lapdog-like dragon seeming overtly cartoony), Parr's script has examples of the kind of humorous banter found in the early comics. At one point, for instance, Magneto disgustedly tells the grotesque Toad to "go play in an airlock." It also accomplishes the difficult task of cutting through a lot of exposition in a non-intrusive way (though the credits, which visually introduce each character, help a great deal in that regard). "We tried to give a kind of introduction, but we didn't want to do an origin story if we could avoid it," Hoberg says. The plan worked: one does not need to have previous knowledge of the X-Men to understand who is who and what is going on.

WOLVERINE 5'3"
4-1-87 *RH* HAIRY VERSION

3-30-87
STORM

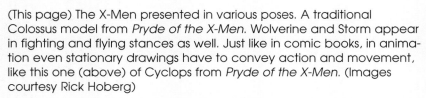

CYCLOPS
RH '87

4-6-87

(This page) The X-Men presented in various poses. A traditional Colossus model from *Pryde of the X-Men*. Wolverine and Storm appear in fighting and flying stances as well. Just like in comic books, in animation even stationary drawings have to convey action and movement, like this one (above) of Cyclops from *Pryde of the X-Men*. (Images courtesy Rick Hoberg)

TOAD

PYRO
3·10·87

EMMA FROST
THE
WHITE QUEEN
3/4/87

BLOB
4·15·87

(This page) The Brotherhood of Evil Mutants—Pyro, the Blob, the White Queen and Toad—made token appearances in *Pryde of the X-Men*, but Magneto was the star bad guy. (Images courtesy Rick Hoberg)

The actor voicing Professor X in *Pryde of the X-Men* was John Stephenson, one of the most recognizable voices in animation, best known for playing "Dr. Benton Quest" in the original *Jonny Quest*. According to Hoberg, he took particular pride in *Pryde*. "Stephenson told me, 'This is the only serious Super Hero adventure cartoon I've done since *Jonny Quest*, and I'm amazed it's taken you this long to get this far!'" he relates. Previously, the actor had provided the voice of Thunderbird for *Spider-Man and His Amazing Friends*.

If there is any kind of stigma attached to *Pryde*, it is that the famously Canadian Wolverine, here voiced by actor Neil Ross (who had also played him in "A Firestar is Born"), blatantly speaks with an Australian accent. Fans at the time were scandalized, though Hoberg reveals that the decision was not only deliberate, but mandated by Marvel!

"I ended up being the voice director on the show, and I was forced to use that Australian version of Wolverine," Hoberg says. "Because all this Australian stuff was so popular at the time—the *Mad Max* films, *Crocodile Dundee*, and so on—it was going to turn out [in the comics] that Wolverine was an expatriated Australian." That direction for the character, however, never actually got beyond the plotting stages, and Logan/Wolverine remained Canadian in the comics. (For the record, Meugniot has a slightly different take on Logan Down Under: "The Australian accent's genesis was simple," he says. "In the wake of *Crocodile Dundee*, New World was trying to develop an Australia-based *Wolverine* movie.")

Despite its success in presenting and handling the characters, and offering an exciting half-hour adventure for kids, *Pryde of the X-Men* did not lead to a series. "None of the networks got it," Meugniot reveals. "It was very different from earlier Super Hero series like *Super Friends* and *Spider-Man and His Amazing Friends*, and the network people were put off by its complexity." At one screening for a network representative, Meugniot says he was asked: "It looks nice, but why is that

(Top and above) In some cases, it is hard to tell these story and design sketches for animation from the original comic book pencils. (Image courtesy Rick Hoberg)

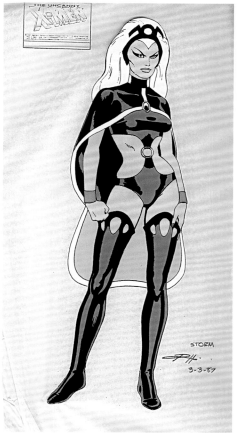

(Top and above) Model cels such as these for Storm and Magneto help to instruct the animation painters how to color the characters. (Image courtesy Rick Hoberg)

Wolverine guy so mean?"

That is not to say that those at Marvel Productions were deterred from trying to sell an *X-Men* series. In fact, it was a top priority for the company's president and CEO, Margaret Loesch. "In all the years that I was at Marvel, my single biggest disappointment was that we could not get an *X-Men* series off the ground, no one was interested," Loesch says. "I did everything but stand on my head to try and sell that series."

The problem continued to lie with network executives (who perhaps should have formed a Brotherhood), who insisted, despite evidence to the contrary, that comic books would not translate to animation. Furthermore, they felt that the target audience for comic books, which they pegged at 18-to-24-year-old men, was not the target audience for Saturday morning, which was in the 6-to-11 demo. "It was flabbergasting to me that, here we had the number one comic book of its day, with thirty-odd years of rich storytelling in its archives, and yet we were confronted with this mindset," Loesch says.

That mindset would quickly change.

X - M E N (1 9 9 2)

After years of dominance by ABC, CBS, and NBC, the fledgling Fox Kids Network arrived on the kidvid scene in 1990 and promptly shook up all of the ossified conventional wisdom regarding children's programming. It was a crusade led by the brand new head of the upstart network…Margaret Loesch! Having moved straight out of production at Marvel, where she had spent the last six years, and into programming at Fox, Loesch was now in a position to green light an *X-Men* series herself. "Once we got Fox Kids up and running, that was the first deal," Loesch says.

The same creative triumvirate returned to the project: Will Meugniot as supervising producer, Larry Houston as line producer and frequent director, and Rick Hoberg as designer and storyboard artist. Graz Entertainment was again involved, this time sharing production duties with Saban Entertainment, a company that would soon become an American television power-house thanks in part to a phenomenon called *Mighty Morphin Power Rangers*. Now that the chance for an X-Men series had finally been realized, all the creative focus was on getting it right.

"Our challenge with *X-Men* was that it had been in the books for thirty years and had gone through so many evolutions, we had to figure out where we picked it up," Loesch says. "So we created sort of an amalgam from the beginning, and tried to be very, very true to the characters."

That included *finally* presenting Wolverine with a proper Canadian accent, courtesy of actor Cathal "Cal" Dodd. Of course, this was not difficult, since Dodd was Canadian. In fact, the entire show was recorded in Canada, where the favorable currency exchange rate saved considerable money in the production budget (Canadian voice recording had also helped stretch the meager budget of 1966's *Marvel Superheroes*, and would become increasingly common in Saturday morning cartoons of the 1990s). The cast of characters was culled from every era of the comic book and included original teammates Cyclops, Jean Grey, the Beast (in his blue and furry form); Storm, from the middle period; and new-comers Rogue, Gambit, and Jubilee, who filled the role that Kitty had in *Pryde of the X-Men*, that of the young-ster looking on in wonderment at the superheroics going on around her. There was also a brand new mutant student of Professor X's named "Morph." The looks of the characters were modeled to favor the style of artist Jim Lee, who was then handling the penciling duties for the team in the comics.

X-Men premiered on Fox Kids' Saturday morning lineup on October 24, 1992 (some weeks after its announced premiere date, because of delays in produc-tion) with the first of a two-part episode titled "Night of the Sentinels," written by Mark Edward Edens. It was structurally similar to *Pryde of the X-Men* in that it focused on young teen Jubilee, whose foster parents are trying to figure out how to handle her emerging

1992's *X-Men* animated series helped put Fox Kids Television on the broadcasting map.

(Top) Professor X working at Cerebro in *X-Men*.

(Above) Jubilee took over the "young girl" role from Kitty Pryde in the *X-Men* animated series.

mutantcy. Her father wants to register her with the governmental Mutant Registry Program, but her mother is hesitant. As for Jubilee herself, she is confused and descending into self-pity. Things in her life are about to get worse, though, when a government-sanctioned, mutant-hunting Sentinel attacks the Salem City Mall, where Jubilee is hanging out in the video arcade. She is rescued by Storm, Rogue, and Gambit, and later taken to the Xavier Institute, where she meets the rest of the team, including Morph, a carefree shape-shifter. Storm tries to explain mutantcy to her, but before she can completely grasp her situation, the Sentinels appear at the Institute and Jubilee is taken away to the Mutant Control Agency, which is operated by Henry Peter Gyrich, whose purpose in capturing unregistered mutants is to probe their brains to learn about other mutants who are out there. Frightened but defiant, Jubilee does what she can to resist.

The X-Men decide to launch an assault on the Mutant Control Agency, rescue Jubilee, and destroy all of the agency's records. They are successful in the latter, but become overwhelmed in a major battle with an army of Sentinels and cannot get to Jubilee. Cyclops, leading the team on the mission, orders a retreat, even though the Beast and Morph are both trapped inside the building. Cyclops reluctantly concludes they are beyond helping. Ever defiant, Wolverine has other ideas and tries to go back for them, but is stopped by Rogue, who with Cyclops's approval, touches him and drains his powers and energy, immobilizing him. The move likely saves Logan's life, but he is not happy about it, particularly after learning that Beast has been captured and Morph has been killed—a death for which he blames Cyclops.

Meanwhile, the president of the United States— a woman—informs Gyrich that she is going to eliminate the funding for his center. Never particularly comfortable with the registry program anyway, she cites the televised news footage of the X-Men fighting the Sentinel in the shopping mall as proof that some mutants are beneficent, and should not be treated as a threat. Gyrich is not about to give up his anti-mutant campaign, though. He rushes back to the center and tells his assistant Trask that they must relocate overseas to continue their work, before the Sentinels are likewise cut from the governmental budget (in a future episode, it would be revealed that Gyrich takes over the island of Genosha, turning it into a mutant slave camp).

However, the X-Men are now on the offensive, and they storm the Center, rescuing Jubilee and destroying the existing Sentinels. Wolverine continues to brood about Morph, as does Cyclops, who is reassured by Jean that he did the right thing by ordering retreat. The fate of Beast is left open, pending a future episode, and the two-parter concludes with Jubilee leaving her foster folks to take up residence at the Xavier Institute.

Overall, "Night of the Sentinels" remains quite close to the comic book mythology, with only minor tweaks (for instance, the X-Men have no idea what the Sentinels are, whereas in the comics, they had been fighting them for more than two decades). What it does capitalize on is the theme of societal paranoia that flourished in the comics storylines. It is revealed that Xavier has scrupulously striven to keep knowledge of the X-Men from the general public, fearing what might befall them if their existence became common knowledge.

In regards to Morph, fans of the comic book who might have been wondering at the episode's start who he was and why he was there soon found out: like Thunderbird before him, Morph was created with the express purpose of being destroyed, the sacrificial lamb offered up to the gods of battle as a way of forcing a major story point that illuminates the shaky relationship between Cyclops, the leader, and Wolverine, the reluctant follower. In fact, the producers had originally intended to use Thunderbird in that role and let history repeat itself, but that idea was nixed at the last minute in fear of protests from the Native American community.

Having a death occur in the first episode was also a way of letting the young viewers know early on *X-Men* was going to offer some headier subject matter than was

(Top) "Read my lips: I'm *not* Australian!" A close up of Wolverine from *X-Men*.

(Above) Rogue's streak of white hair grew into a mane on television.

(Top) The Beast, at his bluest, furriest, and most scholarly, from Fox's
X-Men.

(Above) This robot seems more startled than the Beast, in *X-Men.*

usually found on the Saturday morning lineup, and that
if they wanted sweetness, whimsy, and a happy ending,
they'd better switch the channel over to *Wishkid Starring
Macaulay Culkin.* However, Saturday morning television
being what it then was, and the Marvel Universe being
what it always has been, Morph would rise again.

"We originally intended to let Morph stay dead,"
says Meugniot, "but Fox's broadcast standards and prac-
tices [department] got cold feet about having an actual
death." The producers offered a compromise: if the
network would let Morph *seem* dead at first, so as to
make the story points, they would bring him back as
soon as they could. It worked. "Much to our surprise,"
Meugniot adds, "Morph turned out to be one of the
most popular characters in the early days of the series."

X-Men became the top-rated children's program on
television, and served not only to introduce X-Men
as a franchise to be reckoned with outside of comic book
fandom, it also put the Fox Kids Network at the top of
the heap. "People think that what propelled Fox Kids to
number one was *Power Rangers,* but that's not true,"
says Margaret Loesch. "*Power Rangers* put us in the stratosphere, but we went from number three to number one
because of one event: the premiere of *X-Men.*"

Over the next five seasons, the show would bring in
many other characters from the X-Universe, including
the subterranean Morlocks and their leader, Calisto;
members of the spin-off group X-Force, which included
veteran Sunfire and newer-comers "Strong Guy" and
"Cable"; and nemeses Sinister and Lady Deathstrike.
Nightcrawler would be introduced in a fifth-season
episode that was remarkable for Saturday morning, in its
exploration of the relationship between God and Mutant
(this was during Nightcrawler's evangelical period).

The political themes were sounded time and again
as well, as in an episode titled "The Final Decision,"
in which the X-Men save presidential candidate Senator
Robert Kelly from assassination at the hands of the
Brotherhood, while at the same time joining with nemesis Magneto to battle a common enemy, the robotic

(Top) Ring around a rebel: the 1992 *X-Men* treatment of Wolverine was the first one entirely faithful to the letter of the character.

(Above) Logan out of costume and ready for action in *X-Men*.

(Opposite, top) Storm flies through outer space in the animated *X-Men*.

(Opposite, below) A new look for Jean Grey, from the "X-Ternally Yours" episode of *X-Men*.

leader of the Sentinels, Master Mold, who has been pro-
grammed to eradicate mutants, but who cannot tell
mutants from normal human beings, and so launches on
a campaign to wipe out the entire human race! In this
episode, the long-captured Beast is rescued.

By the time the last original episode of *X-Men* had
been broadcast in 1997, no one at any network doubted
that comic books were an important source for animation, and no one would ever doubt it again.

GENERATION X

The first live-action adaptation from the *X-Men* franchise was *Generation X*, which aired on the Fox network's
primetime lineup on February 20, 1996. Produced
by Marvel Films and its parent company, New World
Entertainment, *Generation X* was based on the
eponymous comic book created by Scott Lobdell and
Chris Bachalo.

The setting is the Xavier School, which is no longer
personally operated by Professor Xavier, who has turned
the organization duties over to his acolytes Sean Cassidy
(here played more for Bond-ish cool than middle-aged
Blarney by Jeremy Ratchford) and Emma Frost (Finola
Hughes), who is enjoying her good mutant phase.
Cassidy and Frost are more than simply business and
teaching partners, but lovers as well.

The new class of students at Xavier School includes
Jubilee (Heather McComb), who can shoot sparks from
her fingertips, but who here is not Asian; "Mondo"
(Bumper Robinson), who can absorb the texture of any
object by touching it; "Monet St. Croix," also known as
"M" (Amarilis), a young African American woman with
an Einstein-sized intellect and something of a superiority
complex; and "Angelo Espinosa," a.k.a. "Skin" (Agustin
Rodriguez), a homey from South L.A. whose limbs
are painfully elastic. While each of these characters have
comic book counterparts, two new ones were created
specifically for the film: "Kurt Pastorius" (Randall
Slavin), who possesses heat and x-ray vision, and "Arlee
Hicks," a.k.a. "Buff" (Suzanne Davis), a typical girl next

(Top) Emma Frost (Finola Hughes) and Sean Cassidy (Jeremy
Ratchford) show off their powers, though not in regulation costumes,
in 1996's *Generation X*.

(Above) Viewers of *Generation X* may have been surprised to
see the White Queen and Banshee in charge of the Xavier School
instead of Xavier, but that reflected what was happening in the
comics at that time.

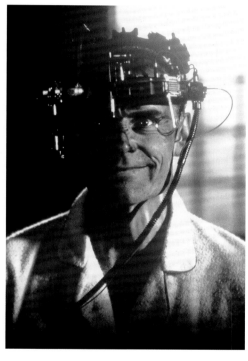

(Top) Russell Tresh's (Matt Frewer) status among the sane was never in question in *Generation X*—he was bonkers from the start.

(Above) The demented genius Tresh built this cranial passport to a different dimension himself.

door who happens to have the physique of Arnold Schwarzenegger, a fact she takes great pains to hide.

Not only do the new students have their hands full attempting to get along with each other, not to mention those from a cross-town rival prep academy, who make it a point not to like the Xavier class (and they don't even know they're mutants!), before long they will be dealing with the kind of problem that only exists in the X-Realm: fighting a deadly, demented genius with the power to enter alternate planes of existence.

The man in question is the seriously bonkers "Russell Tresh" (Matt Frewer), who five years earlier had been working with Sean and Emma on a secret government research project involving young mutants. Tresh was expelled from the project when he tried to extract the X-gene from one of the kids and transplant it into his own brain. Now he's back, with corporate funding to develop a machine through which he can invade people's dreams, which is patterned after a similar machine that Emma had developed earlier. Tresh's corporate pitch was to use this machine as a means of subliminal advertising, but when his personal plans for the device become clear, his financing is pulled. He gets revenge by invading his corporate benefactor's dreams and planting the suggestion of suicide.

But while wandering through the strange netherworld of dreamland, Tresh is startled to run into the restless Skin, who is escaping what he considers to be confinement at the Xavier School by using Emma's prototype dream machine, which he has found in the school's basement. Not realizing how dangerous Tresh is, Angelo forms a bizarre nocturnal alliance with him, and the two continue to see each other in their dreams.

Having gained Skin's confidence, and through the young man having discovered that his hated Emma is now a teacher at the Xavier School, Tresh turns on him and abducts him, planning to pick up his mutant gene extraction experiment where he left off five years earlier. But taking what he has learned from Emma's class in telepathy, Skin sends his spirit to appear before Jubilee that night and desperately pleads for help. Learning of his predicament, Emma and Sean turn the young mutants into a force to fight for Skin's life within the dream world, which Emma has psychically opened. Now comfortable in the netherworld (which is a convincingly eerie environment, enhanced by digital imagery), Tresh proves to be a surprisingly formidable foe. Ultimately it is Skin who brings about his downfall, wrapping his elongated arms around him and plunging with him into dream oblivion. The Generation X team fear that Skin has perished as well, but at the last moment, he reappears to pass back through the portal to reality before is closes for good. As for Tresh, his mind has been destroyed, leaving his uninhabited shell of a body.

Produced on a modest budget in Canada, *Generation X* was a natural fit for Fox, since it had pioneered the teen angst drama genre with such shows as *21 Jump Street*—which had in fact been created by *Generation X*'s writer and co-executive producer Eric Blakeney. In fact, it is the first dramatization of *X-Men* that is not really a Super Hero story per se, rather one that focuses on the problems of its young characters, who are Gen-Xers in both senses. Most of the youngsters do not even have code names, nor are Sean and Emma ever referred to by theirs.

While there are welcome touches of humor here and there, the story is taken seriously by director Jack Sholder and the young actors playing the *Generation X* team (Sholder, incidentally, had previously directed 1985's *A Nightmare on Elm Street, Part 2: Freddy's Revenge*, which was also about an evil presence that haunts the dreams of teenagers). Only the over-the-top turn by Matt Frewer as Tresh seems out of place. While everyone around him is working overtime to suspend disbelief, Frewer plays so broadly as to make one wonder whether he thought he was shooting *Mutants on Gilligan's Island*.

Generation X received high ratings, and there were hopes it might spawn a series. "It was sort of a 'backdoor' pilot," says Avi Arad, Marvel's chief creative officer.

(Above) Skin (Agustin Rodriguez) takes a journey to dreamland in *Generation X*.

(Opposite) The cast of *Generation X*, with Matt Frewer as the insane Tresh featured prominently.

"Then I realized that if you do a live-action television show, you cannot do a live-action [theatrical] movie at the same time. A free show and the big movies could not co-exist."

Four years later, the wisdom of that philosophy would be proven.

X-MEN (2000)

The success of 1998's *Blade*, which had been inspired by Marvel's *Tomb of Dracula* comic book of the 1970s and its later *Blade* spin-off, paved the way for more big-screen Marvel adaptations. Producer Lauren Shuler Donner partnered with Marvel Studios and 20th Century Fox for the production of *X-Men*, and Bryan Singer, who had scored a major hit with his 1995 thriller *The Usual Suspects*, was signed to direct and develop the script along with writer Tom De Santo. Ed Solomon, Christopher McQuarrie, Joss Whedon, Andy Kevin Walker, and David Hayter all contributed to the screenplay, though it was Hayter, an actor-turned-writer, who would receive sole screen credit.

Fan anticipation began to run high as casting was announced. Patrick Stewart, already a cult hero from his role as Captain Picard in *Star Trek: The Next Generation*, was the ideal Professor X, to the point where Stan Lee jokes that he gave Professor X his signature look in 1963 because "I was probably able to read the future and knew that one day Patrick Stewart would be available."

The rest of the cast was equally distinguished. Halle Berry, who had scored the year before playing 1950s star Dorothy Dandridge on television, and who would later win a Best Actress Oscar for *Monster's Ball*, was set for Storm; young Oscar-winner (for *The Piano*) Anna Paquin was cast as Rogue, and Famke Janssen was on board to play the erudite Dr. Jean Grey; James Marsden would be Cyclops; and Rebecca Romijn (then billed as Rebecca Romijn-Stamos) was cast as the nefarious Mystique. Two performers who specialize in action—stuntman Ray Park and 6'10" wrestler Tyler Mane—would take the roles of the acrobatic Toad and

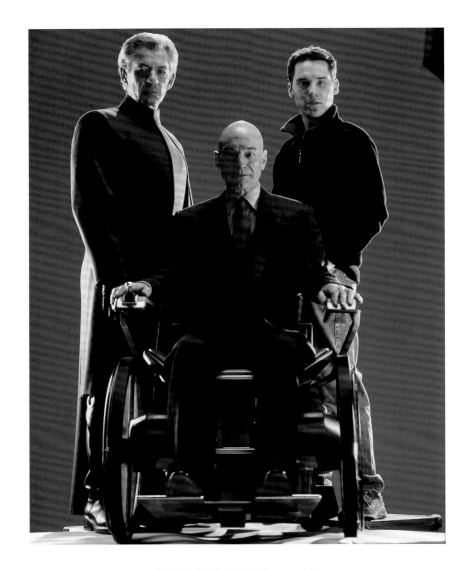

(Top) Sir Ian McKellen as Magneto and director Bryan Singer flank Patrick Stewart as Professor X, in 2000's *X-Men*.

(Above) Interestingly, Professor X never refers to his team as "X-Men" in the context of the first film version.

(Opposite) The *X-Men* theatrical poster played up the paranoia angle.

TRUST A FEW
FEAR THE REST
X-MEN
TWENTIETH CENTURY FOX PRESENTS IN ASSOCIATION WITH MARVEL ENTERTAINMENT GROUP
THE DONNERS' COMPANY/BAD HAT HARRY PRODUCTION A BRYAN SINGER FILM "X-MEN" PATRICK STEWART HUGH JACKMAN IAN McKELLEN HALLE BERRY FAMKE JANSSEN JAMES MARSDEN BRUCE DAVISON REBECCA ROMIJN-STAMOS RAY PARK AND ANNA PAQUIN MICHAEL KAMEN GORDON SMITH
VISUAL EFFECTS SUPERVISOR MICHAEL FINK CO-PRODUCERS JOEL SIMON AND WILLIAM S. TODMAN, JR. EDITED BY STEVEN ROSENBLUM KEVIN STITT AND JOHN WRIGHT, A.C.E. PRODUCTION DESIGNER JOHN MYHRE DIRECTOR OF PHOTOGRAPHY NEWTON THOMAS SIGEL EXECUTIVE PRODUCERS AVI ARAD STAN LEE RICHARD DONNER TOM DeSANTO WRITTEN BY CHRISTOPHER McQUARRIE AND ED SOLOMON
MARVEL
PRODUCED BY LAUREN SHULER DONNER RALPH WINTER
THE EVOLUTION BEGINS ONLY IN THEATRES
DIRECTED BY BRYAN SINGER
www.x-men-the-movie.com
DOLBY
20th CENTURY FOX

the bestial Sabretooth. Veteran character actor Bruce Davison was signed as Senator Robert Kelly, and Sir Ian McKellen, who was best known as a Shakespearean actor on both the stage and screen (and who had previously appeared in Singer's film *Apt Pupil*), was cast as Magneto. Even Stan Lee got into the action, taking the cameo role of a hot dog vender (!) on the beach.

But what fans really wanted to know was who was going to play Wolverine.

Musician and songwriter Glenn Danzig of "The Misfits" was one whose name was mentioned, chiefly because of his physical resemblance to Wolverine—short and muscular—but he lacked an acting resume. Meanwhile, Singer discussed the role with Australian actor Russell Crowe, but Crowe felt aspects of the part were too similar to his recently completed role in *Gladiator* and was not interested. Ultimately it was Dougray Scott who got the nod, signing on to wield Logan's adamantium claws. He would never actually appear before the cameras, though, since the filming of *Mission Impossible: 2*, in which Scott was cast as the antagonist opposite hero Tom Cruise, was running over schedule and conflicted with the start of *X-Men*. With Scott forced to drop out, a last minute replacement was sought. This time thoughts turned to an Australian actor who was then best known for his work in the musical theatre: Hugh Jackman.

Not having been a comic book reader growing up, Jackman was momentarily puzzled when he got the nod. "There's a band in Australia called 'The Uncanny X-Men,'" he says, "and when I first heard about it, I thought, 'They're making a movie about a Sydney pub band? I didn't think they were known at all!' Then I found out it was one of the biggest comic books around."

Filming, which had begun in September 1999 in Toronto, was already a month underway when Jackman arrived on the set to read for Wolverine, and after testing with Anna Paquin, Singer offered Jackman the role on the spot. "I can tell you the exact moment I when I

(Top) Wolverine...? Musician Glenn Danzig (left, with skull and cross-bones) of "The Misfits" was rumored to have been offered the role. (Above, left) Wolverine...? Russell Crowe had the requisite scowl, but not the interest to play Logan. (Photo Steve Granitz/Wireimage.com) (Above, right) Wolverine...? Dougray Scott missed it by *that much* when scheduling problems forced him to abandon the part. (Photo Jeff Vespa/Wireimage.com)

(Opposite) Wolverine! Hugh Jackman was every inch Logan...despite being a lot of inches taller.

LE BERRY: "The message of *X-Men*—finding
ality for all people—is so relevant, and I venture
ay it will probably always be relevant on some
el. This speaks to everybody, especially to
dren. The ones I talk to are very aware of what
movies are all about. They say, mutants are
l, and how silly it is that they're not accepted."

made the decision," Singer recalls with amusement. "We did the screen test in the outer lobby of Roy Thomson Hall [a Toronto concert venue] and I was off sitting in the back of the group, listening to Hugh on headphones, watching through a screen while my assistant director called 'action' and 'cut.' A custodian working at the hall walked up to me, thinking I was a production assistant. He was looking at one of the outer monitors, and he whispers to me: 'Is that the guy they got to play Wolverine?' I thought for a moment, as I was watching and listening to Hugh, and I turned to him and said, 'Yeah.' That custodian was the first person I told when I made the decision. And he didn't even know I was the director!"

In addition to Roy Thomson Hall, other Toronto locations were used extensively, notably Casa Loma, the city's famous Edwardian castle, which provided the settings for the Xavier mansion, and the Gooderham & Worts Distillery, a 19th-century industrial complex that the filmmakers transformed into Auschwitz for the film's grim prologue involving the young camp internee, Erik Lensherr (*Lehnsherr* in the comics), whose mutant powers would emerge at the moment he was being traumatically separated from his mother, who was being taken way to the gas chambers. He responds by nearly pulling down the camp gates with his unseen magnetic force, and this is the birth of Magneto.

As with earlier *X-Men* dramatizations, the film employed the device of a troubled young girl falling in with the X-Men, with Paquin's Rogue now fulfilling the story function that Kitty Pryde and Jubilee had done in different animated versions. But Rogue here is even more crucial to the story: having realized just how powerful she is, Magneto takes her captive and forces her to absorb his power, and use that power to operate a device designed to turn all the leaders of the world, who are gathered in New York for a summit, into mutants— a process that he knows will kill her. The scheme is, of course, thwarted by the X-Men, and Magneto is captured and sent to a high-security, all-plastic prison,

(Top) Toad's (Ray Park) tongue was part practical prop, part digital animation, but all disgusting.

(Above) Bigfoot? No, it's Sabretooth (Tyler Mane) from *X-Men*.

(Opposite) Tyler Mane's experience as a wrestler came in handy for the physical aspects of his role as Sabretooth.

(Prevoius spread) The eyes have it: Halle Berry (left) initially wore uncomfortable contact lenses to opaque her eyes while whipping up a storm in *X-Men*, but later her eyes were digitized white. James Marsden (right), meanwhile, confessed to reporters that the role of Cyclops proved difficult because he usually acted "with my eyes and they took that away from me."

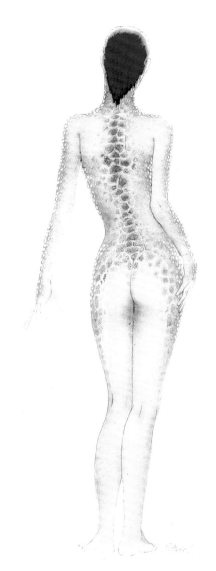

where Professor Xavier still comes to visit him, continuing the two sides of their outwardly civil, but deeply divided mutant debate: can a mistrustful and fearful government be convinced to live peacefully with mutants, as Xavier believes, or is the only solution total forced submission to mutantkind, following Magneto's philosophy?

That question is left unanswered, though director Singer manages to get plenty of political licks in, notably staging a scene of Senator Kelly on the floor of Congress, waving a piece of paper while declaring, "I have a list of names of identified mutants," that chillingly parodies the manner and words of the real Senator McCarthy.

As a high fashion model, Rebecca Romijn was used to spending time in the make-up chair, but nothing like the hours it took four make-up women to apply the one-hundred-plus silicone appliances and blue body dye that turned her into Mystique. "The very first time we tested it took twelve hours," the actress recalls. "Once we started shooting, the make-up took nine hours, which mean that if I had a 9:00 a.m. call, I had to be there at midnight." Because of the heavy make-up workload— it took another two hours to remove—the shoot was scheduled so that Romijn worked in a twenty-four-hour block, then was off for twenty-four hours.

The irony, of course, is that for all those hours being covered, Romijn looks startlingly uncovered. The actress retains her sense of humor about the situation. "I'm in complete denial," she laughs. "I don't feel starkers when I'm in it, but the cast is always reminding me about how naked I am. I'm like, 'You guys, I'm totally not! Look at me, about 70 percent of my body is covered with prosthetics!'"

Halle Berry, meanwhile, was required to wear milky contact lenses that clouded her pupils in the scenes in which Storm is shown changing the weather. "We quickly realized the first time that I could not walk because I couldn't see a foot in front of me," Berry says. "The contacts got thrown out in the first movie and now they do the eyes digitally, and it makes for a much more believable effect, because you can actually see the eyes

(Top) A make-up design sketch showing application details for Mystique.

(Above) Rebecca Romijn as Mystique. "I'm in complete denial!" she laughs regarding the sheerness of her make-up costume.

(Opposite) Mystique (Rebecca Romijn) reverts back to her default form after taking on the guise of Wolverine to fight...Wolverine!

REBECCA ROMIJN: "I'm so proud to be part of it, to be the person that gets to originate this iconic villain that all these *X-Men* fans love so much. It's an honor."

changing, versus one shot with no contacts, and the white eyes in the next shot."

Ian McKellen, who in his career has portrayed some of the world's darkest psyches, from Iago in *Othello* to Adolf Hitler, took an objective approach to the role of Eric Lehnsherr/Magneto. "I don't believe in somebody just being evil, I find that an extremely boring concept of human nature, and very, very difficult to act," McKellen says. "I look for the humanity in the character, and there's plenty in Magneto."

More than anyone else in the film, Xavier is able to respond to Lensherr's humanity. *X-Men* establishes such as strong personal bond between the two one-time friends, despite everything that has come between them, that at times Xavier's referring to Lehnsherr as "Magneto" sounds like an affectionate nickname. Says Singer, "In my own thoughts about their history together, they took the idea of these secret names when they were young and were friends."

While everyone in the cast handled their assignments admirably, it was Hugh Jackman who went out a replacement and came back a star. The actor managed to perfectly capture both the rough, violent side of the character and his more human and humorous side, and even showed a strong resemblance to the comic book image – thanks in part to a great deal of hair spray. And unlike the earlier, criticized Wolverine of *Pryde of the X-Men*, he disguises his natural Australian accent with an American one. The one major difference between the Wolverine depicted on film from his comics counterpart can be measured in inches: at 6'2½", Jackman not only towers over the famously short Logan, but his co-stars as well.

"I spend a lot of time acting with my shoes off," Jackman laughs. "They were particularly sensitive about it on *X-Men*. I felt bad for every other actor, particularly Jimmy Marsden—not that he's short, he's like five-eleven or something—but the poor guy's got these bloody platforms on. Luckily, a lot of the girls in *X-Men* are pretty tall, so we get away with it." (Both Famke Janssen and Rebecca Romijn are also 5'11".)

(Above) The bond between Xavier and Magneto was rarely stronger than in the 2000 film.

(Opposite) Ian McKellen says he sought to portray the humanity in Magneto rather than playing him as a bad guy.

SIR IAN McKELLEN: "What's good about the *X-Men* stories is that they stretch beyond themselves. They ring bells and make connections in people's minds between the world we live in and the world mutants live in."

(Above) Professor X pauses at the theshold to Cerebro.

(Left) Professor X, backed by his team, mans a highly modernistic and sophisticated Cerebro in *X-Men*.

(Opposite) Gaining access to the film's vision of Cerebro was almost like walking the plank.

Likening his character to "a boiling pot with the lid on it," Jackman says that he found a special insight into Wolverine not through boiling, but rather freezing. "I was in Toronto shooting *X-Men* in the middle of winter, and I had a very early call, like five-o'clock, and the hot water wasn't working," he relates. "I had to get into the shower because I had all the hairspray on my hair from the night before, and my wife's asleep, so I had to be quiet. I'm starting this cold shower, and I don't even know how the water is moving, it should have been frozen! It pissed me off, and I thought, 'This is what the character feels like all the time.' So every day when I play the character, I always do it. It's a little physical thing that reminds me what it's like to be Wolverine."

Produced on a budget of $75 million, *X-Men* blazed into movie theatres on July 14, 2000, and went on to become an enormous hit, earning nearly $300 million worldwide. While it was still fresh in people's minds, the next stage of the franchise appeared on the KidsWB television network: *X-Men: Evolution.*

X-MEN: EVOLUTION

Since the beginning, the central idea of *X-Men* had been that the heroes were teenagers who were learning how to use their powers. The animated series *X-Men: Evolution* pushed this idea to a logical extreme, making the show as much about teen drama, which was then a very hot television genre, as crime fighting.

X-Men Evolution is set in an actual high school, Bayville High, which is like any other high school in America except that it has an incredibly high mutant population. Scott, Jean, Kurt, Rogue, and Kitty (who here operates as "Shadowcat") are among the students in the school, though none of the *homo sapiens* students know of their mutancy. They are merely considered the school "goody-goods" by the other kids, and no one more so than the uptight Cyclops. The students live at the Xavier Institute, which serves as a dormitory for good mutants.

(Top) The Jean Grey of *X-Men* is beautiful and forceful, but far removed from her demure "Marvel Girl" pin-up days. Former model Famke Janssen plays Jean.

(Above) At first glance, this ad for a bigoted organization was designed to raise the hackles of readers of alternative newspapers like *The Village Voice*. At second glance, though, it's a deviously clever studio ad for *X-Men*.

(Opposite) A formidable trio from *X-Men*: Storm, Cyclops, and Jean.

FAMKE JANSSEN: "What I like about *X-Men* movies, which sets
them apart from the other comic book adaptations, is I think
they go a little deeper and deal with more meaningful subject
matter. The others ones feel more like they're popcorn
entertainment movies."

Wolverine and Storm, meanwhile are adults on the faculty at the Institute. "Wolverine wouldn't fit into the high school mold without major retooling," explains writer Greg Johnson, who became story editor for the series. "That just didn't seem right for such an iconic character, so keeping him the lone-wolf, forcing him to actually teach the kids, even though it's hard for him to relate, this provided great opportunities for his character without betraying his history." As for Storm, Johnson says: "We felt the team needed a female nurturing presence in the Xavier Institute, and she seemed a natural fit."

The town of Bayville (which is new to the X-mythology) is also inhabited by evil mutants, chiefly Fred "Blob" Dukes, "Todd 'Toad' Tolensky," the cocky Pietro "Quicksilver" Maximoff, and "Lance 'Avalanche' Alvers," all of whom hang out at the run-down Brotherhood of Bayville Boarding House. While Blob, Quicksilver, and Avalanche retain their comic book personalities, Toad represents a major re-thinking of the character, much more of a grungy slacker with disgusting eating habits and hygiene deficiencies, in addition to his lasso-like tongue and hopping ability. Take away the amphibian overlay, though, and this Toad is the sort of kid that everyone had in a class at least once. Adult evil mutants include Sabretooth, whose grudge match with Wolverine rages on, and Mystique, who in her Raven Darkholme persona is the principal of Bayville High. While Mystique is in a position of power—particularly to favor the young bad mutants over the young good ones—she is not really calling the shots at the school: the man ultimately in charge is a very shadowy, very sinister Magneto, who in the first season was glimpsed only as a phantom.

Setting the action in a real high school was just one of the departures from the standard mythology by the *X-Men: Evolution* creative team. Says Boyd Kirkland, the show's producer, "I pressed strongly for going in a public high school even though that was straying from the comic, because we wanted to play up the philosophy

(Above) *X-Men: Evolution* was one of those rare properties that transitioned from television to comic books, rather than vice versa.

(Opposite, top left) A cast shot from the animated series *X-Men: Evolution*

(Opposite, top right) The teenaged dream date Jean Grey from *X-Men: Evolution*.

(Opposite, bottom right) Bayville High, the setting for much of the action in *X-Men: Evolution*.

(Opposite, bottom left) Scott Summers at his coolest, from *X-Men: Evolution*.

of Xavier in the series, his idealistic idea that the survival of mutants depended on them being able to live in normal society and have society accept them."

Rendered as students, most of the characters in the show reflected their usual personalities, though a bit heightened. Nightcrawler, for instance, is now a complete cut-up, to the point of being irresponsible (at least in Scott's righteous opinion). Kurt drops his carefree attitude only when he has to confront his timidity in revealing himself to be different, a fact that is hidden through the use of a device disguised as a watch given to him by Xavier, which masks his real, blue appearance and makes him look like a normal teenager. Rogue, meanwhile, is now a teenaged Goth complete with black clothes and purple lipstick, who reads Bram Stoker's *Dracula* for kicks. Their nicknames echo the banter of the early *X-Men* comics, with Scott dubbed "Slim," Jean "Red," Nightcrawler "Elf," and Kitty "Half-Pint." As the series progressed, other X-Men showed up, notably Hank "The Beast" McCoy, who became a regular, Iceman, Havok, and more recent X-Men such as "Cannonball," "Boom Boom," Forge, and Cable.

X-Men: Evolution also featured an original character "Spyke," a.k.a. "Evan Daniels," who is nicknamed "Porcupine" because he can grow spiny protrusions out of his body. With so many existing X-Men to choose from in the year 2000, why was it necessary to create an entirely new one? "We didn't have quite enough ethnic diversity," Kirkland explains. "We looked at the established characters to try and satisfy that, and just couldn't come up with a good solution to it." Always intended to be an African American character, Kirkland says that Spyke also became Storm's nephew within the mythology of the show in order to point up that the mutant gene tended to run in families, while his blatantly physical power played well visually

During the show's first season the stories centered on the school and the travails of the students, often delving far deeper into teen angst than the Saturday morning norm. "We enjoyed telling those kinds of stories as well

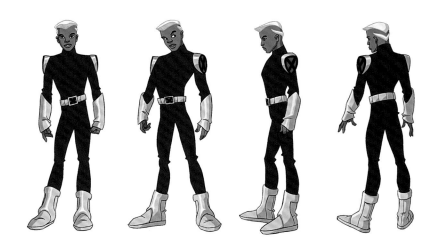

(Top) *X-Men: Evolution*'s Kurt Wagner alternated between a kid with a devilish look and one with a devilish sense of humor.

(Middle) X-23, a young female counterpart to Wolverine, was another character specifically created for *X-Men: Evolution*.

(Above) Evan Daniels, a.k.a. Spyke, was created specifically for 2000's *X-Men: Evolution*.

(Opposite, top) Rogue in Goth mode.

(Opposite, middle left) Can it be…? Yes, in *X-Men: Evolution*, the Xavier Mansion was outfitted with a swimming pool.

(Opposite, middle right) Girlish as ever, Kitty Pryde operated under her "Shadowcat" moniker in *X-Men: Evolution*.

(Opposite, bottom) Mystique as Raven Darkholme, the principal of Bayville High.

Rogue

as the light-hearted ones," says Johnson. "Teenagers experience a ton of angst anyway, and when you add mutant powers to the mix, the results make for good storytelling. But we ultimately did need to mix them up, otherwise the series would have gotten way to heavy."

In subsequent years, *X-Men: Evolution* took on a much more political stance, involving the government witch hunts, Sentinel attacks, and inter-mutant espionage. "By the end of the first season, and especially into the second, Boyd Kirkland, [Marvel executive] Craig Kyle, and I had found the voice we were all comfortable with, and we were eager to shift the tone a bit," Johnson says. "None of us were interested in doing 'X-Men Lite.'" In one of the more intriguing shifts, Mystique, having had a bitter falling out with Magneto, leaves her job as principal of Bayville High, only to be replaced by Robert Kelly! While displaying a characteristic mistrust of mutants, this version of Kelly has yet to embark on a political career, though the seeds of such ambition would be planted in the course of the show.

One more new character would be introduced: "X-23," a female clone of Wolverine—the twenty-third such experiment, hence her code name. As created by Kyle and writer Chris Yost, X-23 sprang into the series virtually fully formed, and enjoyed the rare distinction of moving onto the comic page after having been introduced on television (Firestar had accomplished that earlier). With time, her alternate identity as "Laura Kinney" would be added to the mythology.

X-Men: Evolution enjoyed four successful seasons on KidsWB before stopping production in 2003. While there were X-Men purists who objected to the rewriting of mythology, fans in general seemed to appreciate the fact that the show was a remarkably ambitious, multi-leveled animated "dramedy" that at its best hovered miles above the kidvid norm. "It was a fairly low-budget show, but you wouldn't know it," says Kirkland. "The overall quality of the series was due to a very talented staff and the companies we had overseas doing the animation. Everyone involved went the extra mile."

(Above) The Japanese poster for *X2: X-Men United* suggests who is Japan's favorite X-Man.

(Opposite) *X-Men: Evolution* featured a huge cast, including (clockwise from top), Magneto, at his most shadowy; teenaged Pyro; adult Wolverine; adult Storm; teenaged Toad; teenaged Quicksilver; teenaged Blob; adult Sabretooth, and in the center of it all, Mystique.

X2: X-MEN UNITED

Given its success, there was little question that there would be a feature film follow-up to *X-Men*. *X2: X-Men United* went into production in Canada (Toronto, Vancouver, and Alberta) in June 2002 with Bryan Singer returning as director, and he, Zak Penn, David Hayter, Michael Dougherty, and Dan Harris all contributing to the story and script. Most of the cast was back as well, minus Ray Park and Tyler Mane, whose characters had been killed in the first film, along with several new characters, including Nightcrawler, played by Scottish actor Alan Cumming; "John Allerdyce" (the "St." having been dropped from his first name), a.k.a. Pyro (Aaron Stanford); Yuriko Oyama, otherwise known as Deathstrike (Kelly Hu); Peter Rasputin/Colossus (Daniel Cudmore), and Bobby Drake/Iceman (Shawn Ashmore). Bobby, who had very briefly been seen in *X-Men*, now had a featured part as Rogue's love interest. Even more X-Men could be glimpsed at the Xavier School, chiefly through their powers, such as Kitty Pryde (Katie Stuart). There was even a fleeting, almost subliminal, shot of Dr. Hank McCoy (Steve Bacic), seen being interviewed on television, though no connection was made to his Beast persona.

Surprisingly, the prime antagonist of *X2* was not Magneto, but rather "General William Stryker" (Brian Cox), an ex-Nam vet so gung ho he makes Sgt. Fury look like a draft dodger. Stryker, who is named after, if not exactly based on, the fanatic preacher of *God Loves, Man Kills*, is also a rabid mutant-hater who embodies the truth of Professor X's opening epigram: "Sharing the world has never been humanity's defining attribute."

"In the first movie it was very much mutants against mutants, and now it was time in the second movie to bring in the human element," says Singer. "It goes back to the idea that you don't need to be superhuman to wield power in a bad way, and that's what the Stryker character was all about." Stryker gains the U.S. president's reluctant agreement to invade the recently discovered secret Xavier school, and detain all the mutants they find. The imperative for this has been triggered by a mutant attack on the White House in the person of Nightcrawler. But what President McKenna (Cotter Smith) does not know is that Stryker himself has orchestrated that attack by using mind-control serum on the demon-like mutant, in order to start the mutant wars. The general also has a dark personal secret that is integral to the plot.

Aided by his ultra-cool female assistant, who turns out to be Deathstrike, Stryker sends military forces to the school and takes many of the students there into custody. Most of the X-Men escape, but soon find themselves in the uncomfortable position of allying with the recently escaped Magneto and his evil mutants, to fight their common enemy. Stryker's motivation is fueled by fear and hatred: his own son is a powerful mutant savant, a one-time student at the Xavier School whom Stryker expected to be "cured," and from whom he extracts the mind-control serum. It is also revealed that Stryker was behind the Weapon X experiment that turned Logan into Wolverine, and Yuriko into Deathstrike. But his real goal is to gain control over Xavier and get him to use Cerebro to psychically destroy every mutant on earth!

Stryker's mad plan is defeated, as is the one Magneto hatches: to take advantage of the situation to rewire Cerebro (which, it is revealed, he helped to build), and trick Xavier into destroying all *homo sapiens* on earth. But there is a terrible price for the X-Men's victory: Jean Grey sacrifices herself to save the others, leaving Cyclops inconsolable, and Wolverine (who had come on to her earlier in the film and had been spurned), distraught.

X2: X-Men United was even more serious minded than its predecessor, playing more as a political thriller than a standard Super Hero movie, and was judged by nearly every critic to be even better that the first one. The filmmakers managed to plant some allegorical messages pertinent to modern society—such as the scene in which Bobby "comes out" as a mutant before his

(Top) Professor X and members of the team converge on Washington, D.C., in *X2*.

(Above) Magneto facilitates his escape from an all-plastic prison because his jailer has too much iron in his blood—thanks to Mystique—in *X2*.

(Opposite) The American poster for *X2*. No further title elaboration was necessary.

THE TIME HAS COME
FOR THOSE WHO ARE DIFFERENT
TO STAND UNITED.
X
5·2·03
TWENTIETH CENTURY FOX Presents
In Association with MARVEL ENTERPRISES, INC.
THE DONNERS' COMPANY / BAD HAT HARRY Production
A BRYAN SINGER Film "X2" PATRICK STEWART HUGH JACKMAN IAN McKELLEN
HALLE BERRY FAMKE JANSSEN JAMES MARSDEN REBECCA ROMIJN-STAMOS BRIAN COX
ALAN CUMMING BRUCE DAVISON and ANNA PAQUIN Costume Designer LOUISE MINGENBACH Music by JOHN OTTMAN Co-Producer ROSS FANGER
Special Make-Up Effects GORDON SMITH Visual Effects Supervisor MICHAEL FINK Film Editor JOHN OTTMAN Production Designer GUY HENDRIX DYAS Director of Photography NEWTON THOMAS SIGEL, ASC
Executive Producers AVI ARAD STAN LEE TOM DeSANTO BRYAN SINGER Produced by LAUREN SHULER DONNER RALPH WINTER Story by BRYAN SINGER & DAVID HAYTER and ZAK PENN
Screenplay by MICHAEL DOUGHERTY & DAN HARRIS Directed by BRYAN SINGER
MARVEL
www.X2-movie.com
DOLBY
20th CENTURY FOX

painfully unprepared parents, prompting his mother to ask: "Have you tried not being a mutant?"—as well as some slyly mordant imagery, such as the realization that the government military forces, seen decked out in full commando gear as they attack the Xavier mansion, look far more outlandish than any of the real Super Heroes.

But equally startling is the film's depiction of Nightcrawler. As agile and convincingly devilish as one could hope for (aided by excellent make-up and a digitally animated prehensile tail), he is also religious to the point of fanaticism. Showing virtually no trace of the carefree show-off depicted in the comics, this rendition of Kurt Wagner is so devout that he is compelled to carve Christian iconography into his blue flesh. There is also the intriguing hint that Kurt might have been the victim of Stryker's experiments.

Rebecca Romijn reports that, after their respective hours in the make-up chair, she and Cumming would habitually get together to sing the *blues*. "Alan and I spent a lot of time together and became really good friends, because misery loves company," Romijn laughs. "By day two, he was like: 'What have I gotten myself into?' We would sit either in his trailer or my trailer and just complain to each other [about the make-up ordeal], because we didn't want to be outside complaining to everybody else. We were each other's support system." Through practice, experience, and a few modifications, though, Romijn's make-up ordeal for *X2* was reduced to five or six hours, rather than eight or nine.

McKellen, meanwhile, contributes a subtle but striking, character-defining moment: recognizing a likely kindred spirit in John Allardyce, Magneto asks him his name. "John," the young man replies. "What's your real name?" the older man meaningfully asks, and this time John answers, "Pyro." "[Screenwriters] Dan Harris and Mike Dougherty were very keen on that scene," the actor notes, and this deceptively simple exchange reveals more about Magneto and his philosophy than could an entire page of high-volume expository dialogue.

(Top) Alan Cumming made a creepy and convincing Nightcrawler in *X2*.

(Above) In *X2*, Iceman (Shawn Ashmore) and Rogue (Anna Paquin) share affection, but are prohibited from anything physical because of Rogue's affliction.

(Opposite) The core mutant team of *X2*: Professor X (Patrick Stewart), Rogue (Anna Paquin), Cyclops (James Marsden), Iceman (Shawn Ashmore), Jean (Famke Janssen), Storm (Halle Berry), and Wolverine (Hugh Jackman). In the film, Nightcrawler never actually joins the group.

(Following spread, left top) Hugh Jackman's dance experience as a musical theater performer was called into play for the more physical demands of his Wolverine role.

(Following spread, left bottom) Common enemies make strange bedfellows, as Magneto and Mystique join forces with the X-Men.

(Following spread, right) Kelly Hu as Deathstrike, *X2*'s slightly more refined version of the comics Lady Deathstrike.

Produced at a cost of $110 million, *X2: X-Men United* opened May 2, 2003, on a record 7,500 theater screens worldwide, and went on to outdistance even its successful predecessor, raking in more than $150 million worldwide in its opening weekend, and going for a total of more than $400 million. And that was only the beginning: its home video release later that year earned another $107 million in the first five days alone.

X-MEN: THE LAST STAND

With so much planted, but not quite resolved, in the first two films, there naturally had to be a third X-Men film to complete the trilogy. *X-Men: The Last Stand* went into production in the summer of 2005 in Vancouver, with Brett Ratner directing from a script by Zak Penn and Simon Kinberg. The film's story brings together characters that span the entire history of *X-Men*, from its earliest days—actor Ben Foster appears as the Angel—to its most recent, including "Dr. Kavita Rao," who appears in writer Joss Whedon's 2004 *Astonishing X-Men* run.

The third installment also finally gives Storm a significant role in the action, something that pleased Halle Berry, who over the years had been quite vocal about her frustration that her character was not being fully utilized. "Knowing what role Storm has in the comic books, I kept questioning, 'Why does she never fly? Why does she never fight? Why isn't she part of the action of the movie?'" Berry says. "I think the fans made it clear over the years that they thought Storm should have a more integral part. It is still very much a great ensemble, but I finally get to show her strength in this movie."

One of the early fan buzzes that anticipated *X-Men: The Last Stand* was whether or not Jean Grey was going to appear, having died at the end of *X2*. They should not have worried. "I think everybody's aware that in the comic books, after Jean dies, she comes back as Phoenix," says actress Famke Janssen. "At the end of *X2*, there's the phoenix over the lake, so everybody knew that if we were ever going to do an *X3*, there was a very good

Storm's look in the comics changed repeatedly over the years, as reflected in *X-Men: The Last Stand* by the new hairstyle actress Halle Berry sports.

The rebirth of Jean Grey (Famke Janssen) as Phoenix in *X-Men: The Last Stand* results in the character's inhibitions being thrown off.

chance it was going to be about Phoenix." She is referring to the very last shot of the movie, which is seen under her narration about the forward leap of evolution, in which the nearly subliminal image of a rising phoenix radiates from the waters of Alkali Lake.

Not only does Jean appear in *X-Men: The Last Stand*, she is the one around which the plot revolves. She is first seen as a thirteen-year-old girl in a prologue set in 1985, in which a pre-Magneto Erik Lensherr and a pre-wheelchair Charles Xavier jointly visit her and are amazed by her powers. It will turn out that Professor X has never let on just how powerful she is. Jean Grey is a "Class 5 Mutant," potentially more powerful even than either Xavier or Magneto. And unbeknownst to anyone, Xavier decides to protect both Jean and the world by psychically separating her powers from her conscious mind. Up until her "death," the two sides of her have remained apart, but when a grieving Scott returns to Alkali Lake and discovers Jean is still alive, she begs to see his uncovered eyes. It is one of his optic blasts that breaks down the psychic barriers in her mind, and brings Phoenix into dominance.

Jean is now a creature of pure power and will, and whatever Phoenix wants, Phoenix gets—particularly Wolverine. "There's this sense of a wild animation inside her to a certain extent, and that's the part she connects to Logan," Janssen says. "It's been sort of a constant struggle in her mind to balance that out with the more reserved person who is very much in control of her powers, which is what Xavier has told her to be."

Adds Hugh Jackman: "In the mind of Wolverine, he sees her somewhere in between the two characters. Maybe she's Jean, maybe she's Phoenix, but he feels like he has an insight or connection to her that no one else has. There are fireworks."

Where does this leave Scott? Earlier, when he thought she was still dead, he had been inconsolable. When Wolverine uncharacteristically tries to comfort him, Scott rejects the effort by snapping, "Not everybody heals as fast as you." He is naturally elated upon

(Top) Dr. Henry "The Beast" McCoy (Kelsey Grammer) trades his costume for a suit to fulfill his duties as U.S. secretary of Mutant Affairs in *X-Men: The Last Stand*.

(Above) The Angel (Ben Foster) makes his first appearance in *X-Men: The Last Stand*. The downy wings on the character's back were achieved through a combination of practical costume props and digital animation.

(Opposite) The filmmakers copied Jack Kirby's Angel harness from original comics for the character in *X-Men: The Last Stand*.

Jean's return, but, shockingly, he is destined to be killed by Phoenix!

Having such a powerful loose-cannon mutant at large could not come at a worse time, since the government has finally come to terms with mutantcy. "In *X2*, the villain was the government," says Brett Ratner. "The villain is not the government in this movie. It's a different world when we come into it, more open-minded." In fact, Hank McCoy/The Beast (played by *Frasier* star Kelsey Grammer, inheriting both the guest star status and blue make-up from Alan Cumming) is even part of the president's cabinet, serving as secretary of Mutant Affairs, and for the first time, mutants can claim they are better off now than they were four years ago.

The same can't be said for Magneto, who is living as a terrorist on the run. But he reemerges with a vengeance when the shocking announcement is made that a research scientist, Warren Worthington…the father of the Angel…has developed a vaccine that will eradicate mutantcy—a serum that is being heralded as the *cure*. For some, such as Rogue, the cure sounds inviting, since she would finally be able to touch another human being without fear. For Magneto, however, it is proof that baseline humankind wants to exterminate him and his kind. (The "cure" plotline also "rang a bell" with McKellen, a longtime activist for gay rights. "There are plenty of people around, some in the very higher echelons of the United States government, who think that gays can be 'cured,'" he says. "And so it goes.")

Magneto assembles an army of militant mutants and seeks out Phoenix to join him, which leads to a struggle between him and Xavier over Jean. The movie's biggest shock comes when Jean, having fully transformed into Phoenix, destroys Xavier in the struggle! Even Magneto is upset over his former friend's demise, but he continues his assault.

Having learned that the source of the serum is a young mutant called Leech who is housed at Worthington Laboratories on Alcatraz Island, Magneto and his mutant army, which includes Pyro, Juggernaut

(Vinnie Jones), and Multiple Man (Eric Dane), who can duplicate himself, travel there and launch an attack. *Not* along for the ride is Mystique, who had been shot with a government cure dart while trying to protect Magneto, who then cruelly abandons her. In the final, ground-wrenching battle at the Worthington Lab, however, Magneto suffers what for him is a fate worse than death, as he is also stabbed with cure darts by the Beast. Phoenix, however, remains dangerous as ever, though in her final moments, Wolverine is able to break through to the Jean side of her, and she begs him for release. He complies, killing the woman he has loved with his claws. Order in the world returns as Storm takes over the Xavier School and the Beast is named the U.S.'s ambassador to the United Nations! But the film coda offers a hint of trouble (and the possibility of another sequel?) yet to come as Magneto, now just another old man sitting on a park bench, shows the tiniest hint that his powers may be returning.

"This is a great ending to the trilogy," says Ratner, while acknowledging that the film is also "a much edgier, much more dramatic, much more emotional version of the X-Men." "The story of Phoenix," he says, "has similar parallels to a child in a family going on drugs and losing control and destroying themselves and everybody around them."

One of the most eagerly awaited films of the year, *X-Men: The Last Stand* opened May 26, 2006, setting a record $122 million box office take in its first weekend, and bringing the first big-screen cycle of the *X-Men* saga to a conclusion.

What a ride it was.

(Above) Juggernaut (Vinnie Jones) joins the roster of Evil Mutants in *X-Men: The Last Stand.*

(Opposite) The appearance of sitcom star Kelsey Grammer in full Beast makeup *blue* away the fears of some fans who initially questioned his casting in *X-Men: The Last Stand.*

The Age

# of Mutants

THE UNCANNY X-MEN

| PHOENIX | CYCLOPS | STORM | COLOSSUS | WOLVERINE | NIGHTCRAWLER | SHADOWCAT | ROGUE |

STAN LEE PRESENTS

There's **No** like place **HOME**

CHRIS CLAREMONT
writer
ARTHUR ADAMS
penciler
ALAN GORDON & MIKE MIGNOLA & ART ADAMS
inkers

TOM ORZECHOWSKI, *letterer*   PETRA SCOTESE, *colorist*   ANN NOCENTI, *editor*   JIM SHOOTER, *chief*

GUEST-STARRING THE
NEW MUTANTS

| WARLOCK | MIRAGE | KARMA | MAGIK | WOLFSBANE | MAGMA | CYPHER | CANNONBALL | SUNSPOT |

The Age of Mutants

One can think of the vast roster of X-Men and their various groupings as the comic book equivalents of rock and pop music stars. During their time in the spotlight they shine like supernovas and attract legions of fans, and for a while it seems like they will never be out of the public eye. And some never are: a few become icons who go on year after year, decade after decade, like the graphic literature versions of The Rolling Stones. Cyclops, Jean, Nightcrawler, Storm, and Rogue all easily fit into this category. Others, such as Gambit, leave their groups and achieve new success as a solo act. Still others, like Emma Frost, reinvent their images and parlay the reinvention into a new career (can you say Madonna?). Rarer are those like Wolverine, who shoot ahead of the pack and reach the pinnacle—the Elvis of pencil-and-ink. But a lot of others, no matter how bright their moment in the sun was, are forced to step back after fifteen minutes and make way for the newcomers. They are the Cowsils of the comic book set.

To put in another way, whatever happened to "Maggott?"

MUTANTS, MUTANTS EVERYWHERE

The 1980s was a true mutant boom time, when writers and artists were hustling to think up new mutant powers to add to the rapidly growing roster of characters. By the end of the decade, the entire Universe had started to shake itself up, with individual titles and characters crossing and criss-crossing each other like a four-level freeway exchange. Readers without a road map to the X-superhighway were sure to get lost, and that problem wasn't restricted to the fans. "We were running around like lunatics!" recalls Tom DeFalco, whose tenure at Marvel coincided with the peak years of the Mutant Boom. "We had two offices devoted to that and they could barely keep track. Even within the individual offices there was so much stuff going on it was impossible to keep track of. I can tell you quite honestly, I had no idea what was going on most of the time."

(Opposite) The first offshoot group to be spawned from the X-Men was The New Mutants, depicted here in *X-Men Annual #9*. (Pencils Arthur Adams)

Some of the *X-pansion* of those years was predicated by a detailed long-term publishing plan, though a fair amount of it was spontaneously generated. "During those frantic mid-to-late eighties we were dealing with an army of creative people, and every day someone would say, 'Hey, what if we did this?' or 'What if we did that?'" DeFalco says. "We ended up doing a bunch of those things that were thrown on the fire, and a lot of them worked better than we thought."

Working on all cylinders to keep up with fan demand for new stories and characters, though, did occasionally create problems. "Every once in a while a writer would get confused with the characters and would give a character a new backstory, when they had already given one to that character," says DeFalco. "Later on they would have to go back and try to coordinate it." The point came when it seemed like every ability short of completing the *New York Times* Sunday Crossword Puzzle could be ascribed to mutantcy.

Even now, trying to sort out all the comings and goings of the X-Men of the late 1980s and early 1990s and clarifying the differences between "Skids" and "Skin," "Sage" and "Surge," "Psyche" and "Psylocke," and "Thunderbird," "Thunderbird II," and "Thunderbird III" requires a guidebook.

THE NEW MUTANTS

The first completely new team to be introduced after the mid-seventies revitalization of original X-Men was "The New Mutants," which Chris Claremont and artist Bob McLeod introduced in graphic novel form in 1982, with the follow-up comic book title launching in March 1983. The rationale for the new team was logical: "The 'Uncanny' team that was created for *Giant-Size* were not students," says Chris Claremont. "They were older, tougher, and more experienced. But Xavier's is a school, so how do we answer that? We created new mutants to give Charlie some students to teach."

The New Mutants #1 couched that within an elabo-rately set backstory that had Professor Xavier grieving

(Above) Xavier surveys his newly-assembled "New Mutants" team.

(Opposite) Professor X's second group, from left clockwise: Psyche, Cannonball, Sunspot, Wolfsbane, and Karma.

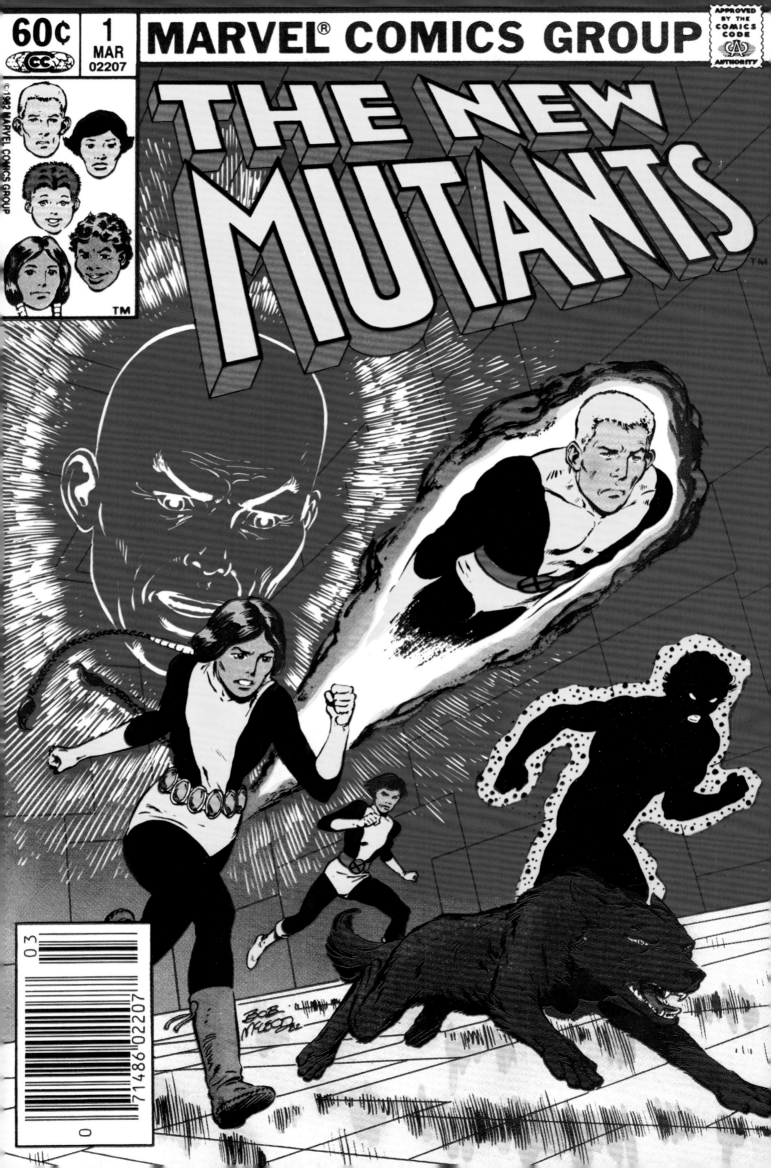

over what he believes is the loss of the original X-Men team in outer space. Broken in spirit, he has to be convinced—almost bullied—by Moira MacTaggart to repopulate the school with new students. He finally does assemble a new team at the Xavier Mansion, once again gathering them from all over the globe, but he steadfastly refuses to create a new team of X-Men, fearing that he will have to endure seeing them all destroyed again. "*That chapter of my life is ended forever,*" he declares, and at the time, he means it. But of course, the original X-Men are not really dead, simply in danger: they have been taken by a parasitic, insectoid alien race called "The Brood," whom they have been battling along with the Starjammers. They would return to Earth and meet their "replacements" in *The Uncanny X-Men* #167 (March 1983).

Despite Xavier's misgivings, the new students back on Earth are chomping at the bit to become a team. They even wear matching uniforms reminiscent of the earliest X-Men outfits: blue-black body suits with yellow tabards and trunks, and red belts with round "X" logos on them. The New Mutants include "Sam Guthrie," a lanky, blond Kentuckian whose code name is Cannonball because he can trigger a thermo-chemical reaction in and around his body and shoots himself through the air like a rocket; Rahne Sinclair, a.k.a. Wolfsbane, a redheaded Scottish girl with a buzz-cut and an accent straight out of *Brigadoon*, who can turn into a wolf; "Roberto da Costa"—"Sunspot"—a short Brazilian boy who draws kinetic energy from the sun and metabolizes it into super strength, during which state he appears to eclipse; "Danielle 'Dani' Moonstar," also known as "Psyche," a Cheyenne girl who can psionically project images, hers and those of people around her, though they often uncomfortably reflect people's most extreme moments of terror or joy; and "Xi'an Coy Mahn," whose codename is "Karma," but whose nickname is "Shan" (the phonetic pronunciation of "Xi'an"), who is the oldest of the New Mutants, if not the most mature. A French-speaking Vietnamese girl with a grenade-like

(Above) The girls of the New Mutants—Wolfsbane, Psyche, Karma and Magma—were a somewhat troubled bunch. (Pencils Josh Middleton)

(Opposite) Charles Xavier's son Daniel Haller, a.k.a. Legion: not a lot of family resemblance.

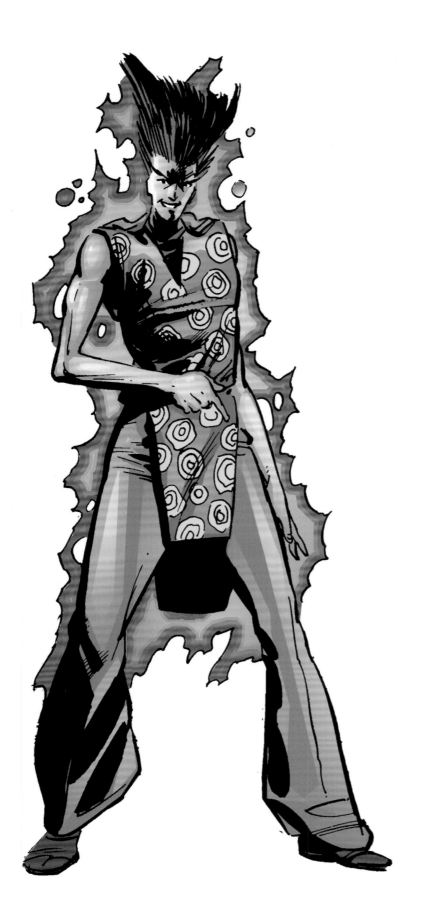

temper, she can control the minds and bodies of other people.

Young and green though they may be, several of them have already led eventful lives. As a young girl, Psyche (who eschews the standard red New Mutant issue belt for a Native American design of silver and turquoise) has seen the deaths of her parents, after which she went to live with her grandfather, the wise Black Star. It was Black Star who sent her from the mountains of Wyoming to the Xavier School, which Psyche is not convinced was a good idea since she holds a fearful view of her powers, feeling they are only good for hurting people she loves. Black Star would later be killed by agents working for Hellfire Club's inner circle member Donald Pierce. (In later years, Dani's teammate Sunspot would also be drawn like a moth to the flames of Hellfire.)

Psyche may be the most brooding of the team, but it is Shan/Karma who carries around the most emotional baggage. Her father was a former Army colonel who was killed as the family fled South Vietnam. Later in the South China Sea, the boat carrying Shan, her mother, and her younger brother and sister was set upon by beast-like Thai pirates, who molested Shan and her mother, who later died. When Psyche inadvertently projects images of these past horrors for all to see, the enraged Shan lashes out at her uncontrollably. *The New Mutants* #1 also contained something of a bombshell for longtime fans of the series: the revelation that Professor Xavier has a son named "David Haller," whose mother is Xavier's former flame Gabrielle Haller, now an Israeli diplomat. A suspected autistic with psi and telepathic powers, David would eventually join the group as "Legion." Even Henry Peter Gyrich shows up in the story, just to let readers know that things would not go easy for the newly formed team.

The New Mutants was an attempt to give the franchise a more mystical flavor, rather than continue a straight action-adventure course. As time and issues went on, more team members would sign up, among them

X-TREME CLOSEUP
Cannonball
TALL IN THE BATTLE

"Until ah get good at maneuverin,' my powers ain't gonna be worth spit to anybody." – Cannonball

Unprepossessing to the point of being yokelish, Sam Guthrie, a.k.a. Cannonball, is nevertheless the breakout member of the New Mutants. He has proven remarkably durable in his career as an X-Man, having even maneuvered himself into membership with the core team. This may be due to the fact that his powers—blasting through the air (complete with exhaust) while protected by an impregnable force field—are more conducive to fighting evil mutants than are projecting one's fears or turning into a wolf. Or maybe it is just proof that still waters run deep.

A one-time Kentucky coal miner, Guthrie's career in the X-Universe started on the bad side, having been discovered and recruited by the Hellfire Club and subsequently sent out to fight Professor Xavier and his team. But the young man just didn't have the evil in him. When Professor Xavier invited him to join the New Mutants, he accepted, and went on to demonstrate a steady, stable personality that rivals even Cyclops's, which has naturally thrust him into leadership roles. Also like Cyclops, Sam has other mutant family members who have worked within the X-Universe.

Cannonball's ability to survive potentially deadly attacks and situations, as well as the startling implication that he was still alive two hundred years into the future (though *which* future is the question), has led other mutants to wonder if he might not be an External, that particular breed of *homo superiors* who are immortal. Maybe he is, or maybe he isn't. But in a period when new mutants were tumbling off of comic book pages like sports equipment out of a closet, humble, laconic Sam Guthrie managed to stand out from the pack.

(Above) The formerly provincial Sam Guthrie acquired a hipper look in later years.

(Opposite, top) Cannonball shooting into action.

(Opposite, below) Cannonball in updated costume, standing next to fellow New Mutant Magma.

"Amara Aquilla" from Britain, known as "Magma" because of her volcanic powers; Colossus's little sister Illyana Rasputin, who as Magik could shoot back and forth through time; and Psylocke, a character who had been on the periphery of *X-Men* since the 1970s in the British comic book *Captain Britain.* Born Elizabeth "Betsy" Braddock, Psylocke was the twin sister of "Brian Braddock," who fought under the name Captain Britain. She is a telepath who can focus her powers into a "psychic knife." Later in her career, through a bizarre mind-swap with a Japanese woman named "Kwannon," Psylocke would emerge as the ninja assassin "Lady Mandarin."

One of the strangest of all heroes in the X-Universe would emerge from *The New Mutants*: "Warlock," an alien "techno-organic" being (a living robot to the uninitiated) who is not strictly speaking a mutant because he is not really human, but who can nevertheless take on the shape and mind of anyone around him. The shape and mind he prefers is that of his human friend "Doug Ramsey," who also joined the New Mutants under the code name "Cypher," and was a mutant translator and interpreter. Years later, it was believed that Warlock had been killed and re-formed (with bits of Ramsey lingering in his memory) into the progenitor of a strange breed called the "Phalanx." But like an unsuccessful transplant, this Phalanx creation rejected the pair's joined psyches (or maybe they rejected it), and it then transformed into "Douglock." This recipe approach to creating characters would become increasingly common in the X-Universe —as would the occurrence of X-Men deaths, including, ultimately, Cypher's.

Even bigger changes were on the way, courtesy of artist and plotter Rob Liefeld, who had taken over the creative reins of *The New Mutants* in 1989. Liefeld would dispense with many of the existing New Mutants and bring in some new amped-up ones, such as "Domino," a woman who can create good luck from nothing; "Shatterstar," a powerful warrior and quick-healer from the alternate dimension Mojoworld; "Feral,"

One of the most bizarre of all X-Men was the techno-organism Warlock, who in time would pass through a series of variant incarnations. (Pencils Bill Sienkiewicz)

also known as "Maria Callasantos," whose is cat-like in both fighting ability and sudden mood swings; and "Thunderbird" —not a return of the original "Thunderbird," but his brother, "James Proudstar," who possesses hyper speed and strength. He would become known as "Thunderbird II," and later still as "Warpath." One of the book's characters would make a more lasting impression: the time-jumping mutant cyborg "Cable," who would appear on the scene in issue #87 to battle a new group of villains titled the "Mutant Liberation Front."

One last notable character would emerge from *The New Mutants*, though he would play on the opposite side: the manic, rambling, Canadian-born mercenary "Deadpool." One of Weapon X experiment's least successful attempts, Deadpool, who also goes by the name "Wade Wilson," is a ruthless combatant who was given Wolverine's healing powers, but at the cost of his body, which was horribly scarred in the process, forcing him to hide within his costume. Deadpool appeared just before *The New Mutants* as a title underwent a major transformation, but more of that later.

The mercenary Deadpool, yet another failed attempt from the Weapon X experiment. (Pencils Patrick Zircher)

X-FACTOR

In 1986, twenty-three years after their debut, Cyclops, Jean Grey, the Beast, Iceman, and the Angel returned for a new series all their own: *X-Factor*, which proved that you *can* go home again, though it takes a little work. It was necessary, for example, for writer Bob Layton and editor Bob Harras to extract Jean from her Phoenix persona, which was accomplished by revising the mythology to now reveal that Phoenix had *never* been the real, physical Jean Grey after all, but rather a duplication created by the Phoenix Force in which to house itself. The *real* Jean had been rescued from the radioactive storm and placed in her state of suspended animation. When she emerged, she seemed to be the Jean Grey of old— she's even called "Marvel Girl" again! (For the record, writer Kurt Busiek also lays claim to contributing this bit of creative legerdemain.)

Like Cyclops, the Angel appears very much his old self in *X-Factor* #1 (February 1986), which was written by Layton and drawn by Jackson Guice (pencils) and Josef Rubenstein (inks), though that would not last long. Iceman, meanwhile, now looks like a slightly more angular version of the Silver Surfer. The most clearly altered from the vintage 1963 team is the Beast, who is still in his blue furry form—at least for the first three issues, after which his human appearance will be restored (temporarily), with the only lingering effect of blue Beasthood a thick thatch of cyan hair.

The team is not headquartered in the Xavier Mansion, but rather a building on the banks of the Hudson in Manhattan—not far from where the comatose body of Jean was discovered. Under the cover of a company called "X-Factor, Inc.," whose public mission statement is to rid society of "the mutant menace," the team members are really seeking out mutants in order to help them. Heading up the operation is Cameron Hodge, a non-mutant who would prove to be a turncoat with ties to the anti-mutant terrorist nation of Genosha. Hodge is not *X-Factor*'s most important bad guy, though. The introduction in issue #5 (June 1986) of arch supervillain Apocalypse would stand as *X-Factor*'s greatest contribution to the X-Universe in general.

With the arrival of a new creative team, husband-and-wife Walter and Louise Simonson, artist and writer respectively, *X-Factor* would get a bit grittier, particularly in regards to the travails of the Angel, who was about to get shoved through the mill. Walt Simonson's brawny graphics wrung every ounce of drama and emotional pain from such episodes as the amputation of the Angel's wings, which had been severely damaged in battle with the Marauders, and which would lead to his startling re-emergence, engineered by Apocalypse, as the metallic-winged, blue-skinned Death, one of the ancient villain's Four Horsemen. (He would ultimately come back to the side of good as the Archangel, though remain blue.)

With time a group of young X-Men "wards" would be added. These included Boom Boom – sometimes

(Top) When the original X-Men were reunited as X-Factor, they went back to wearing matching costumes. Depicted here are Cyclops, the Angel and Jean Grey (the latter two wearing shades for effect, not necessity).

(Above) The quasi-satirical Strong Guy didn't exactly carry the whole magazine on his back, but he was popular.

(Opposite) Reuniting the original team meant figuring out a way to bring the late Jean Grey back to life. The writers not only managed, they even gave her back her old code name, "Marvel Girl."

(Above) X-Factor's matching costumes were not long in fashion. Here the Angel, Jean, Cyclops, the Beast, and Iceman sport new looks.

(Left) The spin-off of a spin-off: a third version of X-Factor, featuring Wild Child, Sabretooth, Mystique, Shard, Forge, and Polaris.

(Opposite) The group known as X-Factor II consisted of newbies Strong Guy and Multiple Man (Men), veterans Polaris and Havok, and New Mutant transferee Wolfsbane.

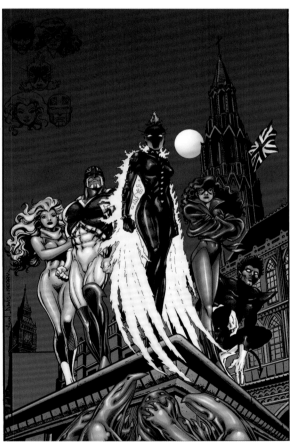

(Top) British heroine Meggan demonstrates the advancing age bracket of comic book readers.

(Above) The London-based Excalibur team: Meggan, Captain Britain, Phoenix II, Shadowcat, and Nightcrawler.

(Opposite) One of the members of the fragmented, dimension-jumping Summers Super Hero dynasty was Rachel Summers, also known as Phoenix II.

called "Boomer," years later rechristened "Meltdown," but who also went by "Tabitha Smith" (scorecards, anyone?), who was a young female mutant who could form explosive orb-like "plasma bombs; "Skids," who was "Sally Blevins," a young woman with the power to encase her body in a force field; "Rictor," in real life Mexican-born "Julio Richter," who could generate shock waves; and "Rusty Collins," one of many in the Marvel Universe who is an orphan, but one of very few in the X-Universe who had no code name. Rusty was a firestarter. Collectively these wards would become known as "X-Terminators."

EXCALIBUR

Meanwhile, on the other side of "the pond," yet another Super Hero group was getting itself established: *Excalibur*. Appearing in October 1988, *Excalibur*, which was created by Claremont and British artist Alan Davis, grew out of *Captain Britain*, a short-lived Marvel UK title that Davis had done with writer Alan Moore in 1976. A kind of cross between Captain America and King Arthur (whose fabled, mystical sword provides the group's name), Captain Britain is the product of a mixed-dimensional marriage—his father was from an unearthly realm called "Otherplace"—and his powers include super strength and flight. Surrounding him in Excalibur were familiar faces Nightcrawler and Shadowcat, along with "Phoenix II," who is also known as "Rachel Summers" (remember that name), and another Brit superheroine called "Meggan," a versatile mutant that can shape-shift, fly, and produce energy blasts. Future members would include the feathery-haired alien "Cerise," the bestial, leonine "Kyllin," and ex-secret agent Peter Wisdom, who can fire stilettos of heat from his fingertips. Colossus and Douglock would also become part of the group. Captain Britain and Meggan would be married in issue #125 (December 1997), which was also the last issue of the title (hopefully the marriage has lasted longer). It should be mentioned that the similarly titled comic book *X-Calibre*, which appeared in March of 1995 as part of the "Age of Apocalypse" storyline, had nothing to do with *Excalibur* except for the presence of Nightcrawler.

ALPHA FLIGHT

Excalibur was not the only team based off-shore. The all-Canadian team Alpha Flight was introduced in *X-Men* issue #120 (April 1979). The group was led by "Dr. James Hudson," who was working with the Canadian government's "Department H," and included northern mutants as siblings "Northstar" and "Aurora," who were super fast; "Shaman," who, like his name implies, was a Native American magic man; "Snow-Bird," who could change into animals (but only those from the Arctic circle); and "Sasquatch," who like the Beast was a former athlete and brilliant scientist named "Dr. Walter Lagkowski," who turned into a gigantic hairy Bigfoot. For a time the peripatetic Wolverine was part of the group as well. The team's own book, *Alpha Flight,* was launched in August 1983 and ran for 130 issues, over which time the cast would expand x-ponentially to include some two dozen new mutant heroes, none of whom made a lasting impression.

THE NEXUS OF '91

The year 1991 was the 50th anniversary of Captain America, which Marvel equated to the birth of the Marvel Universe, at least for marketing purposes. It was also the year that the teams of the X-Universe underwent more player trades than major league baseball in a bad season. The group of wards known as the X-Terminators transferred out of X-Factor and into the New Mutants, while the existing New Mutants scattered. Meanwhile, the main X-Men team divided into two. It was enough to make a fan's head x-plode.

X-Factor got the most complete overhaul, virtually reinventing itself starting with issue #71 (October 1991). There was a whole new team, lead by early X-Men Havok and Polaris, and including, oddly enough, former

(Above) Canada was long a source of mutant characters, but in Alpha Flight they had their own homegrown team. The group included Shaman, Vindicator, and Snowbird. (Pencils John Byrne)

(Opposite) The Amazing X-Men comprised a potluck of characters, including Storm, Quicksilver, Banshee, Iceman, and Dazzler.

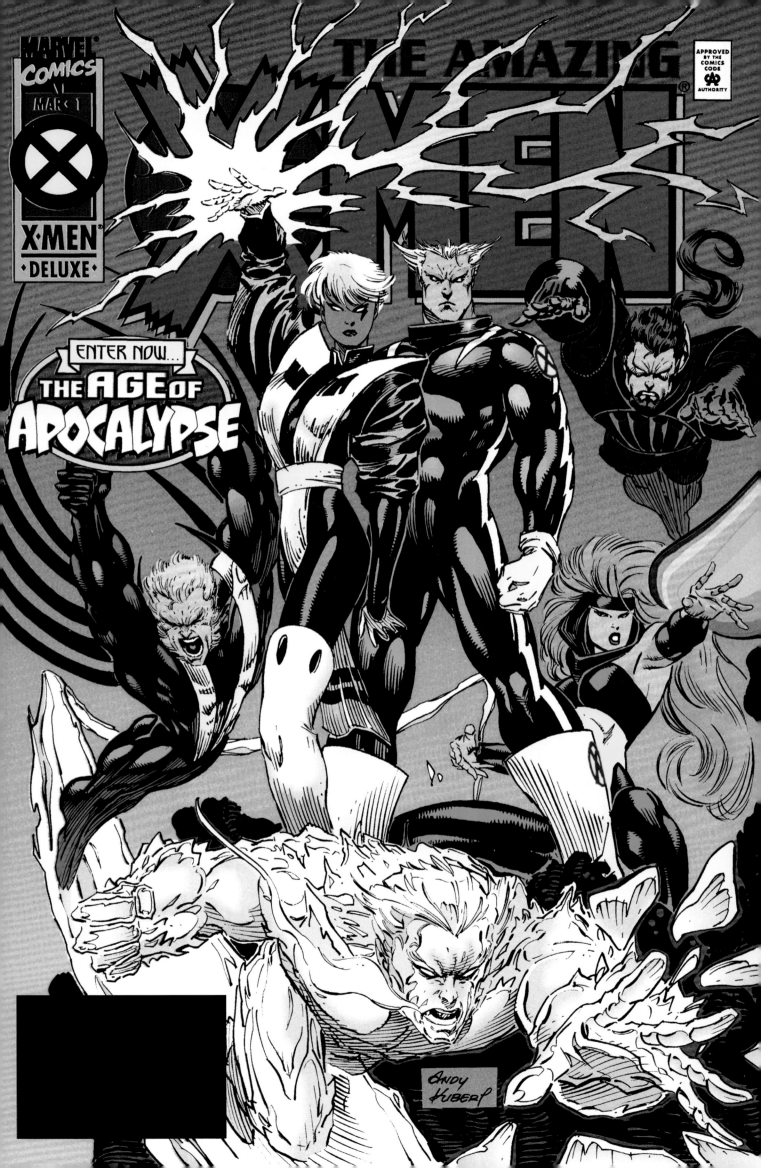

evil mutant Quicksilver, who had recently been a member of The Avengers. Wolfsbane—one of the few survivors from the original New Mutants – was also in the group, as were a couple new characters: Multiple Man, whose real name was "Jamie Madrox," and who could in essence Xerox himself, and Strong Guy, a.k.a. "Guido Carosella," who like his moniker was indeed abnormally strong, due to his ability to store energy in his body like most people store calories. In time, other members would join, including baddies Mystique and Sabretooth, both of whom were reluctant members in the benevolent control of the cyborg sorcerer Forge. This incarnation of *X-Factor*—sometimes referred to as *X-Factor II*— proved successful enough to run until 1998, ending with issue #149.

X-MEN – THE SECOND SERIES

If one *X-Men* title was popular, two would be twice as popular. So a new title, simply called *X-Men* but commonly referred to as the "second series," was launched in October 1991, to run alongside the venerable *Uncanny X-Men*. Artist Jim Lee and writer Whilce Portacio navigated the good ship *Uncanny* while Lee and Chris Claremont were at the helm of *X-Men*.

The idea to add a second regular monthly X-Men title had been Tom DeFalco's, who three years earlier had also spun off Wolverine into a title of his own. "When I joined the staff, I was working on two *Spider-Man* books," he says. "I figured, if *X-Men* is really getting to be a hot book, we should be doing more than one title. There was resistance in the *X-Men* office for the longest time to produce a second title, but when I became editor-in-chief, I didn't care! I thought if we can produce three monthly *Spider-Man* books without harming the character, we could easily produce a second *X-Men* book." (This is, of course, in addition to the various Annuals that came out on a regular basis.)

Among those who had mixed feelings about it was Chris Claremont. "Now we've got six, seven, eight books where there was only one, and even though we're all

(Above) Artist Jim Lee's pages pulsated with energy and action.

(Opposite) One of four covers created for issue #1 of *X-Men* second series (October 1991), which would become the best-selling single comic issue of all time. A Mutant milestone indeed!

(Above) The X-Men "Blue" team featured many A-listers—Rogue, Cyclops, Wolverine, the Beast, and Professor X—along with newer stars Psylocke and Gambit. (Pencils Jim Lee)

(Opposite) Wolverine is incongruously depicted with the X-Men "Gold Team": Iceman, Archangel, Storm, Bishop, and Colossus.

focused on it, the focus is diffused," Claremont says. "The more people, the more books, the more editors, and the more success, the more diffused the beam becomes, until what was originally a laser is now a flashlight. And the beam may go far, it may light up a lot more area, but it's not as intense."

By now official X-Men teams were beginning to resemble the casts of *Saturday Night Live*, in that they were a combination of seasoned veterans with second- or third-generation players, and a few fresh-faced newcomers. *Uncanny X-Men* utilized what was dubbed the "Gold Team," which included Iceman, Jean, the Angel—now the Archangel—Colossus, Storm, and Bishop. The line-up for *X-Men* was called the "Blue Team" and featured Cyclops, the Beast, Rogue, Gambit, Wolverine, Psylocke, and Professor X, who had recently returned from a sojourn in outer space.

Jim Lee was a young (born in 1964) Korean American artist who was already on his way to comics superstardom, thanks to his dynamic way of rendering characters and a visceral, explosive style of staging. Lee penciled (Scott Williams inked) and co-plotted *X-Men* for its first ten episodes, but none topped the initial one, at least in terms of sales. Whether it was the fact that the issue employed the then-unusual marketing gimmick of appearing under four different but interconnected covers, or whether it was the story, the art, the publicity, or just the sense of something historic in the rebirth of the X-Men, the issue went on to sell an incredible *eight million* copies, shattering all existing records.

DeFalco still laughs at the aftermath of printing so many copies. "At one point a bunch of retailers started complaining, because even though they had sold through about 95 percent of them, they had not sold about 400,000 copies," he recalls. "That is a lot of copies, about double what you would normally print of any issue, and they were stuck with them, even though they had sold seven-and-a-half million. I said to one guy, 'What do you think about this?' He said, 'Officially, I have to complain. Unofficially, I bought a Porsche.'"

That 8 million copy statistic, even at 95 percent, stands as a record to this day.

X-FORCE

The same month that *X-Men* #1 was demolishing sales records, another major shift was taking place. *The New Mutants*, whose cast of characters had of late been changing more frequently than a rock diva's costumes, completely transformed after issue #100 into *X-Force*. Cable, Cannonball, Shatterstar, Boom Boom, Feral, Domino, and Warpath all stayed with the new title, as did Sunspot, though it was becoming clear that his allegiance was in question. They were joined by Rictor (late of *X-Factor*) and "Siryn" (pronounced with a long "i"), also known as "Theresa Rourke," the daughter of Banshee, who had inherited her father's sonic scream and could fly. For a time, Siryn worked on the wrong side of mutantcy as an accomplice to her bad uncle Black Tom Cassidy, but finally saw the light. Later, the Morlock Caliban would also join the group.

Within the storyline, this shift had been caused by the fact that Professor Xavier was at that time still on his hiatus in outer space, and in his absence, he had been convinced to leave what he hoped was a new and improved Magneto in charge of his school! (By this time Magneto had undergone a physiological altering at the hands of Moira MacTaggart, which she believed would make him benevolent.) Magneto was certainly *better* than in his old warrior days, but in the final accounting he was no Charles Xavier. So the young New Mutants rebelled and defected, some briefly to the team "The Hellions," which was made up of students from the rival Massachusetts Academy, but many followed Cable into X-Force.

The key creative behind *X-Force* was Rob Liefeld, who segued into the title from *The New Mutants*. Born in 1967 in Southern California, Liefeld was a graduate of the in-your-face school of art, creating panels that leapt off the page and threatened to throttle the reader. Solely in terms of sheer over-the-top brawn, Liefeld's

(Above) X-Force took no prisoners. Clockwise from left: Boom Boom (also called Boomer), Warpath, Cannonball, Shatterstar, Domino, Cable, and Feral.

(Right) Cable and Shatterstar were the breakout heroes from X-Force.

(Opposite, top) The gruesome Caliban was something probably even Shakespeare couldn't have envisioned.

(Opposite, below) X-Force's Siryn was among the growing number of second-generation mutant heroes, being the daughter of Banshee.

Cable

A WARRIOR OUT OF TIME

"I've been staring at my life in the mirror and seeing death reflected back at me – you know...the usual."
—Nathan Summers, a.k.a. Cable

At one time Cable, the cyborg leader of the X-Force, was regarded as "the most mysterious mutant of all." But as the details began to be filled in, it became clear that the taciturn semi-outlaw with the radiating left eye was, if not the most mysterious, certainly one of the strangest mutants in the X-Universe, with one of the most circuitous histories.

The half-machine warrior was in fact "Nathan Summers," the natural son of Scott Summers and Madelyn Pryor! After Madelyn had been transformed into the demented Goblin Queen (in part because of Scott's abandonment of her after Jean had returned), she stole away the child and attempted to sacrifice him to the Dark Side. Young Nathan was rescued by the X-Men, but was then infected with a techno-organic virus by Apocalypse, which began to metallicize his body. This time he was saved by a time traveling member of the "Clan Askani" from two millennia into the future, who promised Scott she would take the boy back with her and cure him.

Now here is where it *really* gets interesting: that member of the Clan Askani who took young Nathan with her back to the 23rd century was called "Mother Askani." But it would turn out that she was really an elderly form of Rachel Summers (remember Phoenix II?), who was the daughter of Scott and Jean, born in a different reality! As a safety precaution in case the virus cure did not work on Nathan and he died, he was first cloned. The cure, though, worked and Mother Askani managed to pull the psyches of Scott and Jean into the future where, as "Slym" and "Redd," they became Nathan's parents. The clone, however, fell into the control of Apocalypse—who had wanted a Summers baby all along—and grew up to be his evil heir apparent "Stryfe," who would lead a villain team called "The New Canaanites." Cable and Stryfe would become bitter, deadly enemies, and their battles would continue to play out when the character received his

(Top) Is this mutant babe Cable or Stryfe? Only Sinister (the one cradling him) can tell. (Pencils Patrick Zircher)

(Above) The time-traveling Cable in middle age.

(Opposite, top) Just like Scott Summers learned his father was a Super Hero, he would discover his son was also. Isn't *anyone* in the family a doctor or lawyer?

(Opposite, below) Cable + Stryfe equals trouble and strife any day.

--I THINK IT'S TIME YOU *SERIOUSLY* CONSIDER CHANGING THE LOOKS ON THE FRONT DOOR.

I'LL TAKE THAT *UNDER ADVISEMENT,* CABLE.

HOW ODD IT FEELS, TO BE CHARGING INTO BATTLE WITH A SON--

--WITH *YOUR* SON--

--OLD ENOUGH TO BE YOUR FATHER.

YES, ODD... BUT VAGUELY FAMILIAR.

A FAMILIARITY THAT COMES, NO DOUBT, THROUGH THE REALIZATION THAT THIS IS HOW IT SHOULD BE.

THAT ALL THE SACRIFICES, ALL THE SOUL SEARCHING... THE SECOND GUESSES AND WHAT IFS... HAVE LEAD TO THIS MOMENT.

A MOMENT WHEN THE FIRST X-MAN AND-- ARGUABLY-- THE "LAST"...

...ARE JOINED TOGETHER IN BATTLE AGAINST A COMMON ENEMY.

WHETHER YOU STAND OR FALL -- WIN OR LOSE --THIS PARTICULAR CONFRONTATION...

...YOU REALIZE YOU'RE ENTERING INTO IT AS SOMETHING MORE THAN MERE COMRADES...

...BUT AS FATHER AND SON.

AS FAMILY.

AND SUDDENLY, YOU START FEELING VERY BADLY FOR THE X-CUTIONER.

characters made Jack Kirby's look like ninety-eight-pound weaklings. While some fans would criticize him for his extreme graphic hyperbole, the truth is that there is no way not to be engaged, even engulfed, by the energy of a Liefield page.

Working with writer Fabian Nicieza, Liefield made *X-Force* an entity that lives up to its name: it is a force, as in "Special Force." It is the Green Berets or Navy Seals of the X-Universe, and the emphasis is always on action. Its prime goal is to bring down the "Mutant Liberation Front," which is a kind of Brotherhood of Evil Mutants with a terrorist bent, with members named "Forearm," "Kamikaze," "Wildside," and "Reaper." Stuck in the middle of all this action, and attempting to represent legitimate law and order, is a huge African American mutant named "G.W. Bridge," a former cohort of Cable's, now working for the law enforcement agency S.H.I.E.L.D., the Supreme Headquarters International Espionage Law-Enforcement Division. "*Hero, villain, human, mutant, none of it matters squat to me,*" Bridge tells an assistant. "*Only right and wrong.*" However, one of the hallmarks of *X-Force* was that "right and wrong" are not that easy to differentiate.

GENERATION X

For years in the pages of *X-Men*, young and often confused and wary mutants had been scouted by two rival establishments: the Xavier School in upstate New York, and the Massachusetts Academy, located in the Berkshire Mountains, which is operated by Emma Frost. The Xavier School and its mission statement are of course well known. As for the Massachusetts Academy, it had traditionally been the front organization for the securing and training of talented young mutants who might grow up to use their powers for the benefit of the prestigiously evil Hellfire Club, which Emma served as White Queen. Incredibly, though, the two joined forces in 1994, when Professor Xavier assumed control of the Massachusetts Academy and installed both Emma and Sean "Banshee" Cassidy as headmasters for his Gifted

(Above) The kids of Generation X might resemble average teenagers on the surface, but they aren't.

(Opposite) Trouble from the start, courtesy of Cable, Feral, and Boom Boom.

(Below) The Xavier School for Gifted Youngsters evolved over the decades into the more formal Institute of Higheer Learning.

Students program. (The old school became the "Xavier Institute for Higher Learning.")

The first class of multi-national newcomers were introduced in issue #318 of *X-Men*. Their own book, *Generation X*, created by Scott Lobdell and Chris Bachalo, launched in October 1994. The comics Gen-Xers differed somewhat in character make-up, traits, and names from the television adaptation made in 1996 (see the *Mutants in the Media* section). Here they consist of Mondo, a Samoan, who absorbs outside textures; Skin—Angelo Espinosa—a kid from East L.A. with a surfeit of pasty gray flesh; "Husk," a.k.a. "Paige Guthrie" (Cannonball's sister), who can shed her skin, snake-like, only to reveal a supernaturally strong body underneath; "Jonothon Starsmore," nicknamed "Jono" but code named "Chamber," an English-born mutant who can radiate energy from his chest, the force of which ruined his lower face, which causes him to wear the fiery blast like a muffler; "Synch," real name "Everett Thomas," a young black man who absorbs the powers of any nearby mutant; M—Monet St. Croix—a powerful, flying telepath who is from the world's smallest sovereignty, Monaco, but who has enough ego and arrogance to fill Montana; "Penance," a puzzling mutant whose skin is knife-edged; and Jubilee, who was transferred in from the main team. The team's recurring opponent was the parasitic "Emplate," who dined on the marrow and the powers of other mutants.

The emphasis of *Generation X* was not so much on heroics as the problems of the youngsters, and as such the title became quite popular. But then in a series of bizarre plot machinations, Emplate would prove to be M's brother, while it would be revealed that M was not M at all, but rather M's two sisters, psychically combined, while the real M was really *Penance*. Monet eventually regained her M-hood, though Mondo would be caught in the plot device of being killed, but not really killed, because it was a secretly created clone that had been killed. Clone-based revelations in comic books are the graphic lit equivalent of identical twin substitutions

(Above) Jubilee (left) was the only established X-Man to join the Generation X team. Flanking her are Husk, Synch, Chamber, M, and Skin.

(Opposite) Banshee and the White Queen (standing in rear) were in charge of the mutant brigade of Generation X. The fact that both had, in their careers, been on the bad side of the law is a testament to the trusting nature of Charles Xavier.

as the solution to a murder mystery, and fans within the Marvel Universe remain polarized as to their validity. No matter; *Generation X* continued until 2001.

Throughout the 1990s and into the new century, various other spin-off titles had been created, often being comic book adaptations of the popular animated series, such as *X-Men Adventures*, which appeared in 1992 and which was based on the Fox show, and *X-Men: Evolution*, which came out in 2001, in the graphic style of that series on KidsWB. Other titles offered revisionist takes on the classic teams, such as 1999's *X-Men: The Hidden Years* and 2000's *Ultimate X-Men*. But by then, a bigger shake-up was underway.

NEW X-MEN

When it seemed like there could not be many undiscovered roads left down which to travel, the X-Universe was rerouted in 2001 by the arrival of British writer Grant Morrison, who took over *X-Men* (the second series) and recrafted it as *New X-Men*, starting with issue #114 (March 2001). Under Morrison's vision (which was executed by such artists as Bachalo, Phil Jimenez, and Marc Silvestri) the days of the longstanding "war" between humans and mutants were numbered because it was revealed that *homo sapiens* are genetically about to become extinct, and the handing of the planet over to their *superior* brethren was inevitable! That knowledge hardly makes things any less settled, though, and under Morrison's entropic vision, everything seems to be going down the tubes: the mutant-haven nation of Genosha is virtually wiped out and Magneto finally seems to be gone (no such luck); Xavier regains the use of his legs, but his malevolent sister Cassandra Nova arrives on the scene to wreak havok; Scott and Jean are having marital problems, which propels him into the waiting arms of Emma Frost; and worse, Jean dies (again). Both Colossus and Moira MacTaggart also die, and just to keep things unpredictable, the Beast emerges as a future-time supervillain.

(Above) The fiery Chamber using an energy blast. (Pencils Georges Jeanty)

(Opposite) Wolverine charges through New York's Times Square in the debut issue of *Ultimate X-Men* (December 2000). As a rule, the X-Men generally stayed out of the Big Apple.

The Morrison revolution came to a conclusion with issue #154 (July 2004), and within a couple more issues the title was changed back to *X-Men* and the world more or less calmed back down.

X-TREME X-MEN

Also in 2001, Claremont returned with *X-Treme X-Men*, a new series featuring mostly familiar characters—Storm, Beast, Rogue, Bishop—along with the recently introduced *third* version of Thunderbird. Unlike his predecessors, this Thunderbird is not Native American, but rather Neal Sharra, a native of India, who can produce heat blasts, and who is in a relationship with Rogue. The title's new character is Sage, who also goes by the name "Tessa," a sultry, raven-haired spy who is blessed with hyper brain-power. There is also a new antagonist, a suave, Spanish anti-mutant named "Diego Sandoval," which might be a nod to the book's Spanish-born artist Salvador Larocca, or it might be an in-joke reference to San Diego, California, the site of the International ComicCon, the world's largest comic book convention. While *X-Men* had long been heralded for portraying more ethnic diversity than any other comic book series, the *X-Treme* team was the most diverse of all.

The premise of *X-Treme X-Men* is as much metaphysical as physical and involves the pseudo-Lovecraftian device of the team looking for ancient volumes of mutant wisdom and prediction written in the form of diaries by the late Destiny. *X-Treme X-Men* would also prove to be the death of Psylocke (though she has recently been revived).

NEW X-MEN — ACADEMY X

In 2004, while the primary X-Universe was being split three ways between *Uncanny X-Men*, *New X-Men*, and *Astonishing X-Men*, which had been launched with writer Joss Whedon (*Buffy the Vampire Slayer*) and artist John Cassaday, yet another limited series emerged, under the name *New X-Men*, subtitled *Academy X*. The first issue

(Above) The adamantium-infused Lady Deathstrike, a.k.a. Yuriko Oyama, was a formidable and vengeful opponent for Wolverine, and proof that not everything to come from his beloved Japan was good for him. (Pencils Salvador Larroca)

(Opposite) The X-Treme team included such favorites Rogue and Bishop, along with newcomers Sage and Thunderbird III (who was no relation to Thunderbirds I and II).

(Top) Relations between Dani Moonstar, Scott Summers and Emma Frost on the staff of Xavier Academy are almost as combustible as those of the students, in *New X-Men–Academy X*. (Pencils Staz Johnson).

(Above) The Xavier class of 2004 is whopping compared to the initial class of five students.

(Opposite) Academy X's "Hellion" team (not to be confused with an earlier grouping called the Hellions), featured Tag, Wither, Mercury, Dust, and Rockslide. Presenting them is grown-up Dani "Psyche" Moonstar, now a teacher at Xavier Academy.

appeared in May and was written by Nunzio DeFilippis and Christina Weir, penciled by Randy Green, with Staz Johnson and Michael Ryan, and inked by Rick Ketcham with Sean Parsons, Scott Koblish, and Avalon Studios (increasingly studios were being listed in the credits in addition to individual artists' names). *New X-Men— Academy X* took place at the Xavier Institute for Higher Learning, where Emma Frost and a post-Jean Scott Summers are in charge, and also romantically involved. The teaching staff includes Dani "Psyche" Moonstar, Rahne "Wolfsbane" Sinclair, and Bobby "Iceman" Drake, who conducts the school's business classes (clearly, the curriculum has expanded). More than one hundred students are registered in a school where the goal seems more geared to teaching young mutants how to control their powers, rather than using their powers as Super Heroes. Professor Xavier himself is away, still fostering his vision of human and mutant coexistence.

The brand-new team, which represents the last entirely original assembly of young mutants to date, includes seventeen-year-old "Noriko Akida," who followed the now-familiar path of running away from home—in her case Tokyo—at the age of thirteen, coming to the states and learning to live by her wits on the streets…and so on. Possessing miles of street kid attitude, which is somewhat of a defensive device to cover her basic insecurity, she has the ability to absorb static electricity and discharge it, giving her super speed. Noriko wears metal stabilizer gauntlets as a way of controlling her energy flow, which must be released periodically, like a body function, and takes on the name Surge.

Others are "David Alleyne," code name "Prodigy," also seventeen, a Chicago-born mutant who has limited telepathy, which allows him to mimic and absorb the knowledge of nearby targets, but only temporarily, and who seems to reject his natural leadership abilities; sixteen-year-old "Sofia Mantega," from Caracas, Venezuela, who can control the air around her, including sounds carried on the air, and who chooses the name "Wind

The White Quee

EMMA GOOD OR EMMA BAD?

"The X-Men were always our primary target."
—Emma Frost, a.k.a. the White Queen

No one in the X-Universe has vacillated between the sides of right and wrong quite as much as beautiful, dangerous Emma Frost. As a result, not even her teammates can always tell exactly where she stands. To paraphrase the satiric 1960s songwriter Tom Lehrer, she is a woman whose allegiance is ruled by *X-pedience*.

A powerful telepath who was born into a wealthy pedigreed family, one of the first to arrive in America from England, Emma increased her inherited wealth through her own business acumen, as chairman of Frost International, and her power base through her association with the Hellfire Club. When introduced into the X-saga (*Uncanny X-Men* issue #129, January 1980), it was as the club's White Queen, a nemesis to the X-Men in general, and the women of X-Men—Storm and Jean Grey (who had then been psychically transformed into the club's "Black Queen")—in particular. She would prove to be a better business-woman than a warrior, though. Since her most effective weapon is her sexual cunning, which she wields like a Bond girl, Emma seems to have little effect on female opponents, and she would lose each confrontation, including a major one with Jean.

Her recruitment campaign was a bit more effective. On behalf of the Hellfire Club, Emma assembled a team of young mutants called the Hellions. But it was because of the Hellions, indirectly, that she would begin to lean toward the side of good. An attack by Sentinels on the Academy left the members of her young team dead and Emma physically weakened and emotionally distraught. In this state she allowed Professor Xavier to take care of her, and later agreed to switch her allegiance to his side as an attempt to atone for the Hellions.

Since then she has remained on the side of right —or so it seems—but her personal and professional fortunes have suffered a definite downturn. During her tenure as co-headmaster of the *Generation X* team, she catastrophically allowed her traitorously evil sister "Adrienne" to infiltrate her school, which resulted in its near destruction, the death of one

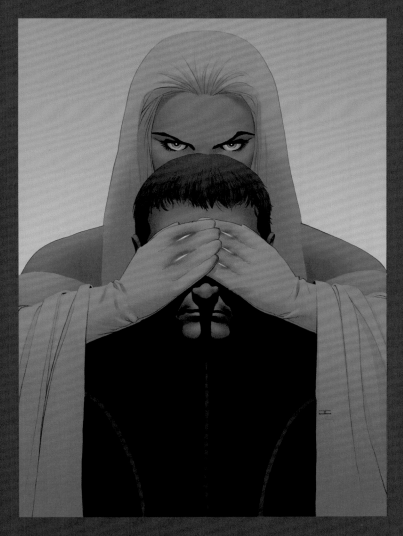

student (Synch), and the team's disbanding. Later she moved to Genosha to teach mutants, but once more suffered through a Sentinel attack.

Amazingly, Professor Xavier gave her another shot at an administrative job in *Academy X*. While many of her coworkers and even some of her students do not really trust her, Xavier clearly does. So does Scott.

In recent years the Hellfire Club has lost a fair amount of its visibility (when the corruption spreads so deeply and transparently into the government itself, a private power club seems redundant), so Emma's White Queen moniker has been provided a new, more physical manifestation, with her development of an additional power that allows her to transform her body into a living diamond. Her early school years have been chronicled in an eponymous title that launched in 2003.

(Above. left) The White Queen first wrapped her little fingers wrapped around Scott Summers while he was still married to Jean. (Pencils John Cassaday)

(Above) Villain or Varga Girl? While it can't be said that whatever Emma wants, Emma gets, it isn't for lack of trying. (Pencils Greg Horn)

(Opposite, top) Emma Frost early in her career. (Pencils John Byrne)

(Opposite, below) For a while, Emma and Banshee were an item—maybe she was drawn to the fact that he appears to get younger by the year.

Dancer"; fifteen-year-old "Laurie Collins" (for whom any potential relation to Rusty Collins is left unstated), a native of Kent, Connecticut, who has pheromone-based manipulations of emotions, though her true nature is summed up by her code name, "Wallflower"; and sixteen-year-old "Josh Foley," from Flushing, New York, who has a healing ability and is called "Elixir."

Also at the school are "Julian Keller," a powerful telekinetic, who seems to walk to a darker beat, and so dubs himself "Hellion"; "Sooraya Qadir" an Afghani who wears a traditional birqua, and who can turn to dust—yes, her code name is "Dust"; "Jay Guthrie," the younger brother of Cannonball and Husk, who has angel wings, and is appropriately called "Icarus"; "Cessily Kincaid," who as "Mercury" transforms into the unique element; "Santo Vaccarro," who is an antagonistic, dark grey Thing-type who can throw off parts of his body, and goes by "Rockslide"; "Brian Cruz," who can immobilize people by touching, or tagging, them, which gives him his name "Tag"; and "Kevin Ford," a previous runaway from the Institute, whose very touch causes death in plants and animals. Possessing an understandably rather morbid outlook on life, he selects the name "Wither."

The students are split into three competing teams within the school: the "Hellions," led by Emma, which consists of Hellion, Mercury, Rockslide, Icarus, Dust, and Tag (and which should not be confused with her earlier doomed Hellions group from the Massachusetts Academy); the "New Mutants," led by Dani, which includes Prodigy, Wind Dancer, Surge, Wallflower, and Elixir (but not the earlier New Mutants, who have long since disbanded); and Scott's group, the "Corsairs," who aren't even identified. Competition is actively encouraged between these squads, with the prize being a championship to be awarded to one group at the end of the semester.

Once again, the story of this limited series has a lot more to do with interpersonal relationships between the students and the faculty of the Xavier Institute than it

(Above) In *Academy X*, the students split into competing groups, not unlike the houses of Hogwarts. The new "New Mutants" included (left to right) Surge, Prodigy, Wind Dancer, Elixir, and Wallflower. (Pencils Randy Green)

(Opposite) All Marvel Super Heroes have interesting real life conflicts; Dust, an Afghani national, is reluctant to remove her traditional birqua to don a costume. (Pencils Clayton Henry)

does with combating Evil Mutants. The pupils—whose powers tend to be more personally invasive than outwardly special—have issues getting along, especially as their respective dark and light sides emerge (in particular, Elixir and Hellion just don't see eye to eye). But in the front office, Dani and Emma are also having problems: Dani simply does not trust the former White Queen, who still might having lingering evil thoughts, as evidenced by her favoritism for the darker students. For her part, Emma seems to enjoy taunting Dani in front of Scott, who is stuck stolidly in the middle. To spice things up, there is even a torrid student/teacher relationship taking place between Rahne and Josh.

And if it is true that Hogwarts owes a debt to the Xavier School for pioneering the concept of a place where special kids can go to learn how to control their powers while keeping off the radar screen of mainstream humanity, then that debt is at least acknowledged, if not repaid, in *New X-Men–Academy X*. While taking a tour of the Institute and seeing the landscaping of the place, Noriko pointedly comments: "*Hedge maze? Someone's read a bit too much* Harry Potter, *huh?*"

THE SCORECARD

The sheer volume and incredible diversity of mutantkind represented in *X-Men* and its dozens of spin-off titles, limited-edition series, one-shots, and black-and-white magazines, which have emerged over the last two decades, has been staggering. In 1999 and 2000 alone, there were twenty-one additional titles created! In the center of this X-plosion of ideas still stands the comic book that started it all in 1963. Now titled *Uncanny X-Men* and once more under the creative control of Chris Claremont, the book that was once almost cancelled for lack of interest is counting down to the landmark of its *five-hundredth* issue.

With all this, it would appear that there is only one thing that mutants could not possibly become: *X-tinct*. Though who knows? Within the expanding X-Universe, anything, technically, is possible.

(Above) Mutant heal thyself...Academy X's Josh Foley, a.k.a. Elixir demonstrates his powers.

(Opposite) By the time of the Age of Apocalypse storyline, mutantcy seemed to be spreading faster than a winter cold, which meant more work for Magneto.

Strange and Alterna

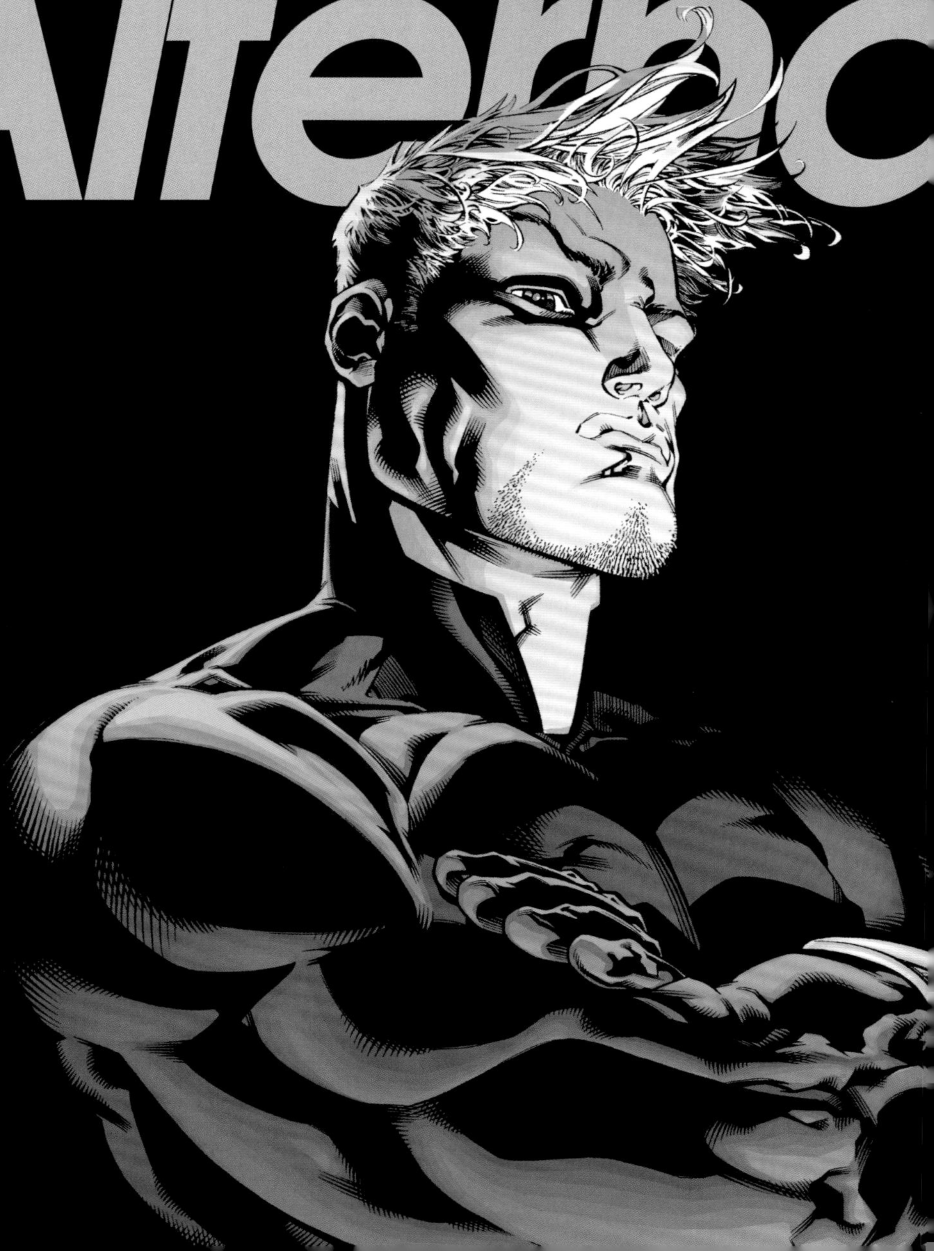

Worlds

Realities

Strange Worlds and Alternate Realities

"I have seen too many conflicting futures to accept only one as inevitable."
—Professor X

All comic book adventures offer a skewed take on reality. In our normal everyday lives, we are not likely to run into someone who can read our minds, fly, pick up trucks, produce fire from their fingertips, or teleport. Neither are we likely to live in a major city inhabited by gaudily clad crime fighters with strange powers who take it upon themselves to look out for the public good. Outside of a comic book convention or on Halloween, anyone walking around in canary-colored spandex, a pointy mask, and clawed gloves would likely be considered suspicious, at the very least.

(Above) Ka-Zar and Zabu have been the Marvel company's answer to Tarzan and Cheetah since the mid-1930s.

(Opposite) Trouble in Savage Land, the inner-earth realm ruled by Ka-Zar. (Pencils Alan Davis)

Comic books establish their own reality, one in which the suspension of disbelief is simply part of the covenant between the writer and artist and the reader. Comedy writers call it "inner and outer logic": the outer logic being acceptance of the fact that an unreal situation exists in the first place, and the inner logic being the fidelity to recognizable reality within that totally unreal situation. But once a particular version of reality becomes totally accepted, no matter how unnatural, the door—or portal—can be opened to counter reality and alternative worlds.

Over the years the Marvel Universe in general, and the X-Men Universe in particular, has offered enough alternate realities, journeys through time, and strange, sometimes alien, places to make a superstring theoretician's eyes cross. These portals have opened onto a series of notable story threads that have become a standard part of the X-Men mythology.

STRANGE WORLDS

Savage Land

One of the odder detours ever taken by the X-Men appeared very early in their saga, in *X-Men* issue #10 (March 1965), when the team journeyed to "Savage

Land," also known as "The World that Time Forgot." A prehistoric realm under the surface of the earth, accessible through an opening in the ice in Antarctica, Savage Land is ruled by a brawny, loin-clothed hero named "Ka-Zar," the "Lord of the Jungle," whose pet is an enormous saber-toothed tiger named "Zabu." Savage Land is also inhabited by a bestial ape man named "Maa-Gor," who is said to be the last of his tribe, not to mention dinosaurs, wooly mammoths, a tribe of "Swamp People," a mysterious pyramid, and the bizarre pterodactyl-like creature Sauron.

If it all sounds very Edgar Rice Burroughs-ish…well, it is. The precedent for Ka-Zar seems plain enough—Burroughs's noble savage Tarzan—and Savage Land appears to derive from that author's prehistoric middle-earth realm, "Savage Pellucidar." And while the cover of issue #10 proudly proclaims Ka-Zar (it rhymes with "quasar") to be "unquestionably the most spectacular new character of the year!" that statement needs qualification. Ka-Zar was spectacular enough, but he was not new. In fact, one could argue that Ka-Zar was the very first Marvel Super Hero, arriving on the scene before Captain America, even before the Sub Mariner.

Ka-Zar was introduced in 1936 in a short-lived series of pulp novels put out by Timely Publications under its "Red Circle" imprint, before the company turned to comic books. After comics became the prime focus, Ka-Zar made a reappearance, in the first issue of *Marvel Comics* (October 1939), receiving special billing on the cover as "Ka-Zar the Great." His exploits in comic book form, though, were no more enduring than his pulp novel form, and Ka-Zar headed back to the land that time forgot and stayed there, forgotten, for the next three decades. Once he had been reactivated, however, Ka-Zar proved popular enough to be awarded his own title in 1970, and he and Savage Land continued to turn up in the pages *X-Men*.

The Shi'ar Empire
Savage Land is located deep within the earth. Another

The bizarre Sauron was surprisingly articulate for a creature that is part flying reptile.

Majestrix Lilandra of the Shi'ar (center) strikes a heroic pose, while Charles Xavier, to the right, remains totally obscured under his galactic mask.

strange realm exists off the earth entirely, one that would have an even greater impact on the X-Men saga. It is the intergalactic Shi'ar Empire, which is the social and political center of the Shi'ar Galaxy (one of the intergalactic Big Three, the others being the "Kree" and the "Skrull" Empires). Shi'ar Princess Lilandra first made her presence known through a recurring troubling dream Professor Xavier began experiencing in *X-Men* #97 (February 1976), though the empire was not fully revealed until seven issues later, when Xavier and the X-Men were drawn into a deadly struggle between the forces of "Majestor (as Shi'ar emperors are titled) D'Ken," who sought to possess a universe-destroying power, and Lilandra, his sister. A side effect of helping Lilandra fight her brother is that Professor Xavier falls in love with the curiously beautiful alien, who possesses such bird-like characteristics as a feather crested head.

D'Ken's perfidy, it would be revealed, went back a generation, to Cyclops and Havok's father, Major Christopher Summers, whose plane had been shot down by Shi'ar warships when the boys were young. Summers and his wife Katherine found themselves transported to the Shi'ar galaxy, where D'Ken imprisoned Christopher and killed Katherine. That was the act that would prompt Christopher into becoming Corsair, leader of the Starjammers, and led to his declaring war on the empire until D'Ken fell, and Lilandra ascended to the throne.

Lilandra would take a more proactive role in history of the X-Men at the climax of the Dark Phoenix saga, acting as the catalyst for Jean/Phoenix's self-sacrifice. Through it all she and Xavier would remain in love. When the Professor disappeared from Earth for a time, he took up residence with Lilandra on her home planet Aerie during her rule as "Majestrix." She in turn would spend time on Earth with him during the period that she was overthrown by her sister "Deathbird." Whatever her relationship to Charles Xavier is at any given moment, Lilandra of the Shi'ar and the X-Men in general remain on friendly terms.

Genosha

Genosha is a small island nation located off the West coast of Africa, and despite its purely terrestrial foundation, most people would consider Genosha an alien environment. Long a habitat for mutants, its history is steeped in evil; Genosha is little better than a scientific death camp where mutants were experimented on and genetically altered—becoming a sub-class called "mutates"—and then enslaved by the state. Rogue, Storm, and Wolverine were among the X-Men who were captured and spent time in the island's slave labor camps. Genosha eventually erupted into full-scale war between mutates and humans—exactly the kind of war that Magneto had dreamed of creating in America. It was therefore ironic that the first governmentally sanctioned ruler of Genosa was Magneto!

It was the United Nations who gave him sovereignty over the war-torn island, in the hopes that dealing with the civil war would either keep him occupied and out of trouble, or kill him. Magneto surprised everyone by ending the war and bringing relative peace to Genosha, making it a sanctuary for mutantkind. The peace did not last long as Magneto once more began to dream of mutant domination of the Earth, using Genosha as his base of operations. But the small island's days were already numbered. Charles Xavier's recently revealed twin sister Cassandra Nova brought about the destruction of the island nation and its millions of mutant inhabitants, and, presumably, Magneto himself. Not surprisingly, it would be revealed that Magneto survived the mutant genocide, and since this is the Marvel Universe, there is always the chance that Genosha will rise once more.

It may look like an inviting metropolis, but the island nation of Genosha has been the site of almost continuous trouble, descending at times into slavery, torture, and genocide.

ALTERNATE REALITIES

Days of Future Past

It has been heard on television a thousand times: "We interrupt our regularly scheduled program to bring you this special report." Claremont and Byrne did just that

"Days of Future Past" presents the last X-Men standing in 2013: Piotr Rasputin, Kate Pryde-Rasputin, Franklin Richards (the son of the Fantastic Four's Reed and Sue), Rachel Summers (daughter of Scott and Jean), and Storm. The wheelchair-bound Magneto is now their leader.

(Following spread) Chaos reigns in the Days of Future Past, to the point where both the present and future incarnations of Kitty Pryde co-exist!

in 1981, stopping the regular flow of the *X-Men* saga for a brief but significant side-track titled "Days of Future Past." Even though this alternate reality story covered only two issues—*X-Men* #141 and 142—it continues to resonate a quarter century later as the first real exploration within the X-Men tapestry of a totally dystopian society in which the mutants are not simply hated and feared, but controlled and interned. If it sounds like Senator Robert Kelly's dream come true, there is good reason for that.

"Days of Future Past" begins in the year 2013, within a North America is barely recognizable. The marauding robotic Sentinels are in power, and they have done their best to eradicate mutantkind from the planet. Whatever mutants are left are living in internment camps and forced to wear inhibitor collars that defuse their powers. They are also forced to identify themselves as members of the new millennium's lowest caste by wearing the letter "M" on their clothing. This is a grim echo of both Fritz Lang's 1931 German film *M*, in which a child murderer, played by Peter Lorre, desperately tries to flee the city, not knowing he has been marked with an identifying chalk letter "M" (for "murderer") on his clothing, and the real-life practice a decade later of the Nazi regime forcing the Jews of Europe (which would have included Peter Lorre, had he stayed in Germany) to identify themselves with a yellow star.

Others within this bleak vision of the future are similarly labeled: "A" signifies "Anamolous Humans," or humans who possess the potential for mutantcy, and "H" is for full humans, the only class of people that the Sentinels allow to reproduce. Most of the X-Men—in fact, most of the Marvel Super Heroes—have already been killed. Headstones mark the graves of Charles Xavier, the members of the Fantastic Four and Peter Parker. The now-middle-aged "Kate" Pryde-Rasputin (in this time stream she is married to Colossus) considers them the lucky ones. The few remaining X-Men—Kate, known once again as Sprite, Colossus, Storm, and

Wolverine, who in 2013 is Colonel Logan of the Canadian Resistance Army—are part of the core of the Anti-Sentinel Resistance. With them is "Franklin Richards," the son of Reed Richards and Sue Storm, and the sole surviving member of the Fantastic Four, and his telepathic/telekinetic lady friend Rachel Summers, who of course is Phoenix II, the daughter of Scott and Jean. Their most unusual ally is Magneto, now called "Magnus," who in a supreme irony is confined to a wheelchair like Xavier. Together they are on a mission to try and save the planet from nuclear annihilation.

How did things get this way? It all goes back to Senator Kelly. On October 31, 1980, while in the last few weeks of his presidential campaign, he has called Professor Xavier and Moira MacTaggart to testify before his committee. But before the day was out the three of them would be assassinated by Mystique's Brotherhood of Evil Mutants, who invade the hearing chambers. The goal of the Evil Mutants is to use the assassination to force conventional humanity to fear and respect them as *homo superior*, though the assault produces the opposite effect: mutants are now regarded as terrorists.

That paves the way four years later for a rabid mutant-hating presidential candidate to sweep into the Oval Office, capitalizing on the anti-mutant mood of the nation. Whereas Kelly might have proven to be a moderate, the new president (who is never identified) takes no prisoners. He pushes through the first Mutant Control Act, only to have it struck down by the Supreme Court as unconstitutional. The president then retaliates by reactivating the Sentinels and sending them out on a campaign to wipe out mutantkind. Before you can say "mission accomplished," the Sentinels have destroyed all Super Heroes, mutant and non mutant alike, and have seized control of America. That remains the situation until 2013, at which time the rest of the world plans to join forces to launch a massive nuclear attack on North America, putting it out of its misery, and annihilating whoever is left in it, human, mutant, or robot.

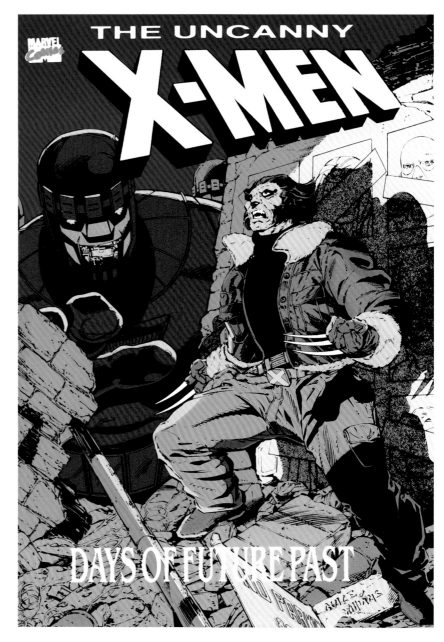

A Sentinel relentlessly pursues Wolverine in this cover for "Days of Future Past."

The cover for part one of "Days of Future Past" warned readers of the dark reality they were about to encounter.

In an attempt to prevent this from happening, Rachel psychically switches the forty-six-year-old mind of Kate Pryde-Rasputin with her 1980 thirteen-year-old self to deliver a warning to her teammates of what is destined to happen. Kate is chosen for this because she had not had enough training at the Xavier school prior to its destruction in the 1980s to learn how to defend herself from psychic attacks. The plan works and the 1980 vintage X-Men speed by jet to Washington, arriving in the hearing chambers just in time to fight the sudden appearance of the Brotherhood of Evil Mutants.

Back in 2013, the remaining X-team decides to hit the Sentinels where they will least expect it: at their headquarters in the Baxter Building (the former headquarters of the Fantastic Four), in the decimated metropolis that was once proud Manhattan. Storm and Wolverine are killed in the battle. But in 1980, things are a bit more successful. The X-Men (joined by the Angel) defeat most of the Brotherhood, though Mystique manages to escape. Meanwhile Destiny, the blind "precog," has Senator Kelly in her crossbow sights. But at the moment she fires, Kitty phases through her, throwing the crossbow bolt off course. Even though Destiny has the power to read the immediate future, the failed assassination attempt comes as a shock because she was unable to detect Kitty's presence because of the time jump.

Kelly, Xavier, and Moira have all escaped assassination, and Kitty's mind is suddenly pulled back into the future to reunite with her 2013 body. The X-Men fly back to Westchester, wondering if they have really altered the course of the future.

While only time will tell for them, the reader is given a hint in a closing coda set in Washington, which shows a secret meeting between the silhouetted, unidentified president, Senator Kelly, industrialist Sebastian "Hellfire" Shaw, and a fourth man. While the president rejects the report of Kelly's Mutant Committee, he agrees that mutantcy is an issue that must be watched. But he insists that it be done covertly. In other words, the matter is now out of Kelly's—and Congress's—hands. The president announces an operation called "Project Wideawake," which is to be run by none other than Henry Peter Gyrich—the fourth man. With the financial and industrial assistance of Shaw, Gyrich is charged with creating a new army of mutant-fighting Sentinels.

And so goes the future.

Fans familiar with all of the television and film incarnations of *X-Men* will recognize "Days of Future Past" as a source for several ideas (the 1992 animated *X-Men* series, for instance, dramatized the assassination attempt of Kelly, and the attempted takeover by Gyrich's Sentinels). And even though readers were warned on the cover of issue #142 that in "This issue: EVERYBODY DIES!" fans were still shaken by the sights of Wolverine being incinerated and Storm lying dead with a spear through her body.

With the real 2013 only seven years away—a year that will also mark the silver anniversary of *X-Men*!—speculations run high as to how Marvel will acknowledge the actual arrival of its onetime landmark "future."

AGE OF APOCALYPSE

If "Days of Future Past" represented alternate reality on a small scale, at least in terms of the number of issues involved, 1995's "Age of Apocalypse" storyline was a major undertaking, an epic that was chronicled in nine freshly launched magazines: *Astonishing X-Men, X-Man, Generation Next, Weapon X, X-Calibre, Amazing X-Men, Factor X, Gambit & The Externals,* and *X-Men Chronicles,* the first issues of which all bore March 1995 stand dates. It was the brainchild of then editor-in-chief Bob Harras, who enlisted the crème of the artists and writers then working for the company—Scott Lobdell, Chris Bachalo, Fabian Nicieza, Larry Hama, John Francis Moore, Jeph Loeb, Howard Mackie, Mark Wald, Joe Madureira, Andy and Adam Kubert, Tony Daniel, Steve Epting, Warren Ellis, Ken Lashley, Mark Waid, Roger Cruz, and Steve Skroce—to execute it.

(Above) Three of the new series that were launched as part of the sweeping "Age of Apocalypse" saga.

(Opposite) New York City lays in ruins in the Age of Apocalypse—who erected a towering monument to himself in place of the Statue of Liberty. (Pencils Patrick Zircher)

The core idea of Age of Apocalypse presents a reality in which Professor Charles Xavier does not exist. For regular readers of *X-Men*, it was almost like *Mutants' Adventures Through the Looking Glass*, a strange realm where conventional good is now bad, black is white, up is down, and nearly everything is reversed, or at least radically altered, from understood reality.

The spark that created this chaotic version of reality was Professor X's mutant son David, whose personal problems include multiple personality disorder. Having decided that all his problems stem from having grown up with a distant, preoccupied father, who was largely out of his life because of his self-appointed duty to shield the world from evil mutants, David comes up with a solution: if he were to go back in time to a period when his father and Erik Lehnsherr were still friends and assassinate Lehnsherr, it would prevent Lehnsherr from ever becoming Magneto. Without Magneto to fight, David figures that Xavier would then have more time to be a real dad to him. He does manage to go back in time and gets Magneto in his sights, but at the last moment his father intervenes and is killed instead! As a result, David ceases to exist, and Magneto, who is suddenly changed by the tragedy, takes up Xavier's cause.

That hardly solves any of the problems, though, since Apocalypse steps in to fill the evil mutant leader void, and succeeds in achieving what had traditionally been Magneto's dream: domination over the human race, much of which he has eliminated through genocide.

Since this altered reality is one in which Xavier was never able to form the X-Men, the individual mutant's lives are radically altered. Nightcrawler is now evil like his mother, and the formerly dead John Proudstar/Thunderbird is still alive. Cyclops, meanwhile, is still the loyal lieutenant, though his boss was now Apocalypse! Even more startling was the perfidy of Dr. Henry McCoy, who has become the "Dark Beast," and whose scientific experiments on humans on behalf of Apocalypse recall those of the Dr. Josef Mengele in Nazi

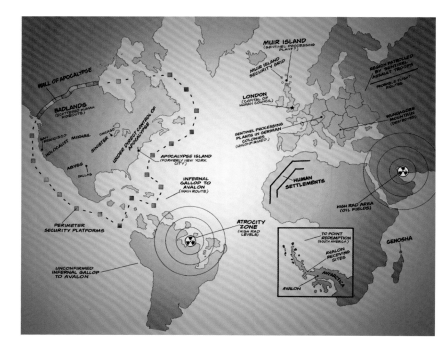

The world in the Age of Apocalypse, showing the extent of Apocalypse's control, and its effects.

Among the startling reversals that occur in the Age of Apocalypse is the fact that the Beast is now a super villain. Here he holds Jean Grey captive.

Germany. Meanwhile, traditional evil mutants Toad and Mastermind are now rebels, traveling with Forge, a pterodactyl creature named "Soaron" (related, apparently, to the earlier Sauron), and "Nate Grey," who is also known as "X-Man," under the cover of a touring Shakespearean company!

Ultimately, Apocalypse and his empire are destroyed by Magneto, and another time jump results in Xavier's being saved from David's attack, though this time, it is David Haller himself who dies.

X-Men 2099

While the Age of Apocalypse was raging, another alternate reality—or at least a future reality—was playing out in *X-Men 2099 A.D.* It had started in 1993 as *X-Men 2099*, without the "A.D.," and was one of a series of century-ahead projections that also re-imagined the lives of Spider-Man, the Punisher, and the Hulk.

In the America of 2099, corporations control everything and Mutantkind has once more been all but wiped out. One who remains, however, is "Xi'an Chi Xan" (not to be confused with *The New Mutant*'s Xi'an Coy Mahn), who is also known as the "Desert Ghost," and whose touch can cause both healing and destruction. Formerly a bad mutant, he has now decided to bring together the remaining mutant heroes to continue the struggle for mutant rights. The new team includes "Timothy Fitzgerald," a.k.a. "Skullfire," who can absorb and release energy (and when he does his skeleton shows through); "Krystalin" (no real name), who can form crystals; "Shakti Haddad," who has a Cerebro-like ability to find mutants, and who goes by "Cerebra"; "Metalhead" (also known as "Eddie"), a walking Philosopher's Stone whose body can become any metal he touches; and "Meanstreak" ("Henri"), who runs so fast he begins to smoke. While not initially part of the team, a woman named "Tina," who has stretching ability, becomes an ally, as does "Bloodhawk," a grotesque, red, bat-winged creature with deadly claws, who was created from underground testing in the desert.

(Opposite, top) The *X-Men 2099* team: Bloodhawk, Krystalin, Desert Ghost, Skullfire, Metalhead, Cerebra, and Meanstreak.

(Opposite, bottom) Home base in *X-Men 2099* was a barren desert outpost – a far cry from the posh Xavier Mansion.

(Top) Alex Summers (prominent left) finds himself in a strange world populated by strange parodies of known X-Men in *Mutant X*. The group, called The Six, include Bloodstorm, The Fallen, The Brute, Iceman, and the Goblyn Queen, who is Alex's wife!

On the evil mutant side are the amusingly named "Rat Pack," a group of mob-like "enforcers" headquartered in Las Vegas, who were formerly employed by the late Sin City corporate mogul "Noah Synge."

X-Men 2099 ceased its regular publications schedule in 1996, though graphic novel treatment emerged in 1998.

Mutant X

The year 1998 also saw the debut of another alternate reality series, *Mutant X*. The protagonist of *Mutant X* (which should not be confused with either the Fox Television series of the same name or the short-lived comic book adaptation of it), is Alex Summers, who of course is Havok in conventional reality, but after his "soul has been transferred to another world," becomes "Mutant X." While Alex's life has mysteriously been turned upside-down, those around him in this strange new world believe he is suffering from some sort of delusion. Only young "Scotty," his son in this reality, seems to understand that Alex is not really his father. But Alex does not find much comfort in the knowledge that the only one who believes him is a small child.

In this strange new world, Alex is part of a group called "The Six," which operate out of the medieval-style Bannerman Castle. His teammates are cracked mirror versions of their familiar parallel version: "Marvel Woman," a telekinetic who is really Madelyn Pryor—here Alex's wife and Scotty's mom—who would transform into the Goblin Queen; "Bloodstorm," a vampiric version of Storm who can still control weather, but can also turn into mist and control vermin; "The Brute," a green, gargoylish Hank McCoy, who developed amphibian characteristics and seriously diminished his intellect after trying unsuccessfully to reverse his mutation; Iceman/Bob Drake (no longer Bobby), whose major difference is that the Norse God Loki altered his powers so that he can no longer control them; and "The Fallen," Warren Worthington III in something akin to his Horseman of Death persona, who now has leather wings and the ability to breathe fire. Other members of the Marvel Universe who appear in twisted form are "Elektra," from *Daredevil*, who is young Scotty's nanny, and the Fantastic Four, who are essentially the same, but now wear body armor. Meanwhile S.H.I.E.L.D.—the Marvel Universe's version of the CIA—is a recognized terrorist organization.

While the Hitchockian man-out-of-place theme was given a moody, sometimes creepy treatment by creators Howard Mackie, Cary Nord, and Andrew Pepoy, *Mutant X* was not a long-lived title, finishing up with issue #32 in 2001.

X-Man

Alternate realities have not only spawned complex storylines, they have also launched new characters that would go forth and carry on outside of their genesis realms. Phoenix II from "Days of Future Past" for example, would reappear as part of the British Super Hero group *Excalibur.* Similarly, Nate Grey, would have a significant impact under the code name X-Man. Does the name "Grey" ring a bell? It should: Nate is the natural (more or less) son of Scott and Jean.

(Above) With the introduction of Nate Grey, yet another scion of the Summers family, the family tree of X-Universe's first family became even more twisted and circuitous.

(Opposite, top) An aged Rachel Summers, in the guise of Mother Askani, caters to baby Cable, who is both her biological stepbrother and surrogate grandson. Behind them in the tank is cloned baby Stryfe.

(Opposite, bottom) Nate Grey, a.k.a. X-Man.

He was genetically engineered by the diabolical Sinister using DNA from Scott and Jean, which makes both Scott and Sinister his father, of sorts. But the person Nate considers his father is fellow mutant Forge. Sinister created Nate as a weapon against Apocalypse, but Nate would ultimately slay Sinister, who killed Forge. A bit more indelicate than his predecessors in the Marvel Universe, Nate's catchphrase is not the boisterous "It's clobberin' time" of The Thing, or the sardonic "I'm the best there is at what I do" of Wolverine, but the bluntly succinct "*Eat this!*" Among the villains X-Man encounters are Caliban, a toad-like, skull-faced, deadly hunter with an ego the size of Texas; Domino, a sleek female assassin (both of whom had "real" universe counterparts); and "Grizzly," an enormous, red, bestial serial killer.

When one considers what happens to Nate Grey once he moves into in the standard *X-Men* timeline, it demonstrates just how tangled the threads of the woven tapestry of the X-Universe can become. In this time stream, Nate Grey confronts Cable, who is really Nathan Summers, the time-jumping son of Scott and Madelyn, who was the clone of Jean Grey and who was brought back to physical life when Nate Grey, Jean's son, connected Madelyn's existing psyche with a brand new body, which makes Nate the consort of both his real mother's clone and the natural mother of his own step-brother, Nathan, who earlier had been transported two millennia into the future by Rachel Summers, who is Scott and Jean's alternate time daughter, which makes Rachel Nate's half-sister from another world, and Nathan's inter-dimensional stepsister.

Got it?

Days of Future

uture:

Days of Future: Future

The extent to which the X-Universe has changed in the forty-three years since the first issue of *X-Men* was sent out to newsstands is monumental. The same can be said for the real world as well. But changes never stop in either realm, and the world of mutants is destined to keep changing, altering, and surprising.

Most of the changes that take place on the publishing side will result from the earth-shaking "House of M" storyline, which came to a climax in late 2005. A major crossover event that extended to all of Marvel's top titles, House of M set off a chain of events that will change the X-Universe forever (or, at least, for the foreseeable future). Briefly, it postulates that Magneto has waged and resoundingly lost the final conflict between humans and mutants. Among the casualties of this war is the fact that his daughter Wanda, a.k.a. the Scarlet Witch, has lost control of her mind, which means she has lost control over her ability to alter reality. As a result, she changes the very fabric of existence, recasting the world as one in which Magneto *won* the war, and now sits in power over a world where mutants are in charge and humans are the minority underclass. In this x-istence all of the characters involved seem to have been granted their heart's desires – Peter Parker even has his long-dead love Gwen Stacy back!

But it is not the world the way it was—it is not "reality"—and Charles Xavier, who remembers the "truth," wrestles with the horrible option of killing Wanda before existence ceases. But by the storyline's climax, the stricken and weakened Wanda, who has desperately wanted to please her distant father and believed that she was doing so, suddenly realizes she has been used by her conniving twin brother Quicksilver, who has been orchestrating the chaos around them. Distraught, she alters reality once more by uttering three words: *no more mutants.* In an instant, the mutant population is all but wiped out from the earth, with only a couple hundred *homo superiors* surviving extinction.

While House of M has an intriguing parallel with its predecessor, Age of Apocalypse, in that at the center of

(Opposite) Mutants roam the streets of New York in *House of M.* Their ranks will quickly diminish. (Pencils, Olivier Coipel)

The world, as a result of the earth-shattering events chronicled in *House of M*, will become a very different place—and if Marvel's editor-in-chief Joe Quesada has his way, it will stay so.

both are a mutant child desperately longing for attention from a preoccupied father, House of M will have far, far greater impact on the Marvel Universe. It has been irrevocably changed, and there is no smiling presence anywhere to step out of the shower and tell us it was all just a crazy dream. And as long as Marvel's editor-in-chief Joe Quesada is in the editor's chair, things will stay that way. Quesada says he saw writer Brian Michael Bendis's premise for House of M as the solution to a long-held problem, a desire to clean house in the X-Universe.

"One of my day-one problems as editor-in-chief was that there were just too damn many mutants," Quesada states. "For a book that relies so heavily on the metaphor of mutants being a minority, they were slowly but surely becoming the majority. House of M gave me a great solution to reducing the mutant population, and have no new mutants appear for quite a long time, so we can bring the specialness back to being a mutant as well as a little bit of the worry, insecurity, and fear that was important when *X-Men* started."

Several new titles emerged and will continue to emerge as a result of the fall of the House of M, including *Generation M* (a four-part miniseries), *Son of M,*

The day after the world alters because of the House of M, the Sentinels still syand tall and threatening.

Deadly Genesis, The Sentinel I Project, and *The 198*—the latter referring to the number of mutants that have been spared in the X-Universe's psychic implosion. A symbol for the kind of changes that readers can expect to see is that the Xavier Mansion, an icon of the X-Universe since the very beginning, alters with the new political tenor of the world and becomes more of a refugee camp than a school.

Quesada called *Deadly Genesis,* written by Ed Brubaker, "the most important series that we're doing after House of M. It really celebrates the anniversary of *Giant-Size X-Men* #1 and it is the story of the greatest mystery in the history of *X-Men*: the true story of the X-Men, Xavier's big secret, the one that he's never told anyone, and it's earth-shattering."

Similarly, the next few years will see the revelation of more of the background of the mysterious Wolverine. "Another one of the offshoots of House of M is that Logan will look around and suddenly break down, because now he remembers everything," Quesada says, "so one of the things that we'll have fun with over the next three to four years is revealing to the fans the true story of Logan. Basically, he knows [his past] and now he'll reveal it to us."

On the media side of things, the situation is not quite so radical. While there might not be a feature film entitled *X4* (though a new comic book series was launched in 2005 under that name, featuring both the X-Men and the Fantastic Four), there will be other X-Men-inspired movies. Screenwriter Sheldon Turner is working the script of *Magneto,* a film that will depict the story of the early years of Erik Lensherr, from his time as a youth in the Auschwitz concentration camp. When the film was announced in late 2004, Turner told the *Daily Variety* that he had "pitched a film that is almost *The Pianist* [Roman Polanski's Oscar-winning 2002 film which is set against the Nazi assault on Europe] meets *X-Men*, about a guy who, after watching his family slaughtered, has an awakening of his powers and seeks revenge."

The film will also cover Magneto's early friendship with Charles Xavier, who reports say will be presented as one of the American soldiers who liberated the camps at the close of World War II (in the comics, of course, Xavier is a Korean-war veteran). Since the roles clearly call for younger men, other actors than Ian McKellen or Patrick Stewart might appear as their characters from the *X-Men* trilogy. McKellen, for one, is philosophical about that: "That would be very much in agreement with the comics, because they are always going back into the past and rewriting their own history," he notes. No targeted release date has been set for the film.

The character of Wolverine is also expected to return in a movie. Hugh Jackman would not only repeat his role in *Wolverine*, which is set in the time before he joined the X-Men, but his company, Seed Productions, is also co-producing the film with Lauren Shuler Donner. "Who knows exactly where we'll go?" Jackman says. "I do have a real desire to make that movie, I think it's just a great character, and a character worthy of a movie. I haven't had enough [of playing him] yet."

The X-Men should return to television as well within the next two years, in a new animated series. "It will be *Wolverine and the X-Men*, but will be centered on Wolverine," says Marvel's man in Hollywood Avi Arad. "It will capture more of the feel of the 1992 animated series."

Universes by their very physical nature tend to expand, and the X-Universe is no different. Coming years, coming decades even, will see many more adventures featuring the unique group of characters that have become part of the collective consciousness of the world. As Joe Quesada puts it, "The stories that we tell can be limitless."

No doubt they will be, leaving readers, moviegoers, television watchers, and gamers with ever more great *X-pectations.*

(Above) Wolverine's years in the wilderness, prior to joining the X-Men, will be chronicled in a feature film prequel starring Hugh Jackman.

(Opposite) Hugh Jackman will bring Logan back to the big screen in a prequel to the *X-Men* trilogy, appropriately titled *Wolverine.*

Chrono
Index

Chronology

1931 Martin Goodman and Louis Silberkleit form Western Fiction Publishing, the progenitor of Marvel.

1934 Martin Goodman becomes sole owner of Western Fiction Publishing.

1936 Ka-Zar, Lord of the Jungle, debuts in his own pulp magazine from Western.

1938 Western Fiction Publishing adopts "Red Circle Magazines" imprint for pulps.

1939 Western Fiction Publishing officially becomes Timely Publications.

Timely launches comic book line with *Marvel Comics* #1 in October. Among the characters is Bill Everett's The Sub-Mariner, arguably the first mutant in comics.

Teenaged Stanley M. Lieber, a.k.a. Stan Lee, joins company as a gofer, proofreader, and copywriter.

1940 Jacob Kurtzburg, a.k.a. Jack Kirby, joins Timely as a staff artist.

1941 Jack Kirby becomes art director for Timely.

Stan Lee publishes first comic book story, a text-filler for issue #3 of *Captain America*.

The Sub-Mariner gets his own magazine.

Kirby leaves Timely along with editor Joe Simon. Lee becomes editor.

1942 Stan Lee leaves Timely for stint in Army. Vince Fago becomes editor.

1945 Stan Lee returns from service to take over as editor.

1947 The designation "Marvel Comic" or "A Marvel Magazine" begins to appear sporadically on the covers of Timely comics.

1951 Martin Goodman creates Atlas News Company as a distribution arm, and as a result, Atlas becomes the name of the publishing company as well.

1954 Publication of the book *Seduction of the Innocent* by Fredric Wertham, M.D., which blames comic books for juvenile delinquency, prompts a Senate subcommittee to investigate the industry.

Artist John Romita (Sr.) joins Atlas.

1956 Jack Kirby comes back to Atlas as a free-lancer.

1961 The publication of the *Fantastic Four* issue #1 (November) sets off "The Big Bang" that creates the Marvel Universe.

1962 The Sub-Mariner reappears as a mutant semi-villain in the *Fantastic Four* #4 (May).

Martin Goodman asks Stan Lee to create new team, ala DC's *Justice League of America*.

1963 Marvel magazines officially are designated "Marvel Comics Group" on their covers.

Issue #1 of *The Avengers*, Marvel's answer to the *Justice League* (September).

Issue #1 of *X-Men*, introducing Professor X, Cyclops, The Beast, The Angel, Iceman, Marvel Girl, and Magneto (September).

1964 First appearance of The Blob in *X-Men* issue #3 (January).

First appearance of The Brotherhood of Evil Mutants in *X-Men* issue #4 (March).

Issue #28 of *Fantastic Four* features the first X-Men cross-over (July).

1965 First appearance of Lucifer in *X-Men* #9 (January).

First comic book appearance of Ka-Zar of Savage Land in *X-Men* #10 (March).

First appearance of Juggernaut in *X-Men* #12 (July)

Writer Roy Thomas joins Marvel.

First appearance of The Sentinels in *X-Men* #14; *X-Men* goes monthly (November).

1966 *X-Men* #17 (February) features Jack Kirby's last interior art for the book. Artist Werner Roth takes over beginning with issue #18.

Writer Roy Thomas takes over *X-Men* scripting from Stan Lee with issue #22 (July)

Artist John Buscema rejoins Marvel on regular basis.

Artist/writer Jim Steranko joins Marvel.

The Marvel Superheroes animated series premiers in syndication; the X-Men appear in a three-segment episode of *Sub-Mariner*.

First appearance of Banshee in *X-Men* #28 (December).

1968 *Avengers* issue #53, X-Men cross-over (June).

First appearance of Polaris in *X-Men* # 49 (October), which is the first of a three-issue run for Jim Steranko.

1969 *X-Men* issue #53 features artist Barry Windsor-Smith's first X-Men story (February).

First appearance of Alex Summers/Havok in *X-Men* #54 (March).

Artist Neal Adams takes over *X-Men* beginning with issue #56 (May).

Writer Chris Claremont interns at Marvel.

First appearance of villain Sauron in *X-Men* #60 (September).

1970 First appearance of Sunfire in *X-Men* #64 (January).

Martin Goodman considers canceling *X-Men*, but instead runs reprints from earlier issues starting with issue #67 (April).

Jack Kirby leaves Marvel.

1971 Issue #1 of *Ka-Zar* (August).

1972 Issue #4 of *Marvel Team Up* features original X-Men out of costume (June).

Company founder Martin Goodman retires. Stan Lee takes over as publisher and Roy Thomas assumes post of editor-in-chief.

1973 Bill Everett, creator of Sub-Mariner, dies at age 55 (February).

John Romita (Sr.) appointed art director.

Writer Len Wein joins Marvel.

1974 Artist Dave Cockrum joins Marvel.

Roy Thomas gets green light to revive X-Men with new team.

First appearance of Wolverine in *The Incredible Hulk* #180 (October).

Roy Thomas vacates editor's chair; Len Wein takes over.

Chris Claremont officially joins Marvel.

1975 Len Wein vacates editor's chair; Marv Wolfman takes over.

Issue #1 of *Giant-Sized X-Men* introduces new team: Nightcrawler, Wolverine, Storm, Colossus, Thunderbird, Banshee, and Sunfire (May).

Chris Claremont and Dave Cockrum take over *X-Men* with issue #94 (August).

Thunderbird dies in *X-Men* issue #95 (October).

First appearance of Moira MacTaggart in *X-Men* #96 (December).

1976 Marv Wolfman vacates editor's chair; Gerry Conway takes over temporarily, followed by Archie Goodwin.

Jim Shooter joins Marvel as associate editor.

First appearance of Lilandra of the Shi'ar in *X-Men* #97 (February)

First appearance of Phoenix, the transformed Jean Grey, in *X-Men* #101 (October).

Issue #1 of *Captain Britain* in the UK.

1977 Artist John Romita Jr. joins Marvel.

First appearance of Corsair in *X-Men* #107 (October).

Artist John Byrne takes over *X-Men* penciling from Dave Cockrum beginning with issue #108 (December).

First appearance of Sabretooth in *Iron Fist* #14.

1978 *X-Men* resumes monthly publication schedule with issue #112 (August).

Jim Shooter takes over as editor-in-chief; Roger Stern becomes *X-Men* editor.

X-Men becomes *The Uncanny X-Men* with issue #114 (October).

First appearance of Raven Darkholme/Mystique in *Ms. Marvel* #18.

1979 First appearance of Alpha Flight in *Uncanny X-Men* #120 (April).

1980 Landmark issue #129 of *Uncanny X-Men* introduces Kitty Pryde, The Hellfire Club, and The White Queen (January).

First appearance of both The Dazzler and Jean Grey's "Black Queen" persona in *Uncanny X-Men* #130 (February).

Marvel buys DePatie-Freleng Productions and forms Marvel Productions, Ltd. to develop and produce animated TV projects.

Jim Salicrup briefly replaces Roger Stern as *X-Men* editor, and in turn is replaced by Louise Jones (Simonson).

Landmark "Dark Phoenix Saga" runs from *Uncanny X-Men* issues #134 through 137 (April–September).

Kitty Pryde joins the team in *Uncanny X-Men* #138 (October).

1981 "Days of Future Past" mini-series in *Uncanny X-Men* issues #141–142 (January–February); first appearance of Phoenix II in #141.

Issue #1 of *Dazzler* (March).

Dave Cockrum returns to *Uncanny X-Men* with issue #145 (May).

First appearance of Rogue in *The Avengers Annual* #10 (August).

Animated series *Spider-Man and His Amazing Friends* premieres on NBC, featuring Iceman and new character Firestar (September).

Issue #1 of *Spider-Man and His Amazing Friends* tie-in comic (December).

1982 *The New Mutants* (Marvel Graphic Novel #4) introduces Cannonball, Wolfsbane, Sunspot, Psyche, and Karma.

Issue #1 of *Wolverine* limited series (September).

Issue #1 of *Vision and the Scarlet Witch*—first series (November).

1983 Issue #1 of *The New Mutants* regular comic book series (March).

Issue #1 of *Alpha Flight* (August).

Issue #1 of *Magic* comic book series; Issue #1 of *X-Men Classics* featuring reprints from the Roy Thomas/Neal Adams period (December).

Artist John Romita Jr. takes over penciling duties on *Uncanny X-Men* with issue #176 (December).

1984 Issue #1 of *X-Men/Micronauts* limited series (January).

Phoenix—The Untold Story (April)

Issue #1 of *Secret Wars* limited series (May).

Ann Nocenti replaces Louise Jones (Simonson) as *Uncanny X-Men* editor with issue #182 (July).

Issue #1 of *Kitty Pryde & Wolverine* (November).

Issue #1 of *Iceman* limited series (December).

1985 Issue #1 of *Vision and the Scarlet Witch*—second series.

Issue #1 of *Secret Wars II* (July).

Issue #1 of *Nightcrawler* (November).

Publication of *Heroes for Hope*, a special charity comic for famine relief; among the writers are Harlan Ellison and Stephen King (December).

1986 Issue #1 of *X-Men/Alpha Flight* limited series (January).

Issue #1 of *X-Factor*, reuniting original team (February).

Issue #1 of *Firestar*, a series based on animated character (March).

First appearance of Apocalypse in *X-Factor* #5 (June).

Issue #1 of *Classic X-Men* reprint series (September).

U.S. debut of Psylocke in *The New Mutants Annual* #2.

1987   Jim Shooter vacates editor-in-chief chair; Tom DeFalco takes over.

Issue #1 of *Fantastic Four vs. X-Men* limited series (February).

Issue #1 of *X-Men vs. Avengers* limited series (April).

First appearance of Sinister in *Uncanny X-Men* #221 (September)

1988   Issue #1 of *Excalibur*, featuring Captain Britain, Nightcrawler, Cerise, Shadowcat, Meggan, and Kylln (April).

Issue #1 of *Havok & Wolverine* limited series.

Issue #1 of *Marvel Comics Presents*, featuring Wolverine in first of many appearances (September).

Issue #1 of *X-Terminators* limited series (October).

Issue #1 of *Wolverine* regular series (November).

Pryde of the X-Men, a half-hour animated pilot for the syndicated series *The Marvel Action Universe* is produced but not sold.

1989   Investor Ronald O. Perleman buys Marvel.

Artist Rob Liefeld joins Marvel.

First appearance of Jubilee in *Uncanny X-Men* #244 (August).

Issue #1 of *Wolverine Saga* limited series (September).

1990   Artist Jim Lee joins Marvel.

Marvel begins long-term partnership with Toy Biz; resulting X-Men action figures serve to popularize franchise.

First appearance of Cable in *The New Mutants* #87 (June).

Classic X-Men renamed *X-Men Classics*.

X-Men Spotlight on the Starjammers limited series.

1991   Chris Claremont leaves Marvel after sixteen-year tenure.

First appearance of Deadpool in *The New Mutants* #98 (May).

First appearance of Gambit in *Uncanny X-Men* #266 (August).

Issue #1 of *X-Force* (August), the revamped version of *The New Mutants*, which ceases after issue #100.

Issue #1 of *X-Men* second series becomes bestselling single issue ever (October).

1992   Issue #1 of *Cable* limited series.

Premiere of *X-Men* animated series on Fox Kids TV (October).

Issue #1 of *X-Men Adventures*, based on animated show.

First appearance of Bishop in *Uncanny X-Men* #282 (November).

1993   *X-Men Unlimited*, *X-Men 2099*, and *Cable* launched as new regular comic book series.

Wolverine & Punisher: Damaging Evidence, *Sabretooth* and *Deadpool* launched as limited comic book series.

1994   Jack Kirby dies at age 76 (February).

Tom DeFalco vacates editor-in-chief chair; Bob Harras takes over.

Scott and Jean finally marry in *X-Men* (second series) #30.

Issue #1 of *Generation X*, featuring Husk, Skin, M, Jubilee, Chamber, Synch, Penance and Mondo (October).

Launch of limited series *Adventures of Cyclops and Phoenix*, *Scarlet Witch* and *Bishop*; and one-shot *X-Men: Alpha*.

1995   Multi-title storyline "Age of Apocalypse" takes over X-Universe (March).

Launch of regular comic books series *The Amazing X-Men*, *Astonishing X-Men*, *Professor Xavier and the X-Men*, and *X-Man*.

Barry Windsor-Smith's limited series *Weapon X* recounts Logan's horrific past.

Other limited series: *X-Men Chronicles*, *X-Men Archives: Captain Britain*, *X-Calibre*, *Wolverine/Gambit: Victims*, *Starjammers*, *Rogue*, *Gambit and the X-Ternals*, *Generation Next*, *Cable & X-Force*, and *Factor X*.

1996   *Generation X* television movie premieres on Fox Network (February).

Issue #1 of *Adventures of the X-Men* based on Fox Kids animated series.

One-shot publications: *Archangel* (black-and-white), *Logan: Path of the Warrior*, *Logan: Shadow Society*, and *Tales of the Age of Apocalypse*.

Limited comic books series: *Magneto*, *Deadpool*, *The Further Adventures of Cyclops and Phoenix*, *X-Men vs. The Brood*, *X-Nation 2099*, and *X.S.E.*

X-Men 2099 is renamed *X-Men 2099 A.D.*

Graphic novel *Xavier Institute Alumni Yearbook*.

Marvel merges with Toy Biz in effort to avoid bankruptcy, but files for Chapter 11 protection on December 27.

1997   Premiere of *Alpha Flight*, second series.

One-shot publications: *Sabretooth*, *Wolverine: Doombringer*, *Juggernaut* and *Generation X/Gen 13* (black-and-white).

Limited comic book series: *Beast*, *New Mutants*, *Wolverine: Days of Future Past*, *Bishop: Xavier's Security Enforcer*, *Gambit*, and *Kitty Pryde: Agent of S.H.I.E.L.D.*

1998   Launch of regular series *X-Men: The Manga*, *Mutant X*, and *Gambit*.

One-shot: *Generation X: Underground* (black-and-white).

1999 Feature film *X-Men* commences filming in Toronto (September).

Launch of regular series: *Bishop, X-Men: The Hidden Years,* and *X-Men Universe.*

Limited series: *Magneto Rex, Wolverine/ Punisher: Revelation, Astonishing X-Men,"* *X-Men: True Friends, X-51, X-Men: Liberators, X-Men: The Hidden Years, X-Men Universe, X-Men: Phoenix,* and *X-Men: Hellfire Club.*

One-shots: *X-Men: The Magneto War* and *Juggernaut: The Eighth Day.*

2000 Bob Harras vacates editor-in-chief seat; Joe Quesada takes over.

X-Men: The Movie comic book tie-in premieres (June).

X-Men feature film opens (July).

Premiere of animated series *X-Men: Evolution* on KidsWB (November).

Limited series: *X-Men: Children of the Atom, X-Men: Black Sun, X-Men: Magik, X-Men: The Search for Cyclops, X-Men Forever,* and *Excalibur: Sword of Power.*

Issue #1 of *Ultimate X-Men* (December).

2001 Grant Morrison takes over *X-Men* (second series), which is renamed *New X-Men* starting with issue #114 (March).

Issue #1 of *X-Treme X-Men* (June).

Origin, six-part limited series in which Wolverine's true history is revealed begins (August).

Issue #1 of *X-Men: Evolution,* based on the animated series (November).

Limited series: *Gambit & Bishop: Sons of the Atom, X-Treme X-Men: Savage Land, Rogue, Iceman, Nightcrawler,* and *Elektra & Wolverine: The Redeemer"* (limited graphic novel series).

2002 John Buscema dies at age 74 (January).

Captain Britain is published, Marvel's foray into trade paperbacks (January).

X2: X-Men United feature film begins shooting in Canada (June).

Launch of regular comic books series *Soldier X, Agent X, X-Statix,* and *Weapon X.*

Limited series: *Wolverine/Hulk, X-Factor, Morlocks, Sabretooth: Mary Shelley Overdrive, X-Men Icons: Chamber, Wolverine/Netsuke,* and *X-Treme X-Men: X-Pose.*

2003 *X2: X-Men United* feature film released (May).

Launch of regular series: *Mystique, Wolverine* (second series), *New Mutants, Emma Frost,* and *Cable & Deadpool.*

Limited series: *X-Men: Ronin, X-Men 2: The Movie, Wolverine: X-Isle, Wolverine: Snikt!, Domino, Wolverine/Doop, Wolverine: The End,* and *1602.*

2004 Grant Morison leaves *New X-Men,* which reverts back to *X-Men* with issue #157 (October); Chris Claremont returns to *Uncanny X-Men;* writer Joss Whedon begins *Astonishing X-Men.*

Limited series: *Alpha Flight, Wolverine/ Captain America, Wolverine/Punisher, X-Men Unlimited* (second series), *Magneto: Dark Seduction, New X-Men—Academy X, Astonishing X-Men, Excalibur, District X, Rogue, Starjammers, X-Force, X-Men: The End, Gambit, Jubilee, Nightcrawler,* and *Sabretooth.*

2005 Issue #1 of *X4* (February).

"House of M" storyline takes over Marvel Universe; the fallout will have lasting effect on X-Universe (July).

X-Men: The Last Stand begins shooting in Vancouver (August)

Launch of regular comic book series: *Mutopia X, X-Factor, New Excalibur,* and *Son of M.*

Limited series: *Generation M* and *X-Men: Deadly Genesis.*

One-shot: *Decimation: House of M—The Day After* (November).

2006 Issue #1 of *X-Men: The 198* (January).

X-Men: The Last Stand feature film released (May).

Index